TEXT, CASES AND MATERIALS

ENGLISH LEGAL METHOD

TEXT, CASES AND MATERIALS

ENGLISH LEGAL METHOD

Second Edition

Erika Kirk LLB, Cert. Ed., Solicitor
Senior Lecturer in Law, Nottingham Law School

BLACKSTONE
PRESS LIMITED

First published in Great Britain 1996 by Blackstone Press Limited,
Aldine Place, London W12 8AA.   Telephone 0181–740 2277

© Nottingham Law School, Nottingham Trent University, 1996

First edition 1996
Second edition 1998

ISBN: 1 85431 826 8

British Library Cataloguing in Publication Data
A CIP catalogue record for this book is available from the British Library.

Typeset by Style Photosetting Limited, Mayfield, East Sussex
Printed by Livesey Limited, Shrewsbury, Shropshire

FOREWORD

The books in the LLB series have been written for students studying law at undergraduate level. There are two books for each subject. The first is the *Learning Text* which is designed to teach you about the particular subject in question. However, it does much more than that. By means of Activities, Self Assessment, and End of Chapter Questions, the *Learning Text* allows you to test your knowledge and understanding as you work. Each chapter starts with 'Objectives' which indicate what you should be able to do by the end of it. You should use these Objectives in your learning — check them frequently and ask yourself whether you have attained them.

The second book is a volume of *Cases and Materials*. This is cross-referenced from the *Learning Text*. It contains the primary sources of law such as statutes and cases plus subsidiary sources such as extracts from journals, law reform papers and textbooks. This is your portable library. Although each volume can stand alone, they are designed to be complementary.

The two-volume combination aims to support your learning by challenging you to demonstrate your mastery of the principles and application of the law. They are appropriate whatever your mode of study — full-time or part-time.

CONTENTS

PREFACE

Learning the law is a lifelong process. The frequent changes in legal rules and the vast volume of legal material means that it is impossible for any individual to be an expert in all areas of law. It is however perfectly possible for you to master the basic principles and skills which form the foundation of all legal study. This book tries to help you to acquire those skills.

By studying the Learning Text, and particularly by using the Cases and Materials section to answer the set questions, you will begin to appreciate the structures and sources of English law. You will also have the opportunity to develop and practice the ability to analyse the raw material of the law: the statutes and reported cases with which all lawyers must engage whatever their chosen field of law.

This book therefore forms the foundation of your study of the law. It is hoped that you will find it stimulating, and that the knowledge and skills which you acquire will be useful to you in all other areas of your legal learning.

ACKNOWLEDGMENTS

Nottingham Law School and the publishers would like to thank the following for permission to reproduce copyright material:

Butterworths & Co. (Publishers) for extracts from the All England Law Reports and Barnard and Houghton, *The New Civil Court in Action*.

The Incorporated Council of Law Reporting for England & Wales for extracts from the Appeal Cases and Weekly Law Reports.

Sweet & Maxwell Ltd for extracts from Smith and Bailey, *The Modern English Legal System*.

Times Newspapers Ltd for extracts from the Times Law Reports.

Weidenfeld and Nicholson for extracts from Anderson and Twining, *Analysis of Evidence*.

TABLE OF CASES

Cases reported in full are shown in heavy type. The page at which the report is printed is shown in heavy type.

TABLE OF LEGISLATION

Statutes, and sections thereof, which are set out in full or in part are shown in heavy type. The page at which the statute or section is printed is shown in heavy type.

TABLE OF SECONDARY LEGISLATION

LEARNING TEXT

CHAPTER ONE

BASIC LEGAL SKILLS

1.1   Objectives

By the end of this chapter you should be able to:

■   explain some of your motives for studying on this course;

■   identify strategies for improving your study skills;

■   distinguish different methods of reading different types of text;

■   apply what you have learned in reading legal materials.

1.2   Introduction

This chapter, together with the chapters on legal reasoning, is intended to help you to discover basic techniques which provide some of the keys to successful study. Some of these techniques are the same whatever subject you are studying, but some techniques are specific to the subject of law, and therefore need to be mastered in order for you to proceed through this course effectively and to the best of your ability.

If this is the first time you have studied by distance learning, or if you have not undertaken any academic work for some years, then read this chapter thoroughly, and return to it from time to time as you progress through the course, to remind yourself of the advice given. If you are accustomed to academic work, or if you already have some legal knowledge, you should nevertheless work through this chapter carefully; you may find that your study skills can be improved, and there may be ways of reading legal materials which you have not considered before. Most important of all, learning new ways of studying may actually enhance your enjoyment and understanding of the course, so take the time to do the exercises set, both in the *Learning Text* and in the *Cases and Materials*, and increase your own capacity for learning!

1.3   Why Have You Chosen this Course?

Our motives for undertaking any course of action are often complex and may not be immediately obvious to us, and there may be a number of reasons behind your decision to study law. It can, however, be very useful to try to identify the motivating factors which have led you to spend your time, money and energy in this way. Knowing why you are studying this subject may help you to persevere when your interest seems to be declining: that will be the time to return to this section of the chapter and remind yourself of why you began the course in the first place.

Turn to *Cases and Materials* (1.1) and read through the list of factors which can motivate our behaviour. Write out below the factors which you feel most closely match your own reasons for joining this degree course. Add any extra reasons which are not mentioned in the list.

It is important to realise at this stage that your own reasons for studying this course will be personal to you, and may not be the same as those of your fellow students. This does not mean that your reasons are less valid than those of other students, although it may mean that you approach your studies differently from them. For example, if your main reason for taking this course is that you find the law interesting in itself, then you may find that you enjoy researching the more difficult points of law and exploring topics which are not on the syllabus. On the other hand, if you are doing this course because you need a degree in order to obtain promotion in your employment, there may be times when you find the legal study a chore. It is at times like these that you will need to return to this section of the book and remind yourself of your personal goals, and re-motivate yourself for the task. Whatever your motivation, you could also try writing out your goals on a separate piece of paper and displaying it in the area in which you do your academic work, to encourage yourself.

1.4   How Do You Learn?

Your success on this course will depend not only on the degree of motivation which you bring to it, but also on your ability to adapt your behaviour in order to learn most effectively. To some extent, the way in which you learn best will vary from the way in which others learn, so again self-awareness is important here.

Research into how people learn has revealed that effective learners have a greater awareness of the techniques which they use in their studies, and adjust these techniques according to the type of task which they are undertaking. To improve your awareness of your own study methods, why not keep a journal or diary of your first few months on the course, noting what, when, where and how you studied, and how effective you felt these study times were for you. Then compare your results with the responses which you give now to the questions set out below, and the advice which follows. You may be able to draw some useful conclusions about how to change your own study habits.

Your study journal can be in any form you like, but if you are not sure how to keep this sort of diary, turn to *Cases and Materials* (1.2) to see an example of an extract from a study diary.

SAQ 1

Based on your previous experience of learning situations, whether at school, college, or in the workplace, consider the following questions, and try to answer them as honestly as you can.

1   At what time of day do you feel most alert and most able to solve problems or read complex texts?

2   For what length of time can you concentrate on the sort of activities referred to in question 1 without your mind wandering?

3   What sort of environment helps you to undertake serious study? For example, do you attempt this type of work with the television or radio on?

The aim of this exercise is to help you become aware of your own behaviour when you are in a learning situation. If that behaviour is helping you to learn well, then it is important to work with it, rather than against it. But if you find that you are behaving in such a way that your learning is hindered, then it may be necessary to modify your behaviour if possible. The following suggestions are obviously based on generalisations about human behaviour, but nevertheless contain a great deal of truth.

For example, if you know that you study best in the morning, and that you need a quiet environment in which to read and think, you may find that getting up half an hour earlier each day in order to study the *Learning Text* enables you to make much greater progress than if you attempt to study for an hour in the evening when you are tired and there may be more to distract you.

Your study environment is important too. Although it can be helpful to make use of short periods of time on public transport and in work breaks for reviewing materials on which you are currently working, you will need a permanent base at home in which to study, with a desk or table, and somewhere to store your books and papers. It is particularly helpful if your family is able to respect this as 'your' space, so that you are able to leave work in progress on the desk without having to put everything away after each study session.

Tidiness is often a matter of personality: you may be the type of person who is not affected by an untidy working environment, and you may be able to work effectively in spite of a cluttered desk on which there are numerous books and papers not related to the task in hand. For a great many people, however, chaos is stressful! You may well feel more in control of the academic work if your study space is clean and tidy. Certainly you should try not to use your desk or table as storage space, but to have on it only those books and papers which are required for the current piece of work.

Try to ensure that you have a good light source over your desk, which does not shine directly in your face, and that the temperature in the room is neither too hot nor too cold. Experiment with the seating arrangements so that you can be relaxed but alert, and if bending your head over books causes your neck or shoulders to ache, try using a reading-stand which props your books open on the desk at an angle. It is worth taking the time to attend to these details, for you will find that you will concentrate much better if your environment is suitable for the task.

By the way, if you find that you can concentrate on your studies with the radio on, all well and good. But some people will find that music can be a distraction, and trying to watch the television whilst studying tends to spoil the enjoyment of both activities!

Here are two more questions which may help you to identify your own preferred style of study.

1   **Do you plan ahead and set yourself goals when you have academic work to do? Do you find that the work often takes longer than you originally estimated that it would?**

2   **Do you prefer to work in a group, rather than on your own, and to exchange ideas with others before coming to your own conclusions?**

For most people, time spent thinking about what you are going to do before you actually start to do it will not be time wasted. Setting targets, both for the long and the short term, will help to ensure that you complete assignments on time, and allocate time to be spent on different topics more carefully. To set long term targets, you will probably want to take account of examination dates, coursework deadlines, and your own holidays or other special events, such as periods when you know that you will be very busy in your job and may have less time to spend on your studies.

Short term targets will help you to structure the week, the day, and even the next two hours ahead. But don't be surprised if you underestimate the amount of time which you need to allocate to a particular task. For example, if you plan to spend two hours working on a particular chapter from the *Learning Text* you may find on some occasions that you cannot complete the amount of reading which you have set for yourself in the time allowed. This is a very common occurrence in any situation, and you need to bear in mind when setting your targets that it is human nature to think (mistakenly!) that a task can be completed in less time than it actually takes. You may need to get into the habit of adding an 'extra time' allowance to your targets.

Finally, remember that your own personality type will affect the way you study. If you enjoy the company of other people, and prefer to work in a group rather than on your own, then you may occasionally find yourself feeling very alone with the work. The amount of written material which must be read in order to study law means that you will have to spend quite a lot of time working alone, and this may be hard for you. If there are other students in your geographical area who feel the same way as you do about this, then you may be able to set up an informal network so that you can have discussions with each other from time to time. But you will also have to come to terms with the fact that studying by distance learning is a solitary occupation.

1.5   How Do You Read?

Just as there are many different styles of learning, so there are a number of different styles of reading which you may need to use according to the nature of the text with which you are working. Whether you spend a long period of time making a careful study of a piece of text, or whether you glance over it quickly, will depend on the type of material it is, and the reasons for which you are reading it.

Consider the different types of text listed below. First ask yourself *why* you would read these items, and then think about *how* you would read them (i.e. quickly, slowly, carefully, selectively etc.). Write your answers in the space provided next to the list.

A newspaper

The index of a textbook

An advertisement in a magazine

A chapter of *Learning Text*

A novel

A train or bus timetable

The contents page of a textbook

You will have discovered from this exercise that your own method of reading already varies more than you may have realised. Some types of text, such as newspapers and advertisements, you probably read out of interest. If you are looking for particular items in the newspaper or advertisement, then it is likely that you will browse through the text first, then concentrate and read more thoroughly the parts that are of particular interest to you. The same may be true when you are seeking specific information from the bus or train timetable, as you will probably skim over the parts that are not relevant to you and study those sections which contain the details you need.

Reading a novel is a different matter. Presumably you are doing this for enjoyment, and therefore you will be reading attentively, trying to absorb details about the plot and the characters in order to follow the story. Attentive reading will also be required when you study the *Learning Text*. Whether you are reading a chapter for the first time and trying to obtain mastery of the subject matter, or whether you are selecting information to use for an assessed piece of work, you will probably be employing a higher level of concentration than when reading the newspaper, and noticing more of the details of the text.

To aid your concentration when studying the *Learning Text* or any other legal textbook, you may find you wish to make notes. This is especially the case if you are gathering information for a piece of written work. In this situation it is most important to include in your notes exact details of the name, date, author, and page numbers of the book you have used. This information will be needed if you have to provide a bibliography to your essay, and in any event, you should always acknowledge the source of your information if you have taken a particular quotation or line of argument from a book. It is really frustrating if you take notes without recording these details, as you will have to search through the books all over again when you come to provide the references for your work.

Reading the contents page or index of a textbook requires a different technique again. In this case, you will probably be looking at the contents page to get an overall picture of what is in the book and whether it is useful to you, and at the index to help you find the answer to a specific question, and so you will probably browse these pages until you find what you are looking for. The point of all this is that you need to be aware of the way in which you read, so that you can use an appropriate technique according to the type of text and the reason why you are reading it.

1.5.1   READING TEXTBOOKS

When reading the *Learning Text* and extracts from the *Cases and Materials* or any other legal book, it is also vitally important that you find some way of maintaining your interest in what you are reading. You will find that legal material is not always easy to read, and there is often a great deal of it! You need to find a way of engaging with the text, so that you think about what you are reading and why you are reading it as you go along, otherwise you will undoubtedly have the all too common experience of reading a paragraph of text without concentrating properly, and then realising that you have no idea what you have just read.

One way in which you can increase your awareness and concentration whilst reading is to set yourself tasks related to the reading, similar to the Self Assessment Questions which are set for you in this *Learning Text*. First, you need to be very clear about the reason why you are reading the text. Are you looking for a specific piece of information to answer a question? If you are, then you will need to have that question at the forefront of your mind, and keep reminding yourself not to get distracted from the specific search.

If you are reading for mastery of a legal topic, before you begin to read thoroughly, skim through the material, and then set yourself some questions which you hope to be able to answer when you have finished reading. For example, if you are learning about the doctrine of consideration in contract law, you might set yourself the task of being able to define consideration in two short sentences, to give three examples of something that constitutes consideration, to name four important cases on the subject, and to identify one area in which there has been debate amongst lawyers about the nature of consideration. This sounds like a lot to do, and you may think it will take a lot longer than simply reading the text in the normal way. But in fact it could save you time, as you will be less likely to have to keep re-reading the text because you did not concentrate on the first read through. It's worth a try anyway!

In *Cases and Materials* (1.3.1) you will find an extract from the text book, *Smith and Bailey on The Modern English Legal System* by Bailey and Gunn. The extract concerns tribunals, that is official bodies which have power to make decisions concerning certain types of dispute, but which are not exactly like courts. Imagine that you are going to write an essay about the nature and functions of tribunals. Look quickly through the extract to get an idea of what it contains, then set yourself some questions to answer from the reading. Write down your questions in the space provided below. Then read the extract with your questions in mind. If you find your mind wandering, remind yourself of why you are reading the extract, and the tasks which you need to complete.

What sort of questions did you ask yourself before embarking on the reading? Although you will no doubt have your own style of asking questions, you might have considered the following points: How might a tribunal be defined? What sort of cases are heard by tribunals? What are the different types of tribunal mentioned in the extract? What is the history of tribunals? What legislation or case law is associated with them? To what extent are tribunals like courts?

If you raised questions such as these, and were able to answer them after reading the extract, then the exercise will have been worthwhile. Whilst reading the extract, you may have noticed words which were unfamiliar to you. This will be a common occurrence once you begin to read legal books more frequently. It is therefore a good idea to have both a reliable English dictionary, and a specialist legal dictionary available, so that you can check the meanings of words which you have not encountered before.

Textbooks are not the only legal materials which you need to read however. Two of the primary sources of law which you will have to be able to handle are statutes (Acts of Parliament) and cases decided by the courts. Later in the *Learning Text* you will learn a lot more about how to analyse these sources, but you need to become familiar with the look of them now, so that you can feel comfortable using them.

1.5.2 READING CASES

Case law as decided by the various courts which constitute the English Legal System (together with case law from the European Court) is vitally important to the development of the law. It is therefore necessary for you to become familiar with the conventions about the way in which reported cases are set out, and that you know how to identify important pieces of information which are provided in the report.

In *Cases and Materials* (1.3.2), you will find a typical report of a case decided by the courts, which you should read through carefully. You could try to ask yourself questions about the case as you read, in the way that you did when reading the extract from the textbook in the previous Activity. When you read the case, there will undoubtedly be many words and concepts which you do not understand at present. Try not to let this worry you too much at the moment. The aim of this exercise is simply to introduce you to a case, and allow you to see for yourself what this important source of law looks like. After you have read the case, try to answer the questions set out below, using your common sense and powers of observation. You are allowed to refer back to the case to do this – you are not expected to do it from memory.

(a) What was the full name of the person who was the subject of this case?

(b) The person whose name you have just given is also referred to in the report by two different technical names – what are they?

(c) When, and in which court, was the conviction originally made, and what was the name of the judge?

(d) In which court was the appeal (which you have just read about) heard, and who were the judges?

(e) What is the significance of the different dates which appear at the beginning of the report?

(f) **Who do you think 'N. P. Metcalfe Esq ' is? (His name appears at the end of the report.)**

(g) **Summarise the point of this case, using one sentence only.**

The answers to these questions can be found in *Cases and Materials* (1.3.2). As you can see from looking at the extract, there are a number of different sections in a law report. Fortunately, a standard format is usually adopted by the publishers of the reports, and this will make it easier for you to find your way round the sections.

The name by which the case is known appears first. This is the name which lawyers will use when discussing the case. Because *R* v *Comerford* is concerned with a prosecution under the criminal law, the case is conducted in the name of the reigning monarch, and the 'R' stands for rex or (in this case) Regina, the Latin for king or queen. If this had been a civil case, the surnames of both parties would have appeared. For example, if Smith wanted to sue Comerford for negligence, the name of the case would have appeared as *Smith* v *Comerford*. There is a convention amongst lawyers which it is important to remember when referring to cases by name. Although in the written reports, the names of the parties are divided by the letter 'v' meaning 'versus' or 'against', this is not the way in which the case is referred to in speech. When discussing the case verbally, it should be referred to as 'Crown *against* Comerford'. If this had been a civil case, it would be referred to as 'Smith *and* Comerford'.

Below the name of the case you will usually find the name of the court in which the reported hearing took place, together with the names of the judges, the date(s) on which the case was heard, and possibly a later date on which the judgment was given, if the court took time for consideration. You will be able to deduce that there was some delay between the hearing and the judgment, if you see the words '*Cur adv vult*' just before the decisions of the judges are set out. These three words are an abbreviation of the Latin phrase '*Curia advisari vult*' which means that the court wished to consider the case before giving judgment.

After the name of the case and the details of the court and the judges, you will see (in italics) a collection of words and phrases which summarise the key issues involved in the case. After that there are two long paragraphs. The first paragraph summarises the facts of the case, and the second (headed 'Held') summarises the decision of the judges. These two paragraphs are together known as the headnote. Once you begin to read law reports regularly, you will find the headnote very useful as a quick way of discovering the important points of a case, but you should not use it as a substitute for reading the case properly yourself. You will often find that the facts are set out at much greater length in the first judgment (the 'leading judgment') and the summary of what was held by the judges will not convey all of the important arguments contained in the report.

Following the headnote, there are some page references for *Halsbury's Laws* and *Halsbury's Statutes* so that anyone reading the report can check legal points in these reference works. Cases referred to in the course of the hearing of the case are then listed, and finally, before the decisions of the judges are set out in full, details of the history of the case are given. You will by now have realised that the information which you need in order to understand what has happened in the case beforehand does not appear at the beginning of the report. You do need to get a sense of the chronological history of the case however, and so the section headed **Appeal against conviction** is a useful one to look at first, when you are reading an appeal case like *R* v *Comerford*.

As you work through the *Cases and Materials* books on this course, do take the trouble to read the cases which are extracted for you, and to ask questions about them as you go along, for this will enhance your ability to understand legal writing and will enlarge your legal knowledge.

1.5.3   READING STATUTES

Acts of Parliament (statutes) are written in a particular form which can make them difficult to understand, and there are certain prescribed rules which have developed over time which are designed to help you interpret them. These rules are explained later in the *Learning Text* but at this stage it is useful for you to see the format of a statute and to appreciate some of its main features.

ACTIVITY 4

Turn to *Cases and Materials* (1.3.3). There you will find the Confiscation of Alcohol (Young Persons) Act 1997. Study the Act, and answer the following questions:

(a)   What is this Act designed to do?

(b)   How is the text of the Act organised and laid out?

(c)   Do you know whether this Act is in force, simply from reading the text?

(d)   Why does s. 1 set out a number of alternative situations?

(e)   From the text of the Act, is it possible to define a 'reasonable excuse' for failing to comply with the Act? (s. 1(3)).

As you will realise, this Act is designed to allow the police to confiscate alcohol which is in the possession of a young person , or which any other person is holding for use by a young person in places prescribed by the Act. The Act is laid out in the standard format for a modern Act of Parliament, with the short title and reference, followed by the long title (beginning, 'An Act to . . .') and the date of Royal Assent. (For the significance of this date, see **2.5.1**).

The text of the Act is divided into a number of sections and subsections. These provide convenient points of reference for those who have to read and interpret the Act. When referring to the provisions of the Act, the convention is to abbreviate the word 'section' to 's.' (as in s. 2, or s. 2(3)).

Although the date of Royal Assent is obvious from the face of the Act, the commencement date is not. Section 2(2) provides that the Act will not come into force until the Secretary of State makes an order to appoint a day for its commencement. There is no way of knowing when that date will be simply from looking at the face of the statute, and this can be a problem when trying to discover whether an Act is in force or not.

One of the difficulties which arises in the process of drafting an Act of Parliament, is the tension which must be held between covering every eventuality by the words of the Act, and making the wording of the Act specific enough to exclude situations which were not intended to be covered by it. You can see this tension at work in s. 1(1) and (3). In s. 1(1) three alternative situations are envisaged which will be included within the scope of the Act. The drafting is quite specific at this point, in order that only the types of behaviour mentioned are caught by the Act. Contrast s. 1(3), which refers to a 'reasonable excuse' for failing to comply with the Act. No definition is given within the Act of what will be regarded as a reasonable excuse, so it will be up to the court to develop an interpretation of this phrase, which may come to encompass many different types of situation.

These are the important features of the Act to note for the present, but you will learn a good deal more about statute law as you work through *Cases and Materials*.

1.6   Legal Writing

This chapter would not be complete without some mention of the skills in the use of the written word which are expected of a potential lawyer.

As this is an academic rather than a practical course in law, we will not be teaching you how to complete court forms, write letters to clients, or draft legal documents. There are particular conventions associated with these tasks, which you will discover later if you decide to practice the law. As a learner, however, your task is to become proficient in writing clearly, grammatically and succinctly, in sentences that are not too long, and without making too many spelling mistakes.

In every module of the course you will be asked to submit written work which will form part of the assessment of this course. It is therefore vital that you learn quickly how to interpret the different requirements for written work which relate to the different modules. On being set a piece of written work, study the instructions carefully. If a word limit is imposed for the essay, you must adhere to it – part of the assessment may well be to test your ability to express yourself concisely.

Be sure that you do not jump to conclusions about the task you have been set. You must answer the question given, not the question you would prefer to have been set. Notice the subtle differences between the words used in essay questions, such as 'discuss', 'describe', evaluate' etc. It is relatively rare for you to be asked to describe something at degree level, as this is regarded as too simple a task. It is more common to be asked to evaluate critically, thus giving you the chance to show the marker that you have not only understood the material, but can also weigh its value and make a critique of it.

Most importantly however, try to express your ideas as simply and clearly as you can. To practise this skill, try writing instructions for an everyday task, like making the bed, or try writing in your own words the facts of one of the cases from the *Cases and Materials* section. Avoid lengthy introductions and conclusions, and try to stick to the point of what you are writing about. Then give your work to a friend who will be honest with you, and ask them to tell you how clearly they have understood your writing!

Because the requirements of the written work vary from module to module, it is difficult to give more specific advice at this stage, apart from emphasising that when you have completed your work *always* read it through carefully, checking for errors, and ensure that you have actually answered the question posed.

1.7   Conclusion

We are never too old or too knowledgeable to discover new methods of learning which will enhance both our enjoyment and our proficiency in studying an academic subject. I hope therefore that in the course of this chapter you will have encountered some techniques which will have helped you to do the following tasks:

■   appreciate the importance of understanding your own motivation for study

■   discover the environment in which you learn best

■ acquire basic skills in reading cases and statutes

■ appreciate the need for careful analysis of the question when writing an essay on a legal topic.

In the chapters of the *Learning Text* which follow, you will have ample opportunity to test these skills. Unusually for this book therefore, there is no assessment question at the end of this chapter, as the skills which you are trying to acquire need some legal material on which they can be practised. But as you attempt the exercises and assessment questions in the following chapters, return to the advice contained in this first chapter, to remind yourself of the good practice which you are trying to develop.

1.8 Further Reading

Lee, S. and Fox, M., *Learning Legal Skills*, Blackstone Press, Chapters 1–5.

CHAPTER TWO

INTRODUCTION TO THE LAW

2.1 Objectives

By the end of this chapter you should be able to:

■ explain how to arrive at a definition of the concept of law;

■ outline a method of classification of the law according to subject matter;

■ apply this classification to a practical example;

■ identify and evaluate the importance of different sources of English law.

2.2 Introduction

In this chapter you will learn about the ways in which lawyers define and classify the law, and the ways in which law is made. You will not find many legal rules in this chapter, nor will you find any case law. This part of the book may therefore seem to contain a great deal of theory, and you may be tempted to skip through it so that you can start work on the more practical areas such as the structure of the courts. Please try to resist this temptation! Although theories of law and methods of law-making may seem of less importance than the legal rules themselves, you will find as your studies progress that you will not be able to understand how legal rules evolve and operate in practice, unless you have a thorough knowledge of the ways in which these rules come into being and the ways in which lawyers categorise them.

As the different types of law are discussed you will need to refer to the *Cases and Materials* section of this book. You will also find it useful to use a good English dictionary, for example *The Concise Oxford Dictionary*, and a good legal dictionary. As you work through this Text, try to get into the habit of looking up unfamiliar words or phrases in your dictionaries.

2.3 Definitions

It is hard to provide a comprehensive definition of the law, for that term can be used to mean many things. For example, some people would use it to refer to the institutions of the legal system, its courts, the Bar, prisons etc. Others would associate the term with the processes of law, its formalities and its rules of procedure, for example the steps which have to be followed when beginning any legal action. Another way of understanding the law would be to define it in terms of the rules laid down by Parliament or by the courts which control our behaviour, for example parking restrictions or the doctrine of privity in contract law. None of these ways of understanding the term 'law' is wrong, but none of them provides a comprehensive definition.

Consult a good English dictionary, such as *The Concise Oxford Dictionary*, and notice the numerous different ways in which the word 'law' can be defined. You might like to note some of these below and refer to them as you progress through the course. You may find that your understanding of these definitions changes as your knowledge increases.

From this activity you will probably have realised that the word 'law' can be understood in many different ways, including those outlined above, but is very often defined in terms of rules. You are probably aware of many rules which people observe in their daily lives which regulate the way that they behave, and yet these are not necessarily referred to as law. Many people also live according to moral rules and abide by religious codes, and yet these are not laws either. So when is a rule regarded as part of the law? Rules are regarded as law when they originate from one of the recognised law-making institutions which you will learn about shortly (see **2.5**). But that is not the whole story, for where does the system of law and its processes fit into the picture?

One way of defining the law so as to take account of all three aspects mentioned above, i.e., the rules of law, the legal system and its processes, is to say that law is a method of social control which maintains public order in society. This definition is useful as a brief and simple way of explaining the concept of law.

From your reading so far and from your general knowledge, which of the following statements are true and which are false?

1   There is no difference between moral rules and legal rules. TRUE/FALSE.

2   Procedural rules, for example, how to begin a breach of contract action in court, are not part of law. TRUE/FALSE.

3   The concept of law is not the same as the concept of justice. TRUE/FALSE.

4   Law is an instrument of social control, fostering social order. TRUE/FALSE.

These questions should have given you some food for thought! You will probably have realised that although many of the rules which we regard as laws are based on moral codes (for example, people must not commit murder), not every moral rule is part of the law of this country. For example, envy, though forbidden by moral codes, is not forbidden by law. Therefore the first statement in the exercise above is false, as law and morality are not the same, although they may overlap.

There is a great deal more to law than this, however, and you will probably realise by now that the law also comprises many procedural rules which must be followed in order for legal issues to be dealt with by the courts. The second statement in the self-assessment question is therefore false, as these procedural rules are also part of the law.

When legal issues are considered by the courts, or when Parliament creates law, one of the aims of those involved in the process is to do justice between people who are affected by the law. Sadly, we know that this aim is not always achieved, and therefore it has to be said that law and justice do not always coincide, and so the third statement in the **SAQ 4** is true.

You should by now have a good idea of what law is, and what is not, and you should also have a good working definition of the law, which appears in the final statement in the **SAQ 4**. This statement is true.

2.4   Classification of the Law

A broad definition of the law is important to your understanding at this stage, but in order to study the law in more detail you need to be able to appreciate how it can be broken up into a number of different component parts. One method of dividing the law into different categories is to classify it as substantive law or as adjectival law.

Substantive law is the term which is used to refer to the rules which govern our rights and duties under the law, for example the cases and statutes which create criminal offences, or the cases and statutes which define contractual obligations.

Adjectival law prescribes how those substantive rules can be used within the legal system, for examples the rules of evidence, procedure and costs which are to be observed when bringing a case to court.

Look at the extract from the Rules of the Supreme Court in *Cases and Materials* (2.1). What type of law is this?

Then look at the extract from the Bail Act 1976 in *Cases and Materials* (2.1). What type of law is this?

The Rules of the Supreme Court contain the detailed procedural steps which must be followed when a case is to be heard in the High Court. This should therefore be classified as adjectival law. By contrast, ss. 3 and 4 of the Bail Act 1976 describe the rights and duties of those involved in criminal proceedings and this is therefore substantive law.

An alternative way of classifying the law is by reference to its subject matter. From the point of view of lawyers and those involved in the legal system, this is the most useful way of dividing the law into categories.

The broadest distinction which can be drawn is between international law and domestic law. International law is concerned with the external relationships between different States and is based on treaties and conventions. A good example here is the Treaty of European Union (also known as the Maastricht Treaty). Domestic law comprises the laws of a particular State, that is the cases or statute law which govern relationships within that country and can be divided into public law and private law.

Public law cases are those cases in which one of the parties to the dispute is the Crown, usually acting through a government department. Public law can be further subdivided into the areas of criminal law and civil law.

Criminal law is concerned with conduct of which society disapproves so strongly that the State must punish the wrongdoer, for example, murder, theft, and driving offences. The major objective of criminal proceedings is to punish the perpetrator of the crime, not to compensate the victim. The Crown Prosecution Service, acting on behalf of the Crown, prosecutes the accused, who will be found guilty of the offence charged if the prosecutor can convince the court beyond reasonable doubt that the accused did commit that offence. Public civil law cases, by contrast, are concerned with problems in constitutional and administrative law. For example, these cases may challenge the legality of actions carried out by central or local government, or may bring test cases on individual freedoms which have been infringed by the government, such as telephone tapping.

As mentioned above, the other branch of domestic law is private law. This involves civil law and is concerned with the rights and duties which private individuals have in relation to each other. There are many different categories of civil law, for example the law of contract, the law of torts (wrongs such as negligence or slander), and the law of property.

The major objective of an action which involves private civil law is to compensate the person who has suffered the wrong, usually by payment of money (damages). A civil action is commenced by the victim, that is, the plaintiff, who sues the defendant in order to obtain a remedy. The plaintiff must prove his or her case on a balance of probabilities, in other words it must be more likely than not that the defendant harmed the plaintiff in the manner alleged.

ACTIVITY 7

On a separate piece of paper, draw a diagram which sets out the categories of law according to subject matter and which shows how these categories relate to each other.

After you have done this you may check your version against that given in *Cases and Materials* (2.1).

This system of classifying the law according to subject matter is not watertight however. One set of facts can have multiple legal consequences and can straddle the various categories outlined above. Road traffic accidents, for example, can result in infringement of rules of the criminal law, and private civil law.

As you progress through your studies you will find that classifying the law in this way begins to be second nature to you. You will not normally need to spell out these classifications when dealing with a case, unless you are specifically asked to do so, as this knowledge is assumed on your part. Another aspect of legal study to which you will need to become accustomed from an early stage is the use of specialised language or jargon. Notice the terminology which is used in the section on classification of the law. You will need to identify the context in which words such as accused, plaintiff, and defendant are used, and learn how to use them appropriately.

2.5   Sources of Law

The last section of this chapter is concerned with sources of law. This provides yet another way of dividing the law into categories, as it can be classified according to the source of the legal rule.

The law of England and Wales has been shaped by many different influences, but a simple way to analyse these sources is to examine the institutions which have formed its rules. Three institutions in particular are relevant here, each one producing a distinctive type of law. They are Parliament, the courts, and the European Community.

2.5.1   PARLIAMENT

Parliament (consisting of the Queen, the House of Lords and the House of Commons) is the originator of statute law (sometimes referred to as legislation). This consists of formally enacted rules dealing with a particular subject matter, produced in the form of an Act of Parliament. An Act of Parliament begins life in draft form as a Bill. This is debated by both Houses of Parliament and must undergo set procedures, until it is finally given the Royal Assent by the monarch. You should be aware that lawyers often use the terms Act, statute, and legislation interchangeably and this can be confusing.

Acts of Parliament are the primary form of legislation, but you will also encounter delegated or secondary legislation. This is legislation produced by a government department or by a local authority to which Parliament has delegated law-making authority in respect of certain matters. This type of legislation is usually published as regulations in the form of statutory instruments, or in the case of local authorities, as by-laws.

Normally, Acts of Parliament are referred to by their short title and the year in which they were enacted, for example, the Police and Criminal Evidence Act 1984.

ACTIVITY 8

Look at the extract from an Act of Parliament in *Cases and Materials* (2.2.1). What is the short title of this Act, i.e., the name by which you would refer to it if you wished to cite it in an essay?

Acts of Parliament have both a short title, and what is known as the long title. You can see the long title of the Act which you have just looked at in *Cases and Materials*, underneath the Chapter number and beginning with the words 'An Act to'. The date which follows immediately after the long title is the date on which the Act received the Royal Assent. This Act is, of course, usually known by its short title as the Law of Property (Miscellaneous Provisions) Act 1989. Acts of Parliament are divided into numbered sections and subsections. In writing, these are abbreviated, and become for example s. 4, or s. 5(1).

However, just because a statute has been enacted and published (which lawyers refer to as 'being on the statute book') this does not necessarily mean that its provisions are in force. This is yet another source of confusion. There may be a lapse of time between the statute receiving the Royal Assent, and the whole statute, or sections of it, coming into force as binding law. The Law of Property (Miscellaneous Provisions) Act 1989 is a good example of this.

ACTIVITY 9

Look again at the Act referred to above in *Cases and Materials* **(2.2.1).**

1   On what date did this Act receive the Royal Assent?

2   Look at the provisions of s. 5: did all of the provisions of the Act come into force on the date of the Royal Assent?

3   What other type of legislation is referred to in s. 5 of the Act?

As you will realise, not all of the provisions of the Act came into force on 27 July 1989, the date of the Royal Assent. Some sections of the Act became law immediately, but s. 5 provided that s. 2 and s. 3 and part of s. 4 would not come into force for two months. Certain other sections were not to come into force until the Lord Chancellor made an order by statutory instrument to that effect. This he duly did, and a statutory instrument was published in 1990, bringing these sections into effect as from 31 July 1990. In your answer to the third question in **Activity 9** above, you should have identified this as delegated legislation.

Once in force, a statute remains operative until it is repealed by another statute. Alternatively, if there are a number of statutes, all of which deal with aspects of the same subject in law, Parliament may decide to repeal all of these statutes and re-enact them in one definitive Act. This is a process known as consolidation of statutes.

In this century, legislation has emerged as the most important source of law, as opposed to the law-making of judges through decisions in the courts. This is partly due to the fact that the social and economic problems of today require far more detailed regulation than can be provided by case law alone. In addition, legislation can be publicised and known in advance by those whom it affects, and it can be put in place quickly when this is necessary.

2.5.2 THE COURTS

It is all very well to say that statute law is the primary source of law in this country, but legislation itself is not enough. As you will discover in later chapters, statutes have to be interpreted and applied to real situations. This is done in the courts of this country, where specially appointed judges preside to make decisions in individual cases. The court system is therefore another important source of law in this country.

In fact the courts are responsible for the creation of two different types of law: common law and equity. The relationship between these two concepts will emerge through an explanation of the term 'common law', which like many other legal terms can be understood in a number of different ways.

First, it can be taken to refer to the system of law which is common to the whole country. This has not always been in existence. Before the Norman Conquest of 1066, many different rules of law operated in different parts of the country. The Norman kings introduced a more centralised system so that common rules were administered by the royal judges through the common law courts in London and throughout the country by the Assize Courts.

Secondly, the term common law is often used in contrast to the term equity. The common law rules which were developed by the courts of Norman England were only designed to cover a limited range of situations. It was said that the common law did not provide a remedy for every wrong. As a result, people who could not pursue their cases at common law turned to the King for help. The King would often ask his Chancellor (a priest) to deal with these petitions, and as time went by, the Chancellor would make decisions on these cases by himself.

By the end of the fifteenth century, a separate court system had emerged, presided over by the Chancellor. This was known as the Court of Chancery, where petitions were dealt with not according to the rules of common law, but according to the Chancellor's principles of equity, from the Latin word 'aequitas' or fairness. Proceedings in Chancery were determined much more on the basis of the discretion of the court to achieve a just result than on the strict letter of the law.

This caused a certain amount of conflict between courts of the common law and the courts of Chancery, but it was never intended that the principles of equity would replace the common law rules, simply that they would fulfil it and make up for its defects. Having a dual system of courts administering different remedies did cause other problems, however, and by the Judicature Acts of 1873–1895, the court system was reformed. The result was that the administration of the common law courts and the courts of Chancery was merged, to create a unified system of courts and procedures. Thus all courts in the modern legal system can use both common law and equitable principles and give either type of remedy. But this does not mean that the common law and equitable rules have merged. These are still recognisably different.

For example, common law rules have a strong influence in contract, tort and criminal law, and common law remedies such as monetary damages are frequently used in the first two mentioned areas. By contrast, equitable principles are influential in land law and in trusts, where discretionary equitable remedies, such as the injunction, may be used.

The third way in which the term common law can be understood is in the sense of the creation of legal principles which evolve from cases decided by the courts. For example, later in the course you will encounter the famous case of *Donoghue* v *Stevenson* [1932] AC 562. In this case it was alleged that a woman had discovered the decomposed remains of a snail in a bottle of ginger beer, after she had consumed some of the contents. She became ill as a result of this, and wished to claim some legal redress. The judges developed a new common law rule, not based on any statutory provision, that a manufacturer of a product can be liable to the ultimate consumer, where the consumer is harmed by the manufacturer's negligence. This principle had not been recognised previously, and is a good example of the way in which the courts can create new law.

Summarise in your own words the different ways in which the term 'common law' may be used in a legal context. You should try to be as concise as possible in your description.

One of the important skills which a lawyer must acquire is the ability to convey information accurately and succinctly. In making a summary of the different meanings which can be attached to the term 'common law', it would be important to include some reference to the early history of English law and the way in which the Norman kings developed a system common to all England. Secondly, the difference between common law rules and equitable principles must be established together with an explanation of the way in which all courts can now administer these rules. Lastly, some reference is necessary to the way in which the term is used to describe the rules created by the judges in the decisions made in court.

2.5.3 THE EUROPEAN UNION

The third source of law of which you must be aware is the European Union. The United Kingdom became a part of the European Communities (the term in use at that time) on 1 January 1973. This has had a radical effect on the sources of English law.

Section 2(1) of the European Communities Act 1972 acknowledged that European Community law would be directly applicable in the United Kingdom. Our national law is therefore subject to, and in some cases superseded by, European law. As the links between the laws of the European Union and its member states become ever closer, you will need to become familiar with the institutions of the Union, and its law making processes. You should therefore study these topics in the *Learning Text*: **European Community Law**.

For now it is important to remember that legislation from the European Union can directly or indirectly alter the law of this country, and cases which involve elements of European law are often referred to the European Court for interpretation of European legislation.

Place the sources of law about which you have been reading, in an order of importance which reflects the way in which they impinge on everyday life today.

This is not an easy task! In fact different lawyers might well give different answers to this question. Ignoring European law for the moment, most lawyers would agree that legislation has become the primary source of law in this country. There is a wealth of statute law which regulates almost every aspect of our lives, and it is a form of law which can be created to respond to situations when the need arises. By contrast, in order to develop the common law, it is necessary to wait for a case concerned with a particular issue to arise and for the parties involved to have the resources to test out the principles in court. Thus common law and equitable principles have become secondary in importance to statute law.

As between common law and equitable rules, in a conflict between these two sets of principles it is a long established rule that equity always prevails over the common law. However, in terms of impact on modern life, the rules of the common law are probably invoked more frequently.

This leaves the question of where the law emanating from the institutions of the European Union fits into this order of importance. European law can supersede our national law, and for that reason it could be regarded as superior to legislation created by Parliament, and to the rules of the common law and equity. However, there are still many areas of domestic law which are not affected by European law, and which will therefore seem more important to those who have to deal with the law of this country. So the answer to this part of the question can vary according to your standpoint.

2.6   Conclusion

By now you should have gained insight into some of the basic features of the legal system in this country. It should be possible for you to:

■   discuss the ways in which law may be defined as a method of social control which fosters order in society;

■   describe the way in which law may be classified according to the subject matter with which it deals;

■   show how the classification of law into public and private law, civil and criminal law, can be used in analysing practical legal problems;

■   classify the law according to its source, i.e., Parliament, the courts (common law and equity), and the European Union;

■   begin to appreciate the interaction of different types of law.

In **Chapter 3**, you will be using this classification system as you discover how the court system is organised and how legal problems are allocated to different courts according to the issues involved.

2.7 End of Chapter Assessment Question

Read carefully through the following story and then identify the different types of legal action which may result from it.

Albert is riding his pedal cycle along a country lane, when a car driven by Brenda hurtles past him and knocks him off his bike. Brenda has for many years harboured a grudge against Albert. Albert sustains serious injuries and is hospitalised for several months.

When he emerges from hospital, he discovers that the landlord of the flat which he was occupying before the accident has let the flat to another tenant. Albert applies to the local authority for accommodation, but he is told that he does not come within the statutory definition of 'homelessness'. Albert wishes to challenge the decision of the local authority.

See *Cases and Materials* (2.4) for a specimen answer.

CHAPTER THREE

THE STRUCTURE AND JURISDICTION OF THE COURTS: CIVIL CASES

3.1 Objectives

By the end of this chapter you should be able to:

- explain the structure of the court system in England and Wales;

- give an account of the jurisdiction of the courts which may hear civil cases;

- analyse the types of cases which can be dealt with by these courts;

- identify the personnel involved in the courts which have civil jurisdiction.

3.2 Introduction

By now, you should be aware of the fact that there are a number of different ways of defining the word 'law' and that there are various ways of grouping together the different types of law that exist within the English legal system. The place where ordinary citizens will come face to face with the machinery of the law is the court system. It is therefore important for you as lawyers in the making (and as lay people) to have a thorough knowledge of the different types of courts which you will encounter in the English legal system. Although you will not be able to memorise all the details which follow, you will find it useful to learn the names of the courts and to be aware of their main functions. This will help you when studying the case law relating to other academic subjects as you will be able to identify the appropriate court and its status within the system.

In this chapter you will be guided through a summary of the functions and jurisdiction of the courts which are capable of dealing with **civil** cases, beginning at the top of the hierarchy and working downwards through the different levels. In **Chapter 4** you will find a similar outline of the courts which are capable of dealing with **criminal** cases. You should be aware, however, of the fact that some courts do not fit neatly into this classification, and may have to be mentioned twice as they have jurisdiction in respect of **both** civil and criminal cases. As usual you will need to refer to *Cases and Materials* to illustrate the points made in this chapter, and you will need to familiarise yourself with the introductory concepts which follow.

3.3 Terms and Definitions

There are a number of different terms and ideas with which you need to be familiar before studying the individual courts in detail.

(a) The system is based on the principle of a **hierarchy**, with courts higher up the hierarchy having greater authority than those lower down in the structure.

(b) Certain courts are thus **superior** courts, for example the House of Lords, the Court of Appeal, the High Court and the Crown Court. Others, that is the magistrates' courts and the county courts, are **inferior** courts.

(c) Certain courts are referred to as **courts of record**; this means that a record of all the business of that court is kept at the Public Record Office. With the exception of the magistrates' courts, all the courts mentioned immediately above are courts of record.

(d) Some courts deal **only** with civil cases, some courts deal **only** with criminal cases, and some courts have jurisdiction to deal with **both** types of cases.

(e) Some courts are limited with regard to the types of cases with which they can deal, according to the **amount** of money at stake, or the **seriousness** of the matter in hand.

(f) Certain courts hear cases at **first instance**, whereas other courts are designated **appeal courts**. Cases are heard at **first instance** when they are heard for the first time and no previous decision has been made in any other court. Courts which hear first instance cases are said to have **original jurisdiction.** Contrary to what you might expect, the courts which hear cases on appeal from first instance courts are **not** referred to as courts of second instance. Instead these courts are said to have **appellate jurisdiction.**

(g) The Court of Appeal, the High Court and the Crown Court together make up the **Supreme Court of Judicature.** This was created by the Supreme Court of Judicature Acts 1873–1875 (known as the Judicature Acts) which were consolidated into the Supreme Court Act 1981.

Turn to *Cases and Materials* (3.1) where you will find two diagrams, one showing the courts which are capable of hearing civil cases and the other showing those courts which have jurisdiction in criminal cases. Using the information given above, you might find it helpful to note on the diagram the courts which are regarded as superior courts, the courts which are classed as courts of record, and those which form part of the Supreme Court. Later in your studies, when you have become more familiar with the names of the different courts, you could try to reproduce the two diagrams from memory, as this will help you to have an overview of the system.

3.4   The Courts which Exercise Civil Jurisdiction

3.4.1   THE COURT OF JUSTICE OF THE EUROPEAN COMMUNITIES (COMMONLY KNOWN AS THE EUROPEAN COURT OF JUSTICE)

■ **Sits in:** Luxembourg.

■ **Personnel:** One judge from each Member State (drawn from those eligible for the highest judicial posts in their own country) and a President of the Court, together with the nine Advocates-General (with the same qualifications as the judges) whose task it is to advise the court on the relevant issues of fact and law and to make recommendations on cases referred to the court.

■ **Jurisdiction:** Civil and criminal law.

The European Court of Justice was brought into being:

(a) to ensure that Member States fulfil their obligations under the Treaties of the European Communities;

(b) to decide disputes between Member States concerning the subject matter of the Treaties; and

(c) to ensure that the institutions of the Communities (i.e., the Council of Ministers and the Commission) act legally and within their powers.

The other aspect of the jurisdiction of this court concerns the interpretation of Community legislation. Under Article 177 of the EC Treaty, the court has the task of giving rulings on references made to it by member states concerning the way in which Community law should be interpreted, and these rulings will then be binding on all Member States.

In *Learning Text: European Law* you will learn more about the work and status of this court, but for now you should note that it appears above the House of Lords in the hierarchy because its rulings are capable of overriding decisions made by the Law Lords.

ACTIVITY 11

Turn to *Cases and Materials* (3.2.1) and look at the extract from the case of *Factortame Ltd and others* v *Secretary of State for Transport (No. 2)* [1991] 1 All ER 70 and then answer the following questions:

1 Which English court or courts referred this case to the European Court?

2 What procedure was used to obtain a decision from the European Court?

3 What effect did the ruling of the European Court have on the *Factortame* case?

The answers to these questions can also be found in *Cases and Materials* (3.2.1).

You should also be aware of the existence of the **Court of First Instance of the European Communities,** a separate court which was created to ease the workload of the European Court of Justice. The Court of First Instance deals with certain specialised cases, e.g., claims by employees of the Community institutions.

Please note that there is yet another European institution which is often confused with the European Court of Justice, and which you must keep separate in your mind. This is the **European Court of Human Rights,** which sits in Strasbourg, and whose function is to interpret and apply the European Convention on Human Rights. The Convention is concerned with the protection of civil rights and freedoms, such as freedom of religion, and freedom of the press.

At the time of writing, Parliament is debating The Human Rights Bill, which will make the European Convention on Human Rights enforceable in English courts. Judges will be able to invoke the rights enshrined in the Convention without the need for individuals to start costly proceedings in the European Court of Human Rights. The enactment of this Bill will thus have far-reaching effects on English Law.

3.4.2   THE HOUSE OF LORDS

- **Sits in:** London.

- **Personnel:** The Lords of Appeal in Ordinary (usually referred to as the Law Lords, or simply the Lords.) Although these Lords are life peers, they are not the same people as the members of the House of Lords who are involved in creating statute law in Parliament. The Law Lords are usually drawn from members of the judiciary who have held 'high judicial office'. The House is presided over by the Lord Chancellor.

- **Jurisdiction:** Civil and criminal law.

The House of Lords has very little original jurisdiction, i.e., it hears very few first instance cases, for its power in this respect is limited to disputed peerage claims. Its main function is to hear appeals from courts lower down the hierarchy and most of its work therefore comes directly from the Court of Appeal. In cases **not** involving a European element, the House of Lords is the final court of appeal for England, Wales and Northern Ireland in both civil and criminal cases and for civil cases from Scotland. Its decisions are therefore binding on all other courts within the English legal system and its judgments can only be overruled either by legislation produced by Parliament, or by the Law Lords themselves choosing to revise their opinion of the law in a later case.

Appeals are usually heard by at least five of the Law Lords, the minimum being three. There is no rehearing of the parties' evidence on appeal; the case is dealt with on the basis of the documents relating to the case and the arguments of Counsel. Decisions made by the Lords are known as speeches or opinions: each judge may deliver a separate opinion, or one judge may speak for all where the decision is unanimous. Where opinion is divided about the outcome of a case, the majority view prevails.

ACTIVITY 12

Look at the extract from the House of Lords case of *Davis* v *Johnson* **[1978] 1 All ER 1132** in *Cases and Materials* **(3.2.2).**

Notice the number of Law Lords who heard this case. Notice also that whilst the case was heard on 16 and 17 January 1978, the Law Lords did not give their opinions until 9 March of that year. You might also wish to read the section headed 'Appeal' and trace the progress of the case from its commencement in the county court in October 1977.

Do not worry if you cannot see exactly how the case has worked its way through the court system, or if the names of the courts are unfamiliar to you. You will understand these things more thoroughly after reading this and the following two chapters, and you will have further opportunities to practise this exercise.

Criticisms have been levelled at the House of Lords on numerous occasions. For example it has been argued that it adds an unnecessary top tier to the legal system, as final appeals could be dealt with by the Court of Appeal. This would have the advantage of saving time and money for litigants, and would mean that there would be less uncertainty and unpredictability about the eventual outcome of cases. To date however the House of Lords has successfully resisted any attempts to abolish it or to reduce its status.

3.4.3   THE JUDICIAL COMMITTEE OF THE PRIVY COUNCIL

■ **Sits in:** London.

■ **Personnel:** The Lord Chancellor and the Lords of Appeal in Ordinary usually constitute this court although other persons who have held high judicial office may be appointed to the Committee.

■ **Jurisdiction:** Civil and criminal law.

As with the House of Lords, the jurisdiction of this court is almost completely appellate. The Committee hears appeals from:

(a)   courts outside the United Kingdom, e.g., the Isle of Man, the Channel Islands and certain of the independent Commonwealth countries;

(b)   prize courts, i.e., the Queen's Bench Division which has considered the ownership of a ship or aircraft captured by an enemy;

(c)   ecclesiastical courts;

(d)   medical tribunals.

The Committee may also have special cases referred to it by the Crown.

What is the link between the House of Lords and the Judicial Committee? What effect do you think this link has on the status of decisions by the Committee?

As you may have realised from the language used in the last few paragraphs, the Judicial Committee of the Privy Council is really a committee rather than a court in the true sense of the word. It therefore gives advice to the Crown rather than giving judgments, and its decisions are not binding on English courts as such. However, because the Committee is largely made up of members of the House of Lords, it is thus linked to the most influential court in the hierarchy and its decisions are treated as having great authority. Cases dealt with by the Judicial Committee are therefore said to be of 'persuasive' value when looking at the status of such decisions. (You will find more detail on the meaning and significance of this last point when you reach **Chapter 9**.)

3.4.4   THE COURT OF APPEAL (CIVIL DIVISION)

■   **Sits in:** London, usually, although technically it may sit anywhere in England and Wales.

■   **Personnel:** The Lord Chancellor, the Lord Chief Justice, the Master of the Rolls (who is the President of the Civil Division of the Court of Appeal), the President of the Family Division of the High Court, the Vice President of the Chancery Division, the Lords of Appeal in Ordinary (if willing to sit), and most importantly, senior judges called Lords Justices of Appeal. Former Court of Appeal or High Court judges and present High Court judges may also be asked to sit.

■   **Jurisdiction:** Civil cases on appeal; there is virtually no original jurisdiction.

When the Court of Appeal was created by the Judicature Act 1873, it was intended to be the final court of appeal, and the House of Lords was to have been abolished as an appellate court. Due to a change of government however, the abolition of the House of Lords did not take place, and so the two tier system of appeal courts remains today.

The Civil division hears appeals principally from the High Court, the county courts, the Employment Appeal Tribunal, and various other tribunals. Normally the appeal will be heard by at least three judges sitting together who rehear the case on the basis of the documents and the arguments of Counsel. The majority decision will prevail in cases where there is not a unanimous opinion. The Court of Appeal has a much heavier workload than the House of Lords, as many cases will not be taken further after the Court of Appeal stage. In order to deal with the volume of work, the Court of Appeal organises itself into divisions, and there may be four or five divisions sitting simultaneously on any one day. Even so there is usually a backlog of cases waiting to be heard, which leads to delay in individual cases.

Think of three arguments that could be put forward for the abolition of the House of Lords (in its judicial, not its legislative capacity) and its replacement by the Court of Appeal as the most senior court. List them below.

As you may remember from the section on the House of Lords, various arguments have been put forward in favour of abolishing it as the final court of appeal in this country. Amongst the points which you might have mentioned above are the cost in terms of both time and money of taking a case right through the court system to the House of Lords, the argument that the Court of Appeal could act as the final appeal court thus making the existence of the House of Lords unnecessary, and the fact that the possibility of further appeal after the Court of Appeal adds a degree of uncertainty and unpredictability to legal proceedings.

3.4.5   THE HIGH COURT OF JUSTICE

■ **Sits in:** London, and other provincial towns.

■ **Personnel:** High Court judges, sometimes referred to as 'puisne' (pronounced puny) meaning lesser, or assistant, judges. Various senior members of the judiciary are also regarded as part of the High Court, e.g., the Lord Chief Justice, the President of the Family Division, the Vice-Chancellor, and a senior presiding judge appointed from the Lords Justices of Appeal.

■ **Jurisdiction:** Mainly civil, with some criminal law. Certain divisions have both original and appellate jurisdiction.

The High Court is divided into divisions which deal with different types of work. Until 1880 there were five divisions but since that date there have only been three. Each division also has its own **Divisional Court** where a number of judges from that division sit together to hear appeal cases. Strictly speaking, these Divisional Courts are of superior status to the divisions themselves, but it is easier to explain the work of the divisions first, before looking at the work of the Divisional Courts.

An important point to note here is that learners often find the distinction between the **divisions** of the High Court and the **Divisional Courts** confusing. It will help you to avoid these mistakes if you remember that on the whole, the three **divisions** of the High

Cour hear cases **at first instance,** with **one** judge sitting alone, whereas the **Divisional Courts** hear cases on **appeal** from other courts and **two** or **more** judges will deal with these cases.

3.4.5.1 Chancery Division

The nominal head of this division is the Lord Chancellor, but in reality the foremost judge is the Vice-Chancellor. The Chancery Division hears civil cases only, and most of its jurisdiction is original. It hears cases at first instance relating to matters such as:

- the sale of land

- redemption of mortgages

- trusts

- the administration of the estates of people who have died without leaving a will

- the granting of probate, i.e., the authority of the Court to administer the estates of people who have died and have left a will which names executors who will deal with the property

- disputes relating to wills and probate

- company and partnership matters

- patents and copyright.

Where two or more judges of the division sit together, this constitutes the **Divisional Court of the Chancery Division.** The work of this court is to hear appeals from the county court relating to bankruptcy and also registered land.

3.4.5.2 Queen's Bench Division

The Head of this division is the Lord Chief Justice. The bulk of the work of this court involves civil cases at first instance, e.g., disputes relating to contracts, and torts such as negligence and defamation. There are also two specialist courts: the Commercial Court which deals with business matters such as banking or insurance, and the Admiralty Court, which deals with various matters relating to ships.

In matters relating to contract and tort, there is an overlap between the jurisdiction of the Queen's Bench Division and that of the county court. Technically, the High Court can deal with any claim of this type, worth any amount of money. In reality, however, there are procedural rules which require less complex cases, or those in which the money claim is less than £50,000, to be dealt with by the county court. A more detailed explanation of this can be found in the section on the county courts (see **3.4.6**).

Many cases which are commenced in the High Court are abandoned or settled out of court, and only a very small proportion of these cases ever comes to trial. Despite this, there is often considerable delay involved in bringing cases to a hearing in the Queen's Bench Division, and considerable cost can be incurred.

The Divisional Court of the Queen's Bench Division consists of two or more puisne judges sitting together to exercise an appellate and a supervisory jurisdiction. The Divisonal Court will hear appeals on points of criminal law from the magistrates' courts and from the Crown Court where that court has heard a case on appeal from the magistrates. These appeals are dealt with by way of case stated, which means that one of the parties has identified a point of law which he or she wishes to dispute, and requires the court against whose decision the appeal is made to 'state a case' by providing all the necessary facts, arguments and decisions for consideration by the court dealing with the appeal.

The Divisional Court also acts as a supervisory court, and has the authority to examine decisions taken by inferior courts, public bodies and tribunals and assess whether the institution concerned has acted within its authority. This process is known as judicial review.

In *Cases and Materials* (3.2.3.1) you will find extracts from two reported cases which were heard by the Divisional Court of the Queen's Bench Division:

(a) *Tucker* v *DPP* [1992] 4 All ER 901; and

(b) *R* v *General Council of the Bar, ex parte Percival* [1990] 3 All ER 137.

Read the extracts from these two cases and then answer the following questions in respect of both cases.

1   What is the nature of the dispute in these cases?

2   In which courts did these cases begin?

3   Is the Divisional Court acting in its appellate or its supervisory capacity in these cases?

You will find the answers to these questions in *Cases and Materials* (3.2.3.2).

3.4.5.3   Family Division

The head of this court is the President of the division.

This court has both original and appellate jurisidiction in respect of all matrimonial matters and also matters relating to legitimacy, adoption, and proceedings under various Acts including the Family Law Act 1996 and the Children Act 1989. There is some overlap between the family matters dealt with by this court and the county courts and magistrates' courts. This is particularly so in relation to matters relating to children under the Children Act 1989. This Act governs the distribution of business between the three courts, which are regarded as one unified court for this purpose, and cases may be transferred between the three courts according to the complexity of the case and the interests of the child. The Family Division will thus deal with the more complex matrimonial and child cases, and in particular, divorce cases which are defended, i.e., where one party does not consent to the divorce being granted, or wishes to dispute some aspect of the divorce.

The Divisional Court of the Family Division has appellate jurisdiction over decisions made by the magistrates' courts in various types of family matters.

SAQ 9

In which divisions of the High Court would the following cases be heard?

  (a) A dispute about contact with the children where one party to a marriage has left the other.

  (b) A dispute about a large debt.

  (c) A dispute about the sanity of a deceased lady who has left a will giving all her money to the Cats' Home.

  (d) A dispute about a decision made by a local authority.

As you will have realised from the preceding paragraphs, the separate divisions of the High Court have distinct functions, and therefore it is not too difficult to allocate cases to the correct divisions. You are more likely to experience problems when trying to decide whether a case should be heard by the High Court, or in the county or magistrates' courts, because of the degree of overlap between these three courts.

As far as the High Court is concerned, disputes concerning contact with children in matrimonial cases (question (a)) will be heard in the Family Division, debts (question (b)) are dealt with in the Queen's Bench Division, matters of wills and probate where there is some dispute about the validity of the will (question (c)) come within the jurisdiction of the Chancery Division, and judicial review cases (question (d)) are heard in the Divisional Court of the Queen's Bench Division.

3.4.6 COUNTY COURTS

- **Sit in:** county court districts throughout England and Wales.

- **Personnel:** Circuit judges and also district judges (formerly known as Registrars). Circuit judges may hear any cases of £1,000 or more in value: district judges hear cases in which the amount claimed does not exceed £5,000. The district judges are also responsible for the administration of the county court, maintaining records, issuing summonses etc.

- **Jurisdiction:** Civil cases at first instance. There is no appellate work apart from the possibility of an appeal from the decision of a district judge to a circuit judge.

The county courts were originally created as local courts which were intended to deal with civil actions involving small amounts of money. Over time, however, the jurisdiction of the county court has been increased until much of its work overlaps with that of the High Court. Its work includes disputes relating to contract and tort, debts, personal injuries, faulty goods and services, bankruptcy, and family matters. The county court does not usually hear defamation actions, actions involving fraud, professional negligence or fatal accidents as these are normally dealt with by the High Court.

Under the High Court and County Courts Jurisdiction Order 1991 (SI 1991 No. 724), the business of the High Court and county courts was distributed as follows.

If the value of the claim (i.e., the amount the plaintiff expects to recover) is **less than £25,000,** then the case is tried in the **county court,** unless the court considers that it should be transferred to the High Court, according to the criteria set out below.

If the value of the claim is **£50,000 or more,** then the case is dealt with by the **High Court,** unless the court considers that the case should be dealt with by the county court, on the basis of the criteria given below.

Claims for amounts between the two sums mentioned are dealt with by either court as appropriate.

The criteria which help the court to determine where a particular case should be heard include factors such as the complexity of the facts or legal issues, the financial substance of the action, and whether the case raises questions which are of public interest.

Turn to *Cases and Materials* **(3.2.4) where you will find an extract from the High Court and County Courts Jurisdiction Order 1991, setting out the criteria for allocation of cases in more detail. You may remember that one of the problems identified in connection with the High Court was the considerable delay that can occur before cases come to trial. How is this problem dealt with by the 1991 Order?**

As you will see from the extract, one of the factors that the court will consider in deciding where a case should be heard is whether the transfer of the case to a different court will result in it being dealt with more speedily, although this factor alone should not decide the issue.

The county courts also have jurisdiction in matters such as trusts and mortgages and partnership law, up to a value of £30,000.

Certain county courts are designated as divorce county courts, and may deal with undefended divorces, i.e., where the divorce is by consent of the parties, certain matters relating to children, and applications for injunctions to prevent molestation. Again there is considerable overlap here between the work of the county courts, the High Court, and the magistrates courts in respect of family matters, including adoption.

SAQ 10

The county courts were originally developed as a forum in which people who were not wealthy could pursue claims for small amounts of money. Given the current value limits for the jurisdiction of the county courts, do you think that this court can still be described as 'the people's court'?

Since the creation of the county courts, the number of cases and the value of the claims dealt with by these courts have increased greatly. It has also become apparent that the most frequent users of the county courts are not individuals trying to obtain justice in small claims, but firms who are suing consumers for non-payment for goods. In fact claims for small amounts of money are now dealt with in a different way from other legal issues in the county courts.

3.4.6.1 Small claims in the county court

Strictly speaking, the small claims court is not a separate court at all, but this is the term used to describe the way in which the county courts deal with claims for amounts of money of £3,000 or less.

Where such a claim is made, the case is not dealt with according to the usual county court procedure, but is automatically referred to the district judge to be dealt with by a process known as arbitration. In arbitration, the aim of the exercise is to settle the dispute in as informal and inexpensive a way as possible. The parties are invited to attend a private, informal hearing, in which the strict court rules of procedure and evidence are set aside in favour of a more 'user-friendly' approach. The parties are allowed to use lawyers if they wish, but this is discouraged by a rule which prevents the winning party from claiming the costs of a lawyer from the losing party.

It is possible for parties to a dispute to ask the court voluntarily to refer the case to arbitration even though the amount claimed is more than £3,000. Similarly, it is possible for a reference to arbitration to be rescinded by the district judge, if the case is more suitable for consideration in the county court, perhaps because it contains a difficult point of law. Certain cases, for example claims for the possession of land, and personal injury cases over £1,000 in value, are not deemed suitable for small claims jurisdiction, and are dealt with according to the usual county court procedures.

3.4.6.2 The Woolf Report

The Civil Justice Review which took place under the chairmanship of Lord Woolf made a number of important recommendations with regard to the distribution of business in the Civil Courts.

These recommendations are likely to be implemented in 1999, and will result in changes to the procedures in the Civil Courts which are designed to reduce the amount of cost and delay involved in litigation. You will need to be aware (through the newspapers and other media) of the alterations which will be made to the information set out above.

3.4.7   MAGISTRATES' COURTS

■ **Sit in:** Local areas throughout England and Wales.

■ **Personnel:** Lay magistrates (i.e., volunteers with no legal qualifications who sit on the bench part-time) sometimes referred to as justices of the peace; stipendiary magistrates (who are full-time, paid and legally qualified); and justices' clerks (one for each bench of magistrates) who are legally qualified and who are employed to advise the lay magistrates on the relevant law and procedure in each case.

■ **Jurisdiction:** Civil and criminal law.

The magistrates' courts are local courts, hearing both civil and criminal cases at first instance. The civil cases that may be heard include the recovery of civil debts such as income tax, council tax, and gas and electricity charges, and the granting or renewing of liquor licences.

The most important part of the civil jurisdiction of the magistrates courts is with regard to family law. When sitting to hear such cases, the court is termed the 'family proceedings court' and it may hear cases concerning financial provision for a spouse or children, personal protection or exclusion orders, and adoption, residence and contact matters. Once again there is quite a degree of overlap here with the work of the county courts and the High Court.

Which of the following statements are true and which are false?

1   **The High Court (Family Division) is the only court which can authorise the adoption of a child.** TRUE/FALSE.

2   **A decree of divorce can be granted by the Family Division of the High Court, or by the county courts, or the magistrates' courts.** TRUE/FALSE.

3   **Where one party to a relationship is violent towards the other, this can be dealt with by the High Court, the county courts or the magistrates' courts.** TRUE/FALSE.

Jurisdiction in family cases is shared between the Family Division of the High Court, the county courts and the magistrates' courts. Many suggestions have been made as to how this overlap in jurisdiction might be rationalised, including the possibility of creating a separate, unified family court to deal with all family cases. One of the confusing aspects of the present arrangement is that although there is overlap between the three courts, the type of work they can do is not identical. This can be seen in the answers to the self assessment questions.

Question 1 contains a false statement. The High Court, the county courts and the magistrates' courts all have power to deal with adoption cases.

Question 2 is definitely a false statement. The Family Division of the High Court has full power to grant a decree of divorce in any case, and certain county courts may also deal with undefended divorces. Magistrates' courts do **not** have power to grant decrees of divorce.

The answer to question 3 if true, in that all three courts have ways of providing protection to applicants who are involved in a violent relationship.

3.5   Conclusion

Now that you have read this chapter, you should have an overview of the various courts which have jurisdiction in civil cases. You will be able to identify the names of the courts and the personnel involved, and it should also be possible for you to:

■   appreciate the significance of the Court of Justice of the European Communities and the relationship between this court and the English legal system;

■   compare the role of the Court of Appeal with that of the House of Lords and make a critical evaluation of the existence of these two appeal courts;

■   identify the overlap in jurisdiction which exists between a number of courts and discuss the desirability of this.

In **Chapter 4** you will undertake a similar exercise in respect of the courts which exercise jurisdiction in criminal cases.

3.6   Further Reading

Ingman, T., *The English Legal Process*, 6th edn, London: Blackstone Press, 1996, chapters 1, 2.

3.7   End of Chapter Assessment Question

It has been said that the organisation of business between the High Court, county courts and magistrates' courts creates anomalies, inefficiencies, and confusion.

Critically examine this statement and consider whether amalgamation of the three courts to create a single civil court would remove these difficulties.

See *Cases and Materials* (3.4) for a specimen answer.

CHAPTER FOUR

THE STRUCTURE AND JURISDICTION OF THE COURTS: CRIMINAL CASES

4.1 Objectives

On completion of this chapter you should be able to:

- give an account of the jurisdiction of the courts which may hear criminal cases;

- analyse the types of cases which can be dealt with by these courts;

- describe the way in which criminal offences are classified;

- identify the appropriate courts in which different types of case will be heard.

4.2 Introduction

The courts described below exercise jurisdiction in respect of cases involving criminal law. Some of these courts are also capable of exercising civil jurisdiction, and have therefore already been mentioned in **Chapter 3**. Where this is the case, the place of sitting and the personnel generally remain the same, and so this information has not been repeated. Learners often experience difficulty, at the beginning of their studies, first, in matching different types of cases to the appropriate courts, and secondly, in following the progress of cases through the hierarchy of courts. This chapter aims to give you some practice in the first of these skills, and the second skill will be tested in **Chapter 5**, when you have all the necessary information to do this properly.

You will need to refer to *Cases and Materials* in order to apply the knowledge which you will gain from the text and to see illustrations and examples of the information given.

4.3 The Court of Justice of the European Communities

In the same way that this court may be asked to give rulings concerning civil law, so references may be made to it for the interpretation of European Community law, where this involves criminal law.

4.4   The House of Lords

The House of Lords may hear appeals on matters of criminal law. These appeals may come either from the Court of Appeal (Criminal Division) or from the Divisional Court of the Queen's Bench Division. Certain conditions must be satisfied before the House of Lords can hear such appeals, and the details of this will be described in **Chapter 5**, which deals with the appeals system in greater depth.

4.5   The Judicial Committee of the Privy Council

In dealing with appeals from courts outside the United Kingdom, as already indicated, the business of this committee is mainly civil. The Committee will not grant special leave for an appeal to be heard in criminal cases, unless there are exceptional circumstances. Leave to appeal will only be granted if there has been a substantial injustice and the accused has been denied a fair trial.

For an example of an appeal to the Judicial Committee from Jamaica, see the extract from the case of *Pratt* v *Attorney-General for Jamaica* **[1993] 4 All ER 769 in** *Cases and Materials* **(4.1).**

Notice the names of the judges, which you will come to recognise as you encounter these names in cases decided by the House of Lords. Notice also (from the section headed 'Appeal') how special leave was required before an appeal could be made to the Judicial Committee from the Court of Appeal of Jamaica. You will appreciate, from reading the headnote and the first paragraph of the opinion of Lord Griffiths, why special leave was granted in this particular case.

4.6   The Court of Appeal (Criminal Division)

Originally, the Court of Appeal was created to hear civil cases only, but the Court of Criminal Appeal, as it was then known, was created in 1907, to hear appeals in criminal cases only. This court was replaced in 1966 by the Court of Appeal (Criminal Division) the name by which it is now known. The head of this court is the Lord Chief Justice. It has jurisdiction to hear appeals against sentence or conviction by persons convicted of offences at the Crown Court, but it does not deal with cases which have been heard by the Divisional Court of the Queen's Bench Division; these cases go direct to the House of Lords. Again you will understand this point more thoroughly when you have read **Chapter 5** on the appeal procedures in the court system.

The Attorney-General (the principal law officer of the Crown) may, on behalf of the Crown, also refer cases to the Criminal Division following a trial in the Crown Court, where the sentence appears to be unduly lenient, or where a person has been acquitted, but some clarification on a point of law is sought.

4.7   The High Court of Justice

4.7.1   THE DIVISIONAL COURT OF THE QUEEN'S BENCH DIVISION

You may find it odd to see the High Court mentioned here as it was dealt with in **Chapter 3** as a court which deals primarily with civil cases. However, as mentioned in **Chapter 3**, this court has jurisdiction in respect of offences which have been tried in the magistrates' courts, and an appeal has been made on a point of law by way of case stated.

ACTIVITY 16

Turn to *Cases and Materials* (4.2.1) and read the extract from the case of *Griffith* v *Jenkins* [1992] 1 All ER 65. As you will see, this was a relatively trivial case, which was considered by three different courts, the last of which was the House of Lords. From the initial hearing in the magistrates' court, an appeal was made by the prosecution to the Divisional Court of the Queen's Bench Division by way of case stated. Because of the difficulties which arose concerning the rehearing of the case, there was then an appeal to the House of Lords. Notice that in order to obtain a hearing before the House, it was necessary for leave (permission) to appeal to be obtained, and the court had to certify that a point of law of general public importance was involved in the case. You will find a further explanation of this in Chapter 5.

4.8 The Crown Court

■ **Important note:** Learners often confuse the names and the functions of the Crown Court and the county courts. Try to memorise now the fact that the **Crown Court** is a court which exercises **criminal** jurisdiction, whereas the **county courts** exercise **civil** jurisdiction.

■ **Sits in:** Court centres throughout England and Wales. The Crown Court in London is referred to as the Central Criminal Court (known popularly as the Old Bailey).

■ **Personnel:** All the judges of the High Court, circuit judges, recorders, and justices of the peace (who will sit with a judge drawn from one of the other categories).

A distinctive feature of the Crown Court is the use of the jury as part of the trial process. The jury consists of 12 men and women selected at random from the electoral register in accordance with statutory rules as to age, occupation and other qualifying characteristics. During a trial in the Crown Court, questions of law will be decided by the judge whereas the jury, with no legal knowledge or training, has the task of deciding questions of fact.

The participation of lay people in criminal trial procedure in this way is an old established feature of the system, but has frequently been criticised on the grounds of lack of suitability of jurors to try the guilt or innocence of another person.

■ **Jurisdiction:** The Crown Court is regarded as one single court which sits in various parts of the country. It was created to replace the previous system of Assizes and Quarter Sessions.

The Crown Court is the only court which has jurisdiction to hear all **trials on indictment** for offences wherever committed. It also hears appeals from persons convicted by way of **summary trial** in the magistrates' courts. It has power to sentence persons convicted by the magistrates, and it also has a small amount of civil jurisdiction, e.g., appeals in liquor licensing cases.

The terms **trial on indictment** and **summary trial** may be unfamiliar to you but it is important that you understand what they mean and that you become confident about using them.

Criminal offences are divided into three categories:

(a) **Offences triable only on indictment.** These are tried only in the Crown Court. These are the offences which are considered too serious to be dealt with by the magistrates' courts and must be heard by a judge and jury. Examples of indictable offences include murder, manslaughter and rape, serious offences against the person, e.g., causing grievous bodily harm with intent, and aggravated burglary. In the main, these are offences which were developed by the common law, rather than by statute. Indictable offences are themselves divided into four classes according to the gravity of the offence, and then matched to a judge of the appropriate status. Thus cases in classes 1 and 2 which include murder, treason and rape, are usually heard by a High Court judge with a jury. Cases in the other classes may be heard by a High Court judge, a circuit judge or a recorder, with a jury in every case.

(b) **Summary offences.** These are dealt with summarily (literally briefly, without a jury) by the magistrates' courts. These are less serious offences including many motoring offences under the Road Traffic Acts, taking a motor vehicle without consent and many other offences created by statute.

(c) **Offences triable either way.** These are crimes which can be tried **either** summarily by the magistrates, **or** on indictment, i.e., before a judge and jury in the Crown Court. They are often referred to as either way offences. They include less serious assaults, criminal damage in excess of £5,000, and many of the offences contained in the Theft Act 1968 but excluding, amongst other things, blackmail and certain burglaries.

An explanation of the way in which summary offences and either way offences are dealt with follows in the section on magistrates' courts (see **4.9**).

Consider the story which follows, and the questions based on it.

Mrs Smith claims that one day last year, she saw Dan point a gun in the direction of his girlfriend, and pull the trigger. The gun failed to fire because the mechanism was faulty, but Dan had not been aware of that until after he had pulled the trigger.

Dan is now being tried for the attempted murder of his girlfriend, under the provisions of the Criminal Attempts Act 1981. He claims that he did not point the gun in his girlfriend's direction as alleged and that Mrs Smith was mistaken or is lying. Secondly, he claims that the act of pointing a gun in this way is not legally capable of falling within the relevant section of the Act.

(1) Who decides whether Dan should be tried for this offence and by what procedure?

(2) In which court would this case be tried and by whom?

(3)   Who will decide whether either Dan or Mrs Smith is lying about what happened?

(4)   Who will decide whether Dan's alleged actions are capable as a matter of law of being within the ambit of the Criminal Attempts Act 1981?

As you will realise from the preceding sections of the text, in order to answer the questions set out above, it is necessary to decide how to classify the offence concerned. As Dan has been charged with attempted murder, this is an offence which is triable on indictment. It therefore falls to the magistrates' court to decide whether there is enough evidence for the case to proceed to trial.

Assuming that the magistrates find that the case should be tried, then the trial will take place in the Crown Court. As murder is a Class 1 offence, it will be heard by a High Court judge with a jury. It is the task of the jury to decide questions of fact, and it is therefore for the jury to determine whether the events really took place as the witness described, or whether Dan is to be believed in preference to Mrs Smith. The legal question, of whether the actions described can be regarded as falling within the wording of the legislation, is for the judge to resolve.

4.9   Magistrates' Courts

In addition to their work in civil cases (described in **Chapter 3**) the magistrates' courts deal with a vast quantity of criminal cases: 98% of all criminal cases are tried summarily by these courts. Magistrates have jurisdiction in respect of **summary offences, either way offences,** and they also have the task of carrying out a preliminary examination of every case in which a person is accused of an **indictable offence.** It is this aspect of the magistrates' work which will be described first.

4.9.1   INDICTABLE OFFENCES

Magistrates undertake a preliminary hearing of most cases where the defendant is charged with an offence triable on indictment. These proceedings are known as **committal proceedings,** in which the magistrates are designated examining justices. The aim of committal proceedings is for the magistrates to establish whether, on a preliminary examination of the evidence, there is a case for the accused to answer.

Originally, committal proceedings involved the witnesses giving evidence in person before the court, i.e., an 'old style committal'. This proved costly, time consuming, and traumatic for the witnesses however, and so a new procedure (the 'paper committal') was developed as an alternative. This simply involved the magistrates making the decision to commit the case to the Crown Court or to discharge it, on the basis of written witness statements.

The Criminal Procedure and Investigations Act 1996 has in effect abolished 'old-style' committals so that in all committal proceedings, evidence is limited to written statements and depositions, and witnesses are not called to give evidence. It is hoped that this will avoid unnecessary time and expense being wasted at this stage of the case.

4.9.2 SUMMARY OFFENCES

Summary offences are dealt with only by the magistrates' courts. Offenders are not entitled to trial by jury in respect of these offences. There are literally hundreds of offences which are triable summarily only, many of them being motoring offences under the Road Traffic Acts. To avoid the court system being totally overwhelmed by minor speeding or parking cases, it is possible for defendants to choose not to appear at court but to plead guilty by post.

Because of the less serious nature of these offences, the magistrates are restricted in the type of sentence which they can impose. Thus an offender can only be given a maximum of six months' imprisonment in respect of a summary offence. Similarly, the magistrates can only impose a fine of £1,000 in respect of summary offences, or such amount as is specified in the statute creating the offence, whichever is higher, up to an overall limit of £5,000.

The magistrates also have power to compensate victims of crime, by ordering a convicted person to pay an amount (again up to £5,000) to the victim of the crime.

4.9.3 OFFENCES TRIABLE EITHER WAY

The third category of offences with which magistates may deal is the group of offences known as 'either way' offences.

The magistrates' court must decide whether the case is more suitable for summary trial in which case it will then deal with the offender itself, or whether the case must be remitted to the Crown Court. To assist the magistrates in their decision-making, in 1990 the Lord Chief Justice produced a Practice Note containing the national mode of trial guidelines which were then amended in 1995. These guidelines require the magistrates to presume that any 'either way' offence should be tried summarily unless there are specified features which make it more suitable for trial by jury, e.g., if an offence is one of a series of similar offences, or if a burglary appears to bear professional hallmarks, or there has been deliberate vandalism. If one or more of these features is present and the magistrates' sentencing powers are considered insufficient for the case, then it can be sent for trial on indictment, after it has been through the transfer for trial procedure.

One interesting feature of this type of offence is that the accused does have the opportunity to express a preference as to mode of trial. Thus if an accused person wishes the case to be dealt with by a judge and jury (and many do so, believing there to be more chance of an acquittal) then he or she can insist on the case being tried on indictment, regardless of the magistrates' opinion as to the suitability of the case for this mode of trial. However, if the magistrates consider that trial on indictment is the most appropriate method, and the accused wishes to choose summary trial, it is the magistrates' view that will prevail: an accused person cannot insist on summary trial. Perhaps a more appropriate title for these offences would therefore be offences triable summarily with the consent of the accused.

You will need to consult *Cases and Materials* (3.1) during the course of studying this chapter. In particular, you may wish to refer to the two diagrams of the court system in order to see how cases move between the different courts.

5.3.1 MAGISTRATES' COURTS

Appeals from the magistrates' courts in family proceedings (the Family Proceedings Court) go to the Divisional Court of the Family Division of the High Court. The Divisional Court has considerable discretion to receive further evidence and to make any order which the court thinks appropriate in the circumstances. From the Divisional Court, cases which began in the Family Proceedings Court follow the same route for appeal as other cases determined by the High Court (see 5.3.3).

5.3.2 COUNTY COURTS

You would probably expect appeals from the county court to lie to the court immediately above in the hierarchy, i.e., the High Court. You may be surprised to learn that in most cases this is not how the appeal system works. The general rule is that an appeal from the decision of a county court judge lies to the Court of Appeal (Civil Division). There are a number of exceptions, however, where this general rule does not apply, and it makes sense to deal with these first.

Where a case has been heard by a district judge, then an appeal lies to the circuit judge in the county court. No further appeal is possible after that, unless leave (permission) to appeal is obtained from either the county court or the Court of Appeal.

Appeals in respect of insolvency matters go to a single judge of the Chancery Division of the High Court.

In all other cases, appeals in respect of proceedings in the county court lie to the Court of Appeal (Civil Division). This does not mean that there is an automatic right to appeal in every case. In a number of cases, there can be no appeal at all unless leave (permission) to appeal is first obtained either from the county court, or from the Court of Appeal. For example, leave to appeal will have to be obtained in order to contest a county court decision in respect of possession of land, or where the value of the claim does not exceed £5,000 in contract and tort cases.

Imagine you have a friend who has a claim against a shop for selling faulty goods. The amount of the claim is £2,500. At the hearing in the county court, the judge finds in favour of the shop and your friend wishes to appeal to the Court of Appeal (Civil Division). You tell your friend that unless leave is granted for the case to be taken further, there will be no opportunity to appeal, but that if the claim were for £6,000, then there would be a right to appeal. Your friend asks you to justify this.

The opportunity to appeal from a decision of the county court has always been limited to some degree. In fact up to 1981, in cases where the amount in dispute was less than £200, if the ground of appeal was a dispute about the facts, then no appeal at all was possible. Gradually this rule has been relaxed, but clearly the scope for appeal is still restricted by the requirement for leave to be given in a number of cases. Your friend's case falls within this category. It was suggested in **5.3** that rules such as this may seem harsh. But as you will discover in the course of learning about the law, time and money are factors which are given a great deal of weight when decisions are made about the handling of litigation. In order to avoid the courts being overwhelmed by appeals which may not succeed, and to avoid expense for the parties involved and for the court system, access to the appeal courts has to be closely monitored and guarded. Where the value of the claim exceeds £5,000, then it is more likely to be worthwhile for the parties to pursue the case to the Court of Appeal, and no leave is required. But in a claim such as that of your friend, it may be that any damages recovered could be swallowed up by the costs, and if the appeal fails this will have been a waste of time both for your friend and for the court.

5.3.3   THE HIGH COURT

Appeals from all three divisions of the High Court and their Divisional Courts lie to the Court of Appeal (Civil Division). In some cases, for example orders made with the consent of the parties and orders concerning possession of land, leave to appeal will be required, either from the High Court or the Court of Appeal. You should pay particular attention here to one very significant category of case in which leave to appeal is necessary. This is where a case which began in a lower court has been considered by a Divisional Court acting in its appellate capacity. If one of the parties wishes to make a further appeal then the permission of either the High Court or the Court of Appeal must be sought.

Appeals to the Court of Appeal are not re-trials: no witnesses are called to give evidence in person. The hearing will be based on the transcripts from the original trial, and on the points of law or fact in dispute at this stage.

There is also an alternative route for appeals from the High Court, although this is rarely used. Known as the 'leapfrog' procedure, this means that appeal cases can be taken directly from the High Court to the House of Lords, provided that certain conditions are satisfied.

In *Cases and Materials* (5.1.1) you will find ss. 12 and 13 of the Administration of Justice Act 1969 concerning leapfrog appeals. Make a list of the conditions which must be satisfied before this procedure can be used. You will find that it is quite complex. Check your list with that given in *Cases and Materials* at 5.1.1.

5.3.4 THE COURT OF APPEAL (CIVIL DIVISION)

Appeals from decisions of the Court of Appeal lie to the House of Lords, but in order to limit the workload of the Law Lords, leave to appeal must be given by one of these courts. There are also certain classes of cases in which any further appeal from the Court of Appeal is prohibited by statute, e.g., an appeal from a county court in probate proceedings.

In all other cases, an appellant may seek leave to appeal from the Court of Appeal and if this is refused, he or she is free to apply to the Appeal Committee of the House of Lords for permission. Appeals may be based on questions of law or fact, although they are usually concerned with matters of law.

5.3.5 THE HOUSE OF LORDS

Appeals to the House of Lords in civil matters usually concern questions of law, although appeals on questions of fact are possible. Generally speaking the House of Lords will only hear appeals involving matters of general public importance, although this is not a statutory requirement, in contrast to criminal cases (see **5.4.2**). Where a case does involve an issue which is of general public importance, this will increase the likelihood of leave to appeal being granted.

5.4 Appeals in Criminal Cases

The system of appeals in criminal cases has been the subject of considerable discussion and criticism in recent years. One reason for this has been the emergence of cases where serious miscarriages of justice have occurred, resulting in the imprisonment of a number of people for crimes which they did not commit.

Partly as a result of such cases, the criminal justice system has been the subject of a Royal Commission which reported in 1993 (the Runciman Commission) and which made a number of recommendations for improvement, some but not all of which have been adopted in the Criminal Justice and Public Order Act 1994. More far-reaching changes have been made by the Criminal Appeal Act 1995, which was enacted as a result of the recommendations of the Royal Commission on Criminal Justice.

There are various routes for appeal in criminal cases, but what must be borne in mind is that **the mode of appeal is always governed by the place of original trial**. This means that if a case was originally tried in the magistrates' court, then the route which an appeal will take will differ from that taken by a case which has been tried before judge and jury in the Crown Court.

5.4.1 APPEALS FOLLOWING SUMMARY TRIAL

The route for an appeal against a decision of the magistrates in a criminal case is initially **either** to the Crown Court **or** to the Divisional Court of the Queen's Bench Division of the High Court.

5.4.1.1 The Crown Court

The defendant may appeal to the Crown Court concerning a question of fact or law, i.e., he or she may dispute either the evidence or a decision on a point of law or both. The prosecution does not, as a general rule, have a right of appeal from the magistrates' court to the Crown Court.

If the defendant pleaded not guilty before the magistrates, then there is a right of appeal against conviction or sentence or both. However, if the defendant originally pleaded guilty, then there is no appeal against conviction, only against sentence.

The appeal will take the form of a complete rehearing with witnesses but without a jury, and the Crown Court may vary the original decision, or confirm it, and has the power to increase the sentence given by the magistrates.

By way of further appeal, either the prosecution or the defence may require the Crown Court to state a case for the opinion of the High Court as described in **5.4.1.2**.

5.4.1.2   The Divisional Court of the Queen's Bench Division

Both prosecution and defence have the right to appeal from the magistrates' court to the Divisional Court, but only on the grounds that the magistrates' decision was wrong in law or that they exceeded their jurisdiction by making an order which was outside their powers.

This is not a rehearing of the case with witnesses; instead, the magistrates 'state the case' in writing and the court works from these written documents. This procedure is known as an appeal 'by way of case stated'. The Divisional Court may confirm, or alter the magistrates' decision. If the prosecution wins the case at this stage, the Divisional Court can direct the magistrates to convict and pass sentence on the defendant.

Further appeal by either party is possible, from the Divisional Court direct to the House of Lords. However, before the House of Lords will hear such an appeal, the Divisional Court must certify that a point of law of general public importance is involved, **and** leave to appeal must be obtained from either court, as required by s. 1 of the Administration of Justice Act 1960.

SAQ 15

Look carefully at the respective rights of the prosecution and the defence to appeal in criminal cases which have been tried summarily, and notice how these vary. Which of the parties has the greater opportunity to challenge decisions of the lower courts?

As you may have gathered, the prosecution and the defence do not have equal rights to appeal against decisions which are adverse to them, in cases which are triable summarily. The defendant is permitted to appeal from a decision of the magistrates' court to the Crown Court, but no such possibility exists for the prosecution. With regard to the other avenues of appeal described above, the parties have the same opportunities as each other, but it does mean that if the prosecution wishes to dispute a decision of the magistrates, then this can only be done by the case stated procedure, on a point of law.

5.4.2 APPEAL FOLLOWING TRIAL ON INDICTMENT

From decisions of the Crown Court, appeal lies to the Court of Appeal (Criminal Division).

Under the Criminal Appeal Act 1968, when a person had been convicted of an offence by a judge and jury in the Crown Court, then there were important differences between the rules concerning appeal against sentence and appeal against conviction, and between appeals based on questions of law, and those based on questions of fact. The defendant had the *right* to appeal against *conviction* where the ground for appeal was a *question of law*. But if the defendant wished to appeal against conviction on a *question of fact* (or mixed law and fact), then *leave* to appeal had to be obtained, or a certificate had to be supplied by the trial judge stating that the case was fit for appeal. It was therefore much easier for a defendant to appeal against a conviction on a point of law, than if the ground of appeal was a question of fact.

This difference between the two types of appeal has been abolished by the Criminal Appeal Act 1995. The requirement of leave to appeal (or a certificate by the trial judge) will apply to all appeals against conviction.

The rules concerning appeal against sentence remain the same following the Criminal Appeal Act 1995. If the defendant accepts the fact of conviction, but wishes to appeal against *sentence*, then *leave* to appeal, or the certificate of the trial judge, must be obtained in every case. When appeal against sentence is made to the Court of Appeal (Criminal Division), the court can vary the sentence, although it cannot increase it. (But see below on the court's power to increase sentence on an appeal by the prosecution.)

There are a number of reasons for these restrictions on the defendant's right to appeal against the outcome of a trial. You will recall that, on a number of occasions in the text, your attention has been drawn to the fact that a balance has to be struck between ensuring that the liberty of the individual is protected and that people are not wrongly convicted of offences, and ensuring that the appeal system is not so overloaded that injustice results from the long waiting period for appeals to be heard.

Probably most of the defendants who are convicted of indictable offences would wish to argue that the jury's finding of fact was wrong and appeal on this basis. But there is a reluctance on the part of the Court of Appeal to question the facts as found by the jury, and so this avenue of appeal is restricted by the requirement of leave. Similarly, many defendants would probably wish to argue that their sentence should not be so severe, and so the possibility of appeal against sentence is limited, in order to ensure that only meritorious appeals reach the Court of Appeal.

From the Court of Appeal, further appeal by the defendant to the House of Lords is possible, but again there are statutory requirements which must be met before the House of Lords will hear such appeals. These are contained in the Criminal Appeal Act 1968. Section 33 of that Act stipulates that an appeal will only lie to the House of Lords if the Court of Appeal certifies that the case involves a point of law of general public importance **and** it appears that the point is one which ought to be considered by the House of Lords **and** either the Court of Appeal or House of Lords gives leave for the appeal to proceed.

Compare the rules concerning appeals from the Court of Appeal to the House of Lords in civil cases with the rules which apply in criminal cases. What significant difference do you see between the two sets of rules?

There is what may seem to be a rather anomalous difference between appeals in these cases, in that in civil cases, there is no statutory requirement that the case involve a question of general public importance, whereas this is a prerequisite for criminal cases. In practice, it is likely that only those civil cases which do contain a point of law of general public importance will be heard by the House of Lords, but the technical difference is still there.

The prosecution has limited rights to dispute the outcome of a case. The Criminal Justice Act 1988 provides that the Attorney-General has discretion to refer an unduly lenient sentence to the Court of Appeal and that the Court of Appeal may then increase that sentence. The prosecution can also refer a point of law to the Court of Appeal for clarification, following an acquittal, but this will not affect the validity of the acquittal in any way. This power is contained in the Criminal Justice Act 1972.

5.4.3 POWERS OF THE COURT OF APPEAL (CRIMINAL DIVISION)

The powers of the Court of Appeal are carefully prescribed by statute. The Criminal Appeal Act 1968 provided three different categories of cases in which the court must allow an appeal against conviction, as follows:

(1) where the Court of Appeal thinks that the decision of the jury was unsafe or unsatisfactory, for example, if fabricated evidence was produced in court or if the trial judge had misdirected the jury;

(2) where there was a wrong decision on a question of law, that is where the trial judge made an error on a point of law;

(3) where there was a material irregularity in the course of the trial, for example, if the trial judge exercised his or her discretion wrongly in discharging a juror for insufficient reason.

In cases which came within these three categories, the Court of Appeal was bound to allow the appeal and quash the conviction.

The Royal Commission on Criminal Justice was of the opinion that these three categories were unsatisfactory. The wording was imprecise, and there seemed to be some overlap between them. The Criminal Appeal Act 1995 therefore abolishes these three categories and replaces them with one ground only. This provides that the Court of Appeal shall allow an appeal against conviction if they think that the conviction is unsafe, and in all other cases, the appeal must be dismissed.

The Court of Appeal also has power to receive fresh evidence which has emerged since the case was determined, and which was not available at the original trial. This may result in the defendant's conviction being quashed, or the court may simply uphold the original decision. Finally the Court of Appeal may order a retrial of the case before a different jury in appropriate circumstances.

5.5 Section 17, Criminal Appeal Act 1968; Sections 3 and 8, Criminal Appeal Act 1995

When all other avenues of appeal were exhausted, a person convicted on indictment could invoke s. 17 of the Criminal Appeal Act 1968. This section empowered the Home Secretary to refer cases back to the Court of Appeal for review. In practice this procedure was restricted to cases in which fresh evidence had been discovered. There was much criticism of this particular provision, relying as it did on the persistence of the appellant and on the discretion of the Home Secretary. Consequently, the Criminal Appeal Act 1995 repeals this section, and replaces the provision with the creation of a new statutory body, the Criminal Cases Review Commission. The Commission will act as an independent review body, able to investigate alleged miscarriages of justice, and refer cases back to the court of trial to be re-heard.

A friend has been convicted of a criminal offence and asks you to which court or courts he will have to appeal in order to challenge the conviction. What is the first question you will have to ask him before you can give your reply to this question?

It will have become apparent to you in your study of the criminal justice system that cases which have been tried summarily, and cases which have been tried on indictment, are dealt with in very different ways by the courts. Your first question, therefore, to any person intending to appeal against the decision of a trial court would concern the place of original trial. As you may remember from the beginning of this section, it is the place of original trial which determines the mode of appeal, and therefore once this is ascertained, you will be able to advise your friend as to the appropriate route for the appeal.

5.6   Conclusion

Now that you have studied **Chapters 1** to **5**, together with the relevant sections of the *Cases and Materials*, you should be well acquainted with the different courts which make up the English legal system and with the ways in which these courts deal with different types of cases. In particular from this chapter you should be able to:

■   distinguish between the courts which deal with appeals in civil cases and those which deal with appeals in criminal cases;

■   comment on the availability of access to the appeal courts in different cases;

■   discuss the reasons for the preconditions which exist to determine whether a case may proceed to appeal stage;

■   chart the progress of a case through the appeal system.

5.7   Further Reading

Ingman, T., *The English Legal Process*, 6th edn, London: Blackstone Press, 1996, Chapter 6.

5.8   End of Chapter Assessment Question

Turn to *Cases and Materials* (**5.1.1**) where you will find extracts from the following two cases:

(1)   *Pepper* v *Hart* [1993] 1 All ER 42; and

(2)   *R* v *R* [1991] 4 All ER 481.

For both of these cases, describe the route by which these cases progressed through the court system, from the first hearing to the final appeal. Include as much relevant information as possible from the report, i.e., dates and places of hearings and names of judges.

See *Cases and Materials* (**5.2**) for a specimen answer.

(b)   What do you think is the point of the Bar student having to dine at the Inn to which he or she belongs?

(c)   How do you suppose Bar students support themselves during the training period?

As you may have realised by now, barristers form a quite exclusive group, with their own rules of conduct and very ancient traditions, and to gain entry to this group is not easy. Their professional rules prohibit them from forming partnerships, but from an economic point of view, it obviously makes sense for them to share expensive resources, such as premises and library facilities – hence the formation of sets of chambers.

Because of the need for students to become acquainted with the customs and etiquette of the Bar, the requirement that they keep terms by dining at their chosen Inn for a specified number of times helps them to discover how the Inns work and the type of conduct which is expected. This does, however, involve a certain amount of expense in addition to the fees required for attending Bar School. Although a limited number of scholarships and bursaries are available, students generally have to support themselves, usually by means of loans, during their training period. This situation is aggravated by the fact that the newly qualified barrister is restricted in his or her earning capacity during the first six months of pupillage, so potential barristers require a great deal of determination and a reliable source of financial support if they are to survive their training.

6.3.1.3   Type of work

If asked to describe the work which a barrister does, most people would think of a man or woman in gown and wig, using their skills of advocacy in the courtroom. However, this is not their only work, for they also spend a lot of time researching points of law and giving advice to solicitors (known as 'counsel's opinion'). Historically, barristers have had a complete monopoly over rights of audience in the higher courts. This situation has been challenged repeatedly in recent years, by solicitors who feel that they have sufficient advocacy skills to represent their clients in court. You will learn more about this in **6.3.2** on the work of solicitors.

Another striking feature about the way in which they work is that with few exceptions, barristers are only permitted to take instruction from 'professional clients', a term which is carefully defined by the Bar Code of Conduct. In practice this means they receive instructions through the medium of a solicitor (or perhaps, for example, an accountant) and are not approached directly by the individual who needs their services. In June 1998, however, the Lord Chancellor published a consultation paper which suggested that the public should be allowed direct access to barristers in order to instruct them, without using a solicitor as an intermediary.

SAQ 19

What do you think might be the advantages and disadvantages of the public being able to make direct contact with barristers?

One of the great advantages from the point of view of the client in allowing immediate access to the barrister is that this might reduce the costs of litigation. Instead of having to pay a solicitor to instruct a barrister, the client can seek the advice of the barrister direct and cut out the 'middle man'. A disadvantage is that the client will not have the experience to select the most appropriate chambers from which to seek advice. From the barristers' point of view, such a change in their professional conduct would require them to make corresponding changes in the organisation of chambers in order to cope with the extra paperwork involved when clients are dealt with direct.

Barristers who achieve prominence through their success at the Bar are eligible to 'take silk', that is to become a Queen's Counsel. All barristers who are not 'silks' are known as junior barristers, and a number of them apply each year to be made QC. Once a barrister has taken silk, he or she will probably be instructed for more weighty cases, and will usually appear accompanied by a junior barrister who will share the work of the case. It is from the ranks of the QCs that most High Court judges are appointed, and so further promotion is possible for those who take silk.

6.3.2 SOLICITORS

The division of the legal profession into two separate branches has its roots in history. But although it can result in duplication of effort, increased cost, and sometimes confusion for the general public, suggestions that there should be fusion of the two branches have never been accepted by the profession.

6.3.2.1 Organisation

The Law Society is the governing body for solicitors, influencing all aspects of training, professional conduct and the organisation of the profession. Numerically solicitors form a much larger body than barristers and are much more accessible, solicitors' offices being found in the high streets of every town. Solicitors are also permitted to advertise their services (within the limits of the professional rules), and this enables potential clients to select a practitioner with experience of their particular legal problem.

A solicitor can choose to work alone as a sole practitioner in their own firm, but most work in partnerships with each other in private practice, offering their services to the general public. A much smaller number are employed in industry, or local or central government.

6.3.2.2 Training

As with barristers, most solicitors are law graduates, or graduates of another discipline who have undertaken a conversion course in law. They must complete a one year course of study (the Legal Practice course) which prepares them for the practical aspects of the work, and then serve a prescribed period of 'articles' (usually two years) attached to a practising solicitor. At this stage, the trainee solicitor is in effect serving an apprentice-ship. Unlike barristers, however, the trainee will be salaried during the term of articles, and although obtaining these training contracts is not easy, because there are far more solicitors' offices than barristers' chambers, more places are available.

6.3.2.3 Type of work

Solicitors are largely occupied in providing legal services to clients on a face-to-face basis, or by telephone or letter. Unlike barristers, they have direct personal contact with clients, and therefore need to employ many personnel to assist in providing this public service.

Increasingly, solicitors tend to specialise in their work in order to gain expertise in particular areas of the law. Within a firm in private practice therefore, you may find different departments specialising in, for example, criminal matters, family law, probate (i.e. dealing with the property of those who have died) land law matters and civil cases such as personal injuries. In the past, solicitors enjoyed a complete monopoly in matters of conveyancing (i.e. transferring ownership of land from one person to another) but in 1985, a significant change occurred. A system of licensed conveyancers was introduced, which allowed non-solicitors to carry out conveyancing work for members of the public, for a fee.

Turn to *Cases and Materials* (6.1) and read sections 17 and 37 of the Courts and Legal Services Act 1990, and consider the following questions:

(a) **What was the purpose of this legislation?**

(b) **What are the implications for the legal profession?**

(c) **In authorising persons to provide conveyancing services, what does it appear were the concerns of the Authorised Conveyancing Practitioners Board (referred to in s. 37(1))?**

As long ago as 1979, the Benson Commission on Legal Services had raised questions about the monopolies which barristers and solicitors enjoyed in court and in conveyancing respectively. As a result, the solicitors' monopoly over conveyancing was broken in 1985, and in 1990, the Courts and Legal Services Act was introduced with the specific aim of developing and improving the way in which legal services were offered to the public. Section 17(1) made it clear that the Act was an attempt to strike a balance between the desire to ensure that justice was administered properly, and the wish to allow people other than members of the two branch profession to carry out some of the work which had hitherto been reserved for barristers and solicitors alone. This meant that for the very first time, the profession was faced with competition for its clients. The hope of those drafting the legislation was that this element of competition would lead to better services being offered to the public, for realistic fees.

It was of course important to ensure that non-solicitors involved in conveyancing work would be suitably qualified, accountable, and insured against the risk of loss to clients. This was the purpose of the rules set out in s. 37.

The Benson Commission had recommended that no change should be made in the rights of audience in the courts, but this position continued to be challenged by the solicitors' branch of the profession. Solicitors who particularly wished to undertake advocacy work did exercise their rights of audience in the magistrates' court, and to a lesser extent in the county court. But the fact that, for example, a case which a solicitor had carefully prepared for a client had to be handed over to a barrister who would be less acquainted with it, for presentation in the Crown Court, caused great frustration to those solicitors who felt that they could have adequately undertaken the advocacy themselves. As a result the Courts and Legal Services Act 1990 introduced some radical changes to the rights of audience rules.

In *Cases and Materials* (6.1) s. 27 of the Courts and Legal Services Act 1990 is set out. Read through this section, and then decide whether the following statements are true or false.

(a) The Courts and Legal Services Act 1990 changes all the previous rights of audience enjoyed by the legal profession. True or false?

(b) Rights of audience can be granted by the court itself, by the general Council of the Bar, by the Law Society, or by any other authorised body under the Act. True or false?

(c) Those who wish to have rights of audience in court must have obtained certain qualifications and comply with an approved code of conduct. True or false?

The aim of the Courts and Legal Services Act 1990 was to preserve the existing rights of audience of barristers and solicitors, whilst making it possible for new rights to be granted and obtained. It is therefore not true to say that the Act changed all previous rights of audience ((a)). Those that already existed remained, but the potential for other people to acquire these rights was recognised.

The Act also established the fact that rights of audience would continue to be granted by an appropriate 'authorised body', which includes the Law Society and the General Council of the Bar, so the statement at (b) is correct. In order to obtain these rights, the person must be appropriately qualified as is indicated in s. 27(a). Statement (c) is therefore also correct.

The most radical part of the Act was the provision for the extension of rights of audience, and in December 1993, the Law Society finally gained the approval required by the Act to allow solicitors in private practice to act as advocates for their clients in the higher courts. A practising solicitor who can demonstrate that he or she is suitably qualified and experienced in advocacy work can apply for certification as a solicitor-advocate, and will then be able to represent his or her clients not only in the magistrates' courts, but also in the Crown Court and in the county courts and the High Court. Further reforms are to follow, as the proposed Modernisation of Justice Bill to be introduced to Parliament in late 1998 will provide that solicitors and barristers will both acquire full rights of audience before all courts, on their qualification. It is too soon to predict what the long term consequences of this change will be, but it raises the possibility that barristers will lose work to solicitor-advocates, and that the Bar will become a much smaller body as a result.

6.4   Paying for Legal Services

It has for many years been recognised that the cost involved in consulting a barrister or solicitor can be prohibitive, and is one of the factors which discourage members of the public from seeking legal advice. This is particularly true of litigation cases, such as personal injury cases, in which the legal costs can be considerable, the outcome of the case may not be certain, and the loser has to pay the costs of the successful opponent as well as his or her own.

Legal Aid in one form or another has been available since the Second World War, to enable those on limited incomes to have access to legal help. But the strict conditions under which it is granted have meant that there is a considerable number of people who may have a genuine legal claim which they are unable to pursue, but are neither eligible for legal aid nor wealthy enough to meet the potential legal costs from their own resources.

How can people who fall in this 'middle income, not eligible for legal aid' trap obtain access to justice?

From your general knowledge, make a list of the different methods of which you are aware which might enable members of the public to be assisted in the payment of their legal costs.

Once you start to think about this question, you will probably find that you know about more schemes of this nature than you thought you did. For example, help with legal matters is often offered by trades unions or by motoring associations to their respective members. It is also possible to obtain insurance to cover legal expenses. Policies are available which enable the insured person to insure against legal costs up to a certain limit in prescribed categories of cases.

Of a more controversial nature are the arrangements which it is now possible for clients to make with their solicitors which are sometimes referred to as 'no win no fee' case arrangements. It seems that these agreements may be of significance to lawyers and their clients in the future, and so they merit closer examination. These agreements are designed for use in contentious cases, that is, legal disputes between parties, which may lead to court proceedings.

6.4.1 CONDITIONAL FEE AGREEMENTS AND CONTINGENCY FEE AGREEMENTS

Although these two terms are sometimes used interchangeably in the textbooks, there are subtle differences between the two types of agreement, and the legal profession treats them differently in practice. The underlying theory is the same, however: that the solicitor undertakes to carry out work for a client on the basis that no fee is payable if the case is lost, but if the client is successful in litigation then the solicitor obtains his or her costs.

Until this century, agreements of this nature have always been regarded as being against public policy because, in effect, they give the lawyer a financial stake in his or her client's litigation which could create a conflict of interest for the solicitor. However, given the rising costs of litigation and the increasing difficulty in obtaining legal aid, it has been recognised that agreements of this nature enable clients to pursue legal claims for which they could not pay by any other means, so giving access to justice which would be denied to them otherwise.

The first type of agreement of this nature to be sanctioned by law was the **conditional fee agreement**.

At *Cases and Materials* (6.2.1) you will find an extract from s. 58 of the Courts and Legal Services Act 1990. Read the section provided and then answer the following questions:

(a) In what type of cases may conditional fee agreements *not* be made?

(b) What format must the parties use for such an agreement?

(c) How will the client know how much money the solicitor will be allowed to claim if the conditions for payment are satisfied?

The success of conditional fee agreements depends upon the client recovering sufficient money from the litigation with which to pay the solicitor's costs and so it is inappropriate for such agreements to be made in cases where no damages are payable. Section 58(10) of the Courts and Legal Services Act 1990 therefore expressly excludes a number of types of cases from the operation of such agreements. These are cases concerned with divorce and other matrimonial matters, domestic violence cases, and cases involving children such as adoption cases. You may have noticed from s. 58(1) of the Act that before conditional fee agreements could be used by the legal profession, it was necessary for the Lord Chancellor to prescribe certain rules which were to be observed in all cases. The current rules issued by the Lord Chancellor permit conditional fee agreements to be used only in personal injury cases, insolvency cases, and matters involving the European Court of Human Rights.

Conditional fee agreements must also comply with the requirements of s. 58(1) by being in written form, stating the circumstances in which the legal fees will be payable, and specifying the percentage by which the standard fees will be increased in the event of successful litigation. This latter point is a significant feature of this type of arrangement, and the percentage 'uplift' on the fees must be stated in this way so that the client is aware of how much more they may be required to pay as a result of using this method. The Lord Chancellor has provided that the allowable uplift on fees is 100%, and thus solicitors may agree with their clients that the client will pay no fee to the solicitor if the case is lost, but will be liable to pay double the standard fee if the litigation is successful.

Conditional fee agreements are not to be used in cases in which a client has been granted legal aid. Given the proposed withdrawal of legal aid in personal injury cases, and the possibility of the extension of conditional fee agreements to all civil non-family cases, it would seem that conditional fee agreements and contingency fee agreements may replace legal aid in this type of litigation.

Contingency fee agreements are not at present covered by any statutory framework and therefore operate on a different basis to conditional fee agreements. In fact until very recently, contingency fee agreements remained unlawful despite the legalisation of conditional fees. The case of *Thai Trading Co. (a firm)* v *Taylor and another* [1998] 3 All ER 65 (which can be found in *Cases and Materials* (**6.2.1**)) established that agreements which did not comply with s. 58(1) of the Courts and Legal Services Act 1990 and therefore did not qualify as conditional fee agreements, might nevertheless be valid as contingency fee agreements.

In order for this agreement to be acceptable for the court, however, it appears from the judgment that the solicitor must seek no more than his or her ordinary profit costs if the case is won. The solicitor may therefore agree to undertake litigation (other than personal injury litigation) on the basis that no fee will be payable if the case is lost, but the normal fees can be recovered from the client if the case is won.

The arrangements for payment of legal fees discussed in the previous sections have largely been concerned with the funding of legal services by private means. As indicated earlier, however, it is possible in some cases to gain assistance from public funds in order to obtain legal aid and advice, and these methods will be discussed next.

6.4.2   THE PUBLIC FUNDING OF LEGAL CASES

The concept of making public funds available in order that people of limited financial means might have access to legal services is not new, the legal aid system being introduced after the Second World War in parallel with the National Health Service. As with the Health Service, however, it soon became apparent that demand for such services would increase far beyond the expectations of the founders of the scheme, and since the 1980's, attempts have been made by the Government to reduce the cost of legal aid, largely by severely limiting its availability.

Although legal aid is a convenient term to use in this discussion, you should distinguish carefully between legal aid which is granted to assist parties involved in litigation, and Legal Aid and Advice (often referred to as the Green Form scheme) which is the provision of legal assistance to clients in non-contentious matters.

The Green Form scheme has been used extensively in private practice, particularly for undefended matrimonial cases. It is means tested, so that only the poorest clients gain free advice, all others having to pay a contribution to the cost of the advice on a sliding scale according to their means. In return the client receives advice from the solicitor, limited to two hours of his or her time.

At the time of writing, however, the scheme is under attack because of the vast cost of operating it. Undefended divorces have been removed from its scope, and the Legal Aid Board, which is ultimately responsible for the provision of funds for legal services, appears to be in favour of replacing it with a system of contracting out legal advice and assistance work to a limited number of firms of solicitors. Time will tell whether this proposal will prove acceptable to the legal profession.

For the client with a civil matter which will involve court work, civil legal aid is available to those who can satisfy both a means test and a merits test, which is administered by the Legal Aid Board. Again, only the poorest can obtain free legal aid, all others being assessed to pay a contribution. As has already been noted, eligibility for legal aid has decreased markedly in the past 20 years, thus leaving a large number of people with income and capital in excess of the legal aid financial limits, but insufficient to meet the potential cost of litigation.

Legal aid is also available to defendants in criminal cases and a means test and a merits test are imposed before financial help is given. In criminal cases, however, the grant of legal aid is in the hands of the court clerk.

6.5   Alternative Means of Resolving Legal Disputes

Given the cost of conducting litigation, the uncertainty of the outcome of court cases, and the long periods of delay which can be involved, some clients and their legal advisers have begun to look to other ways of resolving legal arguments, rather than commencing court proceedings. In the final part of this chapter, we will consider methods of **alternative dispute resolution (ADR)** as it is known, beginning with the method which has been established the longest, that is, arbitration.

6.5.1   ARBITRATION

You have already encountered the concept of arbitration in **Chapter 3** when the work of the county court was discussed. However, the type of arbitration you are going to learn about in this section has a totally different basis to the automatic references to arbitration which you read about earlier. Arbitration in the county court is a process which can be imposed upon the parties, and it is an event which they may never have foreseen or desired. By contrast, the arbitration procedure under discussion here is something which the parties involved have planned for, possibly years in advance, when a contract was made between them.

Arbitration is a procedure which has found favour between parties to commercial contracts. When the contract is drawn up, the parties agree a form of arbitration clause which provides that if a dispute occurs concerning the performance of the contract, then instead of commencing a court action, the parties will take the dispute to an independent arbitrator. This avoids the cost, delay and publicity involved in court appearances.

ACTIVITY 21

A recent statute has consolidated the law in this area. In *Cases and Materials* (6.3.1) you will find extracts from the Arbitration Act 1996. Study the sections set out and then answer the following questions.

(a)   **What is the underlying philosophy of the process of arbitration?**

(b)   **In order for the agreement to be covered by the Act, what format must be adopted for it?**

(c)   **Who chooses the persons who will act as arbitrators?**

(d)   **What happens if one of the parties thinks that the arbitrator is acting unfairly and is biased against him or her?**

(e)   **What sort of remedies can be awarded to a party to arbitration?**

(f)   **If one of the parties to the original contract begins court proceedings instead of going to arbitration, what will happen?**

Section 1 of the Arbitration Act 1996 sets out the purpose of arbitration, which is to ensure that parties can choose how to settle their legal disputes fairly and without unnecessary delay or expense. In order for the Act to apply, the arbitration agreement must be in writing, although it need not necessarily be signed by the parties (s. 5). Section 16 allows the parties to agree a method for the appointment of the arbitrator, and the Act itself provides a procedure to be followed if the parties' own arrangements fail for some reason. The arbitrator selected by the parties does not have to be a person with legal qualifications. The parties may prefer to select someone who has technical knowledge relating to their business.

If in the course of the arbitration one of the parties has reason to believe that the arbitrator is not acting impartially, then under s. 24 of the Act, that party can apply to the court to have the arbitrator removed. Under normal circumstances, however, after the parties have made representations to the arbitrator, he or she will make a decision which is binding on the parties. The parties cannot seek to overturn the arbitrator's decision through the courts unless there has been a clear denial of justice.

The parties can specify in the original agreement the types of remedy which the arbitrator may award (s. 48), including the types of award normally made by a court. The aim of the exercise is to avoid court proceedings, and thus if one of the parties breaches the arbitration agreement by starting a court action, s. 9 of the Act provides that the other party can apply to have the proceedings stayed. The court is under a duty to stop the proceedings unless it appears that the arbitration agreement is invalid. The Act therefore recognises that this method of dispute resolution takes priority over court proceedings where the agreement has been validly made.

6.5.2 MEDIATION AND CONCILIATION

Two other methods of alternative dispute resolution of which you should be aware are mediation and conciliation.

Mediation is set to become an important feature of divorce proceedings, as the Family Law Act 1996 makes provision for the court to direct the parties to a divorce to take advantage of mediation services. The mediation process gives parties the opportunity to discuss points of conflict either together with the mediator or by using the mediator as a channel of communication. The mediator thus tries to help the parties find their own solution to their difficulties without resorting to the courtroom.

In conciliation, the person offering the conciliation service may be more proactive, and put forward ways in which the parties may be able to reach a particular agreement. Conciliation has in the past proved particularly useful in industrial disputes.

Like arbitration, both of these methods can avoid the necessity of the parties battling out their differences in court, but mediation and conciliation share the drawback that a satisfactory conclusion is not always reached, and the parties may in the end resort to court proceedings.

6.6 Conclusion

As you will realise from this chapter, the law relating to legal services is in a state of flux at the moment. Changes in the rights of audience rules may have far-reaching effects for the legal profession, and the increasingly restricted scope of legal aid means that litigants must seek other methods of funding their court actions, or find other ways in which to resolve their legal conflicts.

So after reading this chapter, you should be able to:

■ discuss the changes which are currently taking place within the legal profession;

■ appreciate the problems faced by the legal aid system;

■ give examples of ways in which litigation may be privately funded;

■ give an account of developments in the field of alternative dispute resolution.

6.7   Further Reading

Bailey, S. H., and Gunn M. J. *Smith and Bailey on the Modern English Legal System* 3rd edn, London: Sweet and Maxwell, 1996, Chapters 3 and 8.

6.8 End of Chapter Assessment Question

Refer to *Cases and Materials* (**6.2.1**) and read the case of *Thai Trading Co. (a firm)* v *Taylor and another* then answer the following question: What particular features of the English legal system today have led to the decision in this case, and what are the implications for the future?

See *Cases and Materials* (**6.5**) for a specimen answer.

CHAPTER SEVEN

STATUTORY INTERPRETATION (OR STATUTORY CONSTRUCTION)

7.1 Objectives

By the end of this chapter you should be able to:

■ identify the difficulties involved in understanding statute law;

■ appreciate the differing roles of Parliament and the courts in this process;

■ compare the different conventions used by the judiciary in the process of statutory interpretation or construction;

■ identify the aids and presumptions used by the judiciary when considering the meaning of an Act of Parliament;

■ analyse decided cases with a view to identifying the methods of interpretation or construction adopted by the judiciary.

7.2 Introduction

From your work on the previous four chapters and the accompanying exercises in *Cases and Materials,* you will by now have formed a picture of the different sources of law, the different courts which deal with various types of cases, and the personnel involved. It is now time to make a closer study of the way in which statute law and case law are both applied and developed by the judges in the courts of England and Wales. In this chapter, we will analyse the methods by which judges interpret case law and give meaning to the complex words and phrases which can be found in Acts of Parliament. In order to obtain the most benefit from your study of this chapter, you will need to refer to *Cases and Materials* and a good quality dictionary.

7.3 Understanding Statute Law: Interpretation and Construction

As the major source of law in England and Wales, statute law, in theory, ought to be easily understood by those to whom it is addressed. Nothing could be further from the truth. As anyone who has tried to read any sections of any statute will know, legislation is not easy to understand, and we require specialist help if we are to grasp its meaning. This specialist help is provided by solicitors (the 'front line' lawyers who provide advice on legal matters generally) and by barristers (the more specialist lawyers who represent clients in the higher courts and who provide legal opinions in complex cases). Ultimately, if the resolution of a legal dispute depends upon the meaning of a piece of statute law, then it may be necessary for the parties to commence court proceedings, and obtain a definitive interpretation from a judge, of the meaning of the words used in the legislation.

Over time, the judges have developed conventions which guide them in finding the meaning of the laws which Parliament and other rule-making bodies produce. It is these conventions which will be examined in this chapter.

In order to begin the process of understanding a piece of legislation, first of all the words used have to be given meaning, rather like interpreting a foreign language. This process of **interpretation** is one with which we are all familiar, as we constantly assign meaning to the words used in any document we read. But statute law may also be **construed:** this is the process whereby uncertainties and ambiguities in the application of the statute are resolved, otherwise known as **statutory construction.**

So, for example, if the word **credit** appears in a statute, firstly we need to **interpret** the word, i.e., give it meaning so that we can comprehend it, but secondly we may need to **construe** it, i.e., decide whether the word as used in the statute applies to a particular situation with which we are concerned, or whether the word should be understood in such a way that it does not have any relevance to the particular case we are considering. In practice, however, you may find that the two terms, interpretation and construction, are used interchangeably, and this technical distinction between the two becomes rather blurred.

But why is this process so complicated? There are a number of reasons why statute law presents such difficulties both to the ordinary individual in attempting to understand it, and to judges who have to make decisions as to its legal meaning, and apply it to particular cases.

7.3.1 THE GENERALITY OF STATUTE LAW

Case law is based on the facts of **particular** situations, but legislation is drafted in **general** terms. Rules which are set out in statutes have to be capable of application to different classes of people and situations. The draftsman has to create a rule which is general enough to cover all foreseeable circumstances which may fall within the scope of the rule. This is a difficult task, which is rendered even more complicated by the fact that the draftsmen and legislators may not be able to predict developments in society and in technology which ought to be covered by the scope of the statute in question, but do not fall within the wording used.

ACTIVITY 22

Turn to *Cases and Materials* (7.1.1), you will find an extract from the Obscene Publications Act 1959. Section 2 of the Act creates the offence of publication of an obscene article, and s. 1 attempts to provide a definition of an 'article'.

What sort of articles do you think were in the draftsman's mind when these sections were prepared?

What developments in technology might not have been foreseen at the time?

Can you think of any items which were not mentioned in these sections but which ought to have been included?

At the time of its enactment, the sort of articles which were in the contemplation of the draftsman appeared to be items such as books, magazines, tape recordings and films. Apparently, the draftsman did not consider the problem of photographic negatives (which cannot be shown to the public without further processing), nor could the development of video cassettes, or access to pornographic material on the Internet have been foreseen.

The first of these problems (photographic negatives) had to be solved by additional legislation: the Obscene Publications Act 1964 was enacted to close this loophole in the law. The second problem was solved when the courts decided that the word 'article' could be interpreted in such a way as to include a video cassette. But it remains to be seen how the language of a statute which was drafted in 1959 can be interpreted to include data available on the Internet.

From this example, you will appreciate the necessity for statute law to be drafted in wide, general terms; but there is a further problem in that if the language is too broad, then the Act may encompass people and situations which were not intended to be affected by this particular law. So in addition to trying to cover all possible circumstances, the draftsman must also include sufficient detail within the sections, so that the meaning is clear and unambiguous. It is difficult for the draftsman to meet both of these objectives.

SAQ 21

Although there are obvious drawbacks with legislation which is drafted in general terms, there are actually some advantages too. Can you think of at least two (possibly more) of these?

Although it is vital that every Act of Parliament should describe legal rules in clear and certain terms, there are some areas of law where clarity of drafting seems more important than it does in other areas. For example, in tax law and in criminal law, it is vital that the detailed provisions of the law be unambiguous in order to protect individuals from the serious consequences which flow from any breach of this type of law. However, in other areas of law, it may be beneficial for statute law to be drafted in much more general terms. This then allows the judge in an individual case a certain amount of discretion in the application of the rule which may lead to a more just outcome. A second advantage conferred by a more general style of drafting is that the legislation may encompass more cases, and so avoid litigation, as it will be apparent to the parties in dispute that their case falls within the terms of the statute, thus avoiding the need to test the matter in court. A third advantage is that legislation which is drafted in wide terms may not need to be amended with every new development in technology, as the words of the statute in its original form may be deemed to apply to new situations, thus saving valuable time in Parliament.

7.3.2   THE LIMITATIONS OF LANGUAGE

The second problem which may be encountered in dealing with statute law is the difficulty which has often been referred to as the limitations of language. All language is capable of ambiguity, and to a large extent our understanding of the language with which we communicate depends upon our having values and background in common. As the values and background of the people to whom the law is addressed vary greatly, then it becomes even more difficult to resolve these ambiguities.

One of the greatest problems which has been identified in the use of language in drafting statutes is that words do not always (if ever) have a fixed meaning, and may be understood in different ways according to the context in which they are used and the values and background of the audience to whom they are addressed. As a result, when judges are required to apply statute law, they have to make choices about how a particular word should be understood in a particular context.

ACTIVITY 23

Look up the word 'bar' in a good quality dictionary (for example *The Concise Oxford Dictionary*) and note the many different meanings of this word. A judge attempting to interpret a statute containing this word would assign a different meaning to it acccording to whether the context and subject matter of the statute was concerned with premises licensed to serve alcohol, the professional work of the barrister, or the provision of safety guards to protect people from dangerous machinery.

7.3.3   STYLE OF DRAFTING AND STRUCTURE OF STATUTES

Because of the difficulties of drafting mentioned in the previous sections, the language and sentence structure used in statute law tends to be very elaborate. Long sentences, with numerous sub clauses, are often used, in a way which would not be acceptable to a teacher, marking a learner's essay! The arrangement of sections in a statute is not usually designed in a way which is helpful to the reader.

As a result of these problems, the judges have, over the years, developed a number of presumptions which are used to assist in the task of providing an authoritative interpretation or construction of a particular statute. These are often referred to as the **rules** of statutory interpretation, although they are not binding rules in the true sense of the word. More properly they are referred to by writers as the **canons of construction** or **approaches to statutory interpretation,** and these will now be examined.

7.3.4   THE JUDICIAL TASK

There is one further factor which must be borne in mind, as the approaches to statutory interpretation are studied: what **exactly** is the task of the judge when reading a statute? Is the judge's task merely to give meaning to the words which Parliament has used, i.e., to give the words their plain meaning regardless of what Parliament may have intended? Or should the judges be seeking for the meaning which Parliament **intended,** rather than relying simply on the words which have been used?

The answer to this question will depend to a great extent on the approach to interpretation which is adopted by a particular judge, and will therefore begin to emerge as the case law is analysed.

7.4   The Approaches to Statutory Interpretation or Construction

7.4.1   THE LITERAL RULE (THE ORDINARY MEANING APPROACH)

According to this approach, the words used by Parliament in a statute should be given their ordinary or usual meaning. Where this approach is adopted, the task of the judge is regarded as that of ascertaining the intention of Parliament (if Parliament can be said to have such a thing) by looking at the words which have actually been used. This approach emerged strongly in the nineteenth century, and is still widely used as the appropriate starting point in determining the meaning of a statute. The logical consequence of this rule, however, is that if the words used are clear, and the ordinary English meaning can be assigned to them, then that meaning must be applied however hard or unjust the result.

For example, in the case of *Puhlhofer* v *Hillingdon London Borough Council* [1986] AC 484 the court was required to decide on the meaning of the word 'accommodation' in the Housing (Homeless Persons) Act 1977. This Act provides that a person is not homeless if he is occupying 'accommodation'. By using the literal or ordinary meaning approach, the House of Lords drew the conclusion that a person was occupying accommodation, even though the premises in question had no cooking or washing facilities, and he therefore had to eat out and to use a launderette to wash his clothes.

This approach to interpretation can therefore result in hardship, and has been criticised on the grounds that it is not always possible to ascertain the ordinary or natural meaning of a word. In addition the approach has been condemned for taking too narrow a view of the function of the judiciary.

ACTIVITY 24

For an explanation of this attitude to the respective roles of the judge and of Parliament, turn to *Cases and Materials* (7.2.1). There you will find an extract from the speech of Lord Diplock in the case of *Duport Steel Ltd* v *Sirs* [1980] 1 All ER 529 at page 541. Amongst judges who adopt the literal rule of statutory interpretation, how do the respective roles of the judges and Parliament in the law making process appear to be regarded?

As you will see from Lord Diplock's speech, those judges who adopt the literal rule appear to frown upon the use of creative thinking in judicial interpretation of statutes; Parliament and not the judiciary is regarded as the ultimate law-maker.

7.4.2 THE GOLDEN RULE — AN APPROACH TO INTERPRETATION TO AVOID ABSURDITY

As can be seen from the discussion above, the literal rule does not address the question of the problems which may arise as a result of the strict application of the plain meaning approach. The traditional response to this criticism has been that if the judicial interpretation of the words of a statute leads to undesirable consequences, then it is the task of Parliament to amend the law and remove the difficulties which have emerged. However, over time the judges developed a way of dealing with this problem without recourse to Parliament, and this strategy has become known as 'the golden rule'. The essence of this convention is that if the wording of the statute is ambiguous, and the application of the ordinary meaning or literal approach leads to some 'absurdity or inconvenience', then the ordinary meaning can be departed from, and another less usual meaning adopted in its place. The literal rule thus remains the starting point, but a secondary meaning can be assigned to the words in question where the use of the ordinary meaning will lead to some inconsistency or absurdity.

The golden rule may also be employed in cases where there may be only one possible interpretation which can be applied to the words of the Act under consideration, but public policy demands that an alternative interpretation is found.

A discussion of the use of the golden rule can be found in the case of *Adler* v *George* [1964] 1 All ER 628.

ACTIVITY 25

Read through the case of *Adler* v *George* in *Cases and Materials* (7.2.2) and then consider whether the following statements are true or false:

(a) This case was decided on the basis of an ordinary, natural meaning approach to statutory interpretation. TRUE/FALSE.

(b) Lord Parker felt that the purpose of the Act and the context of the words were important factors in reaching a decision. TRUE/FALSE.

(c) Lord Parker felt that it would be wrong for the court to alter the language of the statute by reading words into the section. TRUE/FALSE.

As I hope you will have gathered from the judgment, in this case a literal interpretation of the words of the section would produce an absurd result. A natural meaning approach would mean that an offence would be committed if an obstruction took place outside the station, but not if it took place within it. The first statement above is therefore false, as the golden rule was applied in this case.

It is interesting to note that Lord Parker CJ, who delivered the judgment in this case, took what might be termed a liberal approach to the task of interpreting this statute, and was prepared to look at what conduct the statute was designed to prevent, and also at the context in which the meaning of the words should be ascertained. The statement at (b) above is therefore true.

Any judge who felt that the literal rule was the only appropriate method of statutory interpretation would be horrified to find that, in this case, Lord Parker actually altered the wording of the statute, by reading into it words which Parliament had not expressly included in that section. Thus the words 'in the vicinity of' were interpreted to mean 'in or in the vicinity of' in order to avoid the absurd result referred to above. This suggests that, in this case, the court took a much less restrictive view of the role of the judge, than would a judge who only approved of the ordinary meaning approach.

7.4.3 THE MISCHIEF RULE — INTERPRETATION ACCORDING TO THE STATUTORY PURPOSE

It may seem from the previous paragraphs that members of the judiciary have a very limited role in terms of law-making, and that they are restricted to the task of declaring the meaning of the words which Parliament has used in the statutes which it has enacted. However, in recent years, it has been possible to detect a willingness amongst some judges to adopt a more liberal approach. It is becoming evident that judges are now intrepreting legislation in accordance with what is perceived by them to be the purpose of the statute, rather than performing a mechanical operation of assigning meaning to the words which Parliament has actually used.

This is often referred to as the **purposive approach** to statutory interpretation. In this approach, the judges seek the interpretation which will promote the underlying purpose or social goal of the statute, rather than being content to apply an ordinary meaning or interpretation to the words used.

Although the term 'purposive approach' is a relatively recent invention, the concept itself is not new; it can be seen to have its origins in what is known as the mischief rule which was developed from *Heydon's Case* (1584) 3 Co Rep 7. In this case, four questions were posed which have become the classic statement of the mischief approach. In using this approach, the court has to consider:

1st.   What was the Common Law before making of the Act,
2nd.   What was the mischief and defect for which the Common Law did not provide,
3rd.   What remedy the Parliament hath resolved and appointed to cure the disease of the commonwealth, and
4th.   The true reason for the remedy; and then the office of all the judges is to make such construction as shall suppress the mischief, and advance the remedy . . .

This rule therefore allows the court to look at the state of the law as it was before the statute was passed, in order to discover the mischief which the statute was designed to remedy. In attempting to discern the purpose of the legislation, the judges may also wish to undertake research into the legislative history of the Act, for example, by examining Hansard, the official report of proceedings in Parliament. Until relatively recently, the consultation of Hansard by any court was not regarded as a legitimate aid to statutory interpretation, but the case of *Pepper (Inspector of Taxes)* v *Hart* [1993] 1 All ER 42 reversed this state of affairs. For a fuller discussion of this case, see **7.3.2**.

An example of the use of the mischief rule can be found in the case of *Royal College of Nursing of the United Kingdom* v *DHSS* [1981] AC 800. This case involved the interpretation of the Abortion Act 1967. This Act requires termination of pregnancy to be carried out 'by a registered medical practitioner' in order for that termination to be lawful. The question arose as to whether a termination could be said to be carried out 'by a registered medical practitioner' in circumstances where the physical acts which caused the abortion were actually carried out by a nurse, acting on the instructions of a registered medical practitioner.

In order to construe the words of the statute, the court looked at the mischief which the Abortion Act 1967 was designed to remedy, and at the policy and purpose behind the Act. The court came to the conclusion that this statute was designed to ensure that abortions took place under qualified medical supervision and that this was indeed the case where a doctor took responsibility for the operation, even though the physical acts were performed by a nurse. The terminations were therefore lawful.

ACTIVITY 26

Extracts from the speeches of members of the House of Lords in the case of *Royal College of Nursing of the United Kingdom* v *DHSS* are provided at *Cases and Materials* (7.2.3). Read carefully through these extracts, and then try to answer the following questions:

(a)   Which approaches to statutory interpretation can you identify in the extracts set out, and by which members of the House of Lords were they used?

(b)   If an ordinary meaning approach to the words of the statute had been adopted by a majority of the judges, what would have been the outcome of this case?

(c)   What does this case reveal about the way in which different approaches to statutory interpretation are based on different philosophies about the role of the judge?

This case established a number of important points about methods of statutory interpretation and about the role of the judge in the law-making process. These points emerge particularly clearly, because the members of the House of Lords who heard the appeal were sharply divided in their opinions. The first point to note is that the dissenting speeches of Lord Wilberforce and Lord Edmund-Davies seem to be based on an ordinary meaning approach to the statute, and any liberal approaches to interpretation are rejected. Lord Diplock's speech, by contrast, contains clear reference to the mischief rule, and explores the history of the legislation relating to abortion. If you have been able to discern these approaches, then you have answered question (a) above, correctly.

Another important point to notice is that if the judges, in interpreting the words of the statute, had seen their role only in terms of giving meaning to what Parliament had actually said, then the ordinary meaning approach to the words used would have been regarded as conclusive. The result of this case would then have been very different. In answer to question (b) above, a literal interpretation of the words of the statute would have meant that, as the acts which induced the abortion were not carried out by a person with the qualifications specified in the statute, the abortions did not fall within the terms of the Abortion Act 1967, and were unlawful.

From your reading of the extracts in *Cases and Materials,* I hope you will have drawn the conclusion that the Law Lords who adopted the literal approach, did so as a result of their view that it is not for the courts to 'redraft' legislation to achieve a more acceptable outcome in a particular case, or fill in any gaps in the statutory provisions. Any such defects in the legislation must be corrected by Parliament itself according to this philosophy. This view of the judicial role was adopted by the dissenting minority in the *Royal College of Nursing* case. The majority of the Law Lords saw their role in a different, more interventionist, light however, and were prepared to take into account the history and policy of the statute, and to read the provisions in a wider sense, in order to achieve a just result in the case concerned. Members of the judiciary who adopt this philosophy, regard themselves as having a law-making role alongside Parliament, and would not see their task in purely mechanical terms, applying the words of a statute without question. Your answer to question (c) should reflect this divergence of opinion amongst the judiciary.

7.4.4   THE UNITARY (OR CONTEXTUAL) APPROACH

For many years, the three rules outlined above have been regarded as the classical theory of statutory interpretation. However, academic writers have identified the emergence of a fourth approach which Farrar and Dugdale in *Introduction to Legal Method* have called the unitary approach, or the contextual approach to the construction of statutes.

By examining the judgments of many cases, writers on statutory interpretation have observed that the three traditional approaches seem to be merging, and that greater emphasis is being placed on the importance of the context of the statute, in ascertaining its meaning. As a result, it is becoming even more difficult to identify which method of interpretation a particular judge may have used in arriving at a conclusion as to how the words of a statute should be construed.

7.4.5   THE EUROPEAN DIMENSION

The rules described above are those which apply to legislation which has been prepared and enacted in the Houses of Parliament and which forms part of English law. There is, however, a vast and constantly growing body of legislation which is being produced by the law-making bodies of the European Union. Different considerations and different procedures apply to the interpretation of legislation which emanates from the European Union, because this legislation is drafted in a very different way from the statutes produced by the United Kingdom Parliament. The legislation of the EU is based on the statement of broad general principles, which must then be interpreted and applied by the courts as appropriate. A literal approach to the interpretation of such material would not be helpful, as there may be insufficient detail to make this method meaningful. It is the practice of courts within the English legal system to adopt the purposive approach when interpreting treaties and conventions which have their origin outside this legal system, and similarly, the purposive approach is adopted when a court interprets legislation produced by the UK Parliament in response to initiatives from the European Union.

These points should be borne in mind when studying cases which involve points of interpretation of European law.

7.5   Aids to Statutory Interpretation or Construction

To complete your understanding of the process of statutory interpretation and construction, it is necessary to examine briefly a number of assorted 'rules' or conventions which the judges employ in conjunction with the main approaches referred to above. These can be categorised under the general heading of internal and external aids.

7.5.1   INTERNAL AIDS

Sometimes referred to as intrinsic aids, these consist of material found within the printed copy of the Act itself, which may give clues as to the correct understanding of the law. Thus, the long title of the Act, whilst not to be used to contradict anything in the body of the Act itself, may be a useful indicator of the scope of the statute if there is a debate as to this. (Have you remembered the difference between the long title and the short title of an Act? If not, refresh your memory by referring back to **Chapter 2**.)

Similarly, the way in which the sections of an Act are punctuated will give clues as to how that section is to be understood. Perhaps most useful is the definition section of the Act, which is an increasingly common feature of modern legislation. This provides definitions of words used in the Act and their meaning in the particular context of the Act.

ACTIVITY 27

Refer to the extract of s. 205 of the Law of Property Act 1925 in *Cases and Materials* **(7.3.1). What type of section does this appear to be?**

As you will realise, this is the definition section for the Law of Property Act 1925, and contains numerous sub-sections which define words used in the Act, in order to clarify the interpretation of the statute.

A number of presumptions are also relied upon by the judiciary in construing legislation. Mostly these are of a general nature, for example, that a statute must be read as a whole, and that words take their meaning from the context in which they are used. (This is sometimes referred to as the *noscitur a sociis* rule, i.e., words are known by the company they keep!) Other important presumptions are that statute law does not make any fundamental change to the common law unless this is clearly intended, and that it does not have a retrospective effect unless this is expressly stated. A statute creating a criminal offence will normally require a guilty mind or criminal intent (known as mens rea) to be proved as an element of that offence, before any person can be convicted of the alleged crime. There are certain crimes (known as crimes of strict liability) which do not have this requirement of intent in order for a crime to be committed, but this must be clearly indicated in the words of the Act which creates the offence.

There are in addition some more specific rules of interpretation, for example, the *ejusdem generis* rule. This rule applies in situations where a section of a statute contains a list of particular words, which taken together might be said to form a class (a genus). If the list is followed by a general word, then that general word must be interpreted in such a way as to fall within the class created by the specific words. A famous example of this can be found in the case of *Powell* v *Kempton Park Racecourse Co.* [1899] AC 143 HL. This case concerned the interpretation to be applied to the Betting Act 1853 (since repealed). The Act prohibited the keeping of a 'house, office, room or other place' for the purpose of betting with others, and the question to be resolved was whether this could include an open air racecourse. By applying the *ejusdem generis* rule the court concluded that the genus or class created by the words was one which referred to indoor places. The words 'or other place' at the end of the list had to be construed in accordance with this and therefore an open air venue was not included in the scope of the Act.

7.5.2   EXTERNAL AIDS

Sometimes referred to as extrinsic aids, these are devices which assist in the interpretation of the statute concerned, but which are not contained within the printed copy of the Act. Examples of external aids are English dictionaries, which judges may use when seeking the ordinary meaning of the words used, and academic authorities in the form of textbooks, which may be consulted to help with an opinion on a particular point.

Two forms of external aid which have caused much debate are, first, the preparatory materials which precede legislation (e.g., Law Commission Reports, or reports of Royal Commissions, sometimes collectively referred to as *travaux préparatoires*) and, secondly, Hansard, the official report of the proceedings of the Houses of Parliament. There has been a good deal of discussion concerning the extent to which these materials should be consulted by the judiciary when considering the interpretation of legislation.

Before any major piece of legislation is put before Parliament, a group of eminent lawyers may be gathered together in the shape of a Royal Commission, or as members of the Law Commission, to consider how the law should be reformed. The report which is produced by this group may contain a draft bill, or other suggestions as to how a statute might be framed to create new law. The extent to which such materials can be consulted by the courts as part of the process of statutory interpretation was considered in the case of *Black-Clawson International Ltd* v *Papierwerke Waldhof-Aschaffenberg AG* [1975] 1 All ER 810. This case revealed quite wide differences of opinion amongst the members of the House of Lords but the outcome seems to be that it is legitimate for judges to consult this sort of material in order to establish the mischief which the legislation was intended to cure. The use of such reports to ascertain the meaning of legislation is not, however, regarded as permissible.

As far as the use of Hansard is concerned, the position has been clarified by the case of *Pepper (Inspector of Taxes)* v *Hart* [1993] 1 All ER 42 HL. For years there had been a strict rule which forbade counsel to quote from, or judges to consult Hansard as an aid to statutory interpretation, even though it may have helped considerably in identifying the intention of Parliament. As a result of this case, it is now possible for judges to refer to Hansard in certain circumstances.

7.6   Conclusion

You will by now have realised that statutory interpretation is not an exact science. The judges vary considerably in their approach to this judicial task, and it is often difficult to discern from a judgment exactly which approach to the construction of the statute a particular judge has adopted. Unfortunately, the judges do not, as a rule, announce whether they are using one particular method of interpretation, or an amalgam of them all.

You should, however, feel able to:

■ give an account of the different methods of statutory interpretation in use in this country;

■ identify the different approaches to the law which underlie these different methods;

■ give examples of cases in which these different methods have been used; and

■ describe other aids to interpretation in common use and the historical background to these.

In **Chapter 9** we will continue to look at the role of the judge in the legal system, but this time the focus will be on case law, rather than statute law.

7.7   Further Reading

Ingman, T., *The English Legal Process*, 6th edn, London: Blackstone Press, 1996, Chapter 8.

7.8   End of Chapter Assessment Question

Refer to *Cases and Materials* (7.3.1), where you will find extracts from the speeches of the House of Lords in *Pepper* v *Hart*.

You will already have looked at part of this case in an earlier exercise in Chapter 4. Now read the extracts again, with a view to answering the following questions:

(a)   What reasons are given for the former rule which prohibited reference to Hansard as an aid to statutory interpretation?

(b)   What conditions are imposed by the Law Lords on those who wish to consult Hansard as an aid to statutory interpretation?

(c)   What implications does this have for modern methods of statutory interpretation?

See *Cases and Materials* (7.5) for a specimen answer.

CHAPTER EIGHT

LEGAL REASONING

8.1 Objectives

By the end of this chapter you should be able to:

- distinguish between law and fact, between fact and evidence, and between fact and inference;

- appreciate the importance of standpoint when analysing factual material;

- organise factual material in a logical fashion;

- appreciate the process of inductive reasoning and its application in a legal case.

8.2 Introduction

Earlier in this *Learning Text* (**1.5.2**) you discovered that the ability to read and understand case law is a fundamental skill which it is vital for a student of the law to acquire. It is now time to consider the process of understanding case law in more detail, for this will help in your study of the final chapter, concerning the doctrine of precedent.

You will recall that a reported case usually contains details of the facts which led to the legal dispute, statements of the law relating to the dispute, and reasoned discussion by the judges of the way in which the law is applied to the facts. The judges may also refer to the rules of evidence which determine whether or not particular facts may be heard by the court. In this chapter we are only interested in the facts, and in the way in which legal arguments can be constructed based on those facts. You are not expected to know anything about admissibility of evidence in court or any detailed rules of court procedure. The aim of the chapter is to introduce you to a particular method of analysing facts in a logical way, and this will help you both to read case law more critically and to compose your own arguments about cases in a more organised way.

The techniques which are discussed in this chapter are based on those developed by Terence Anderson and William Twining in *Analysis of Evidence*, from the work of an American lawyer, J. H. Wigmore. The methods outlined in this chapter are very much simplified, however, and much of the detail has been omitted. If you find that you enjoy this type of reasoning, and that you want to learn more about it, then you should consult *Analysis of Evidence*.

8.3   What are the Facts?

Before analysing the way in which facts are presented in legal cases, it is worth considering what we understand by the word 'facts'. Most people would identify well known historical events as 'fact', for example, we would say that the outbreak of the First World War in 1914 is a 'fact'. But as you will have noticed in some of the cases which you have already read in *Cases and Materials*, it is not always so easy for the court to determine the 'facts' which have resulted in a legal dispute.

How might you define a 'fact'? (You might want to consult a dictionary to help you answer this question).

Give examples of three things which you would regard as facts. Show your examples to another person and ask if they agree that the things you have chosen are 'facts'.

If the other person does not agree about your 'facts', how else might you classify these items?

It is not too difficult to define the word 'fact'. If you consulted a dictionary you would probably find that it is usually referred to as something which is known to have occurred, or something which is known to be true. But once you begin to look for examples of things which people generally would agree to be facts, then problems can begin. For example, if you have stated some well known historical event as a fact, then other people will probably agree with you that this is indeed a fact which actually occurred. But if you present as one of your facts, the statement that 'England has an excellent football team', others might point out to you that this is not fact, but is merely an opinion. But what is the difference between the two types of statement? How do you know that one is fact and the other is opinion?

How would you demonstrate to someone that your date of birth is a fact, and not simply your own opinion about the date when you were born?

In order to convince someone that you were born on a particular date, you would need to collect evidence which would provide sufficient proof to satisfy that person that your date of birth was a fact. Statements from your parents or other members of your family would be helpful, but might not be completely reliable. What if they are all mistaken, or are lying for some reason? Presumably the best form of proof would be your official birth certificate. This would provide documentary evidence that what you are claiming as a fact is true.

8.4   Facts and Evidence

By now you should be realising that the simple definition of a 'fact' which the dictionary provides is not sufficient for all purposes. It now begins to appear that a fact is only a fact if it can be *proved* to have happened or *proved* to be true. This is particularly true of the facts which are alleged in legal disputes. As you read more and more case law, you will begin to see that the 'facts' of the case are treated as propositions which the parties seek to prove. The material which they produce to support these propositions is the evidence.

Read the case of *R v Stratford-upon-Avon Council Housing Benefit Review Board and Another, ex parte White, The Times,* 23 April 1998), in *Cases and Materials* (8.1), and answer the following questions:

(a)   From the information given in the report, what 'facts' do you think the Council would have had to establish in order to show that the applicant was not entitled to housing benefit?

(b)   What evidence would the court have accepted as proof of such facts?

(c)   Was such evidence available?

This case illustrates the way in which the facts of a case can be seen as propositions which must be proved by evidence of such weight that it will persuade the court to come to a particular conclusion. In order to convince the court that the applicant was not entitled to housing benefit, the Council would have had to establish as a fact that the applicant had contrived to place himself under a legal liability in order to take advantage of the housing benefit scheme.

The sort of evidence which would be taken to support this proposition might be, for example, that the applicant had entered into the arrangement to pay board and lodging for himself and his family with the sole purpose of making the claim for benefit, and would not otherwise have agreed to live in community in this way. Timing was evidently important to the court, so if the applicant had terminated the agreement after a successful application for housing benefit, this would have been evidence suggestive of bad faith on his part.

Another factor which the court took into account was the intention of the applicant and the landlord to create a legally binding relationship concerning the occupation of the property. Thus if the Council had been able to show that the agreement to live in the community house and pay board and lodging was not intended to create a legal obligation, then this also would have been evidence that the supposed legal liability was contrived with the intention of taking advantage of the system. In the event, the court could find no evidence of this nature, and therefore the facts which were required to be present in order to establish a breach of the law could not be made out.

The result in this case reveals another important feature about fact and evidence and the way in which the process of arguing a case works in practice. The aim of the parties involved in a legal case before a court is to persuade the court that there is sufficient evidence to support the facts which the parties seek to prove. The party that can provide the greater weight of evidence to support their argument will win the case. As a prospective lawyer, it is therefore vitally important that you become skilled in distinguishing fact from evidence and organising both in such a way that you will convince a court of the rightness of your case. You will learn more about this process of organisation later in the chapter.

8.5   Facts and Law

When analysing a reported case, you will sometimes find that not only do you have to try to distinguish facts from evidence, but you will also have to determine whether the issues raised by the case concern questions of fact or questions of law. You would think that this process would be fairly straightforward, but it is actually more difficult than it looks. This is because cases can raise questions which are a mixture of law and fact, and also because the way in which the factual issues are presented can affect the nature of the legal issues and vice versa.

As a first step, in order for any court to resolve a legal dispute, it must investigate the facts of the case, and the evidence which is said to support those facts. The court cannot decide upon the legal rights and duties of the parties without establishing the order of events which led to the dispute, and testing the evidence adduced to prove the facts.

Imagine that you are a judge in the High Court, and that you are hearing a case in which a worker in a textile factory has been injured whilst using a sewing machine provided by the owner of the factory. In order for you to decide the legal rights and liabilities of the parties involved, what findings of fact do you think you would need to make? (Remember you are not being asked about the law applicable to this situation – simply use your imagination to make a list of the sort of factual information which would be necessary in order for you to ascertain what has happened in this case).

Obviously if you are going to come to some conclusion about how the accident occurred, you will want to establish a detailed account of the events surrounding the incident, and of the way in which the accident occurred. This will involve hearing the stories of the various witnesses involved and trying to form a composite history based on those stories which you believe to be accurate. You will probably also want to know about matters such as the condition of the machine, the training which the worker had been given, and whether the worker was using the machine in the appropriate fashion.

These findings of fact will help to define the legal issues involved and thus the rights and duties of the parties. For example, if it can be shown that the owner had provided a faulty sewing machine for the worker to use, and it was the defect in the machine which caused the accident, then a particular line of legal argument can be pursued by the injured worker. In this way, finding the facts concerning the condition and operation of the machine will be a necessary preliminary to identifying the legal rules which are applicable.

But it is also true to say that the legal issues which are selected for argument in court can determine which of the available facts are regarded as vital to the case. For example, if the facts show that the worker had been properly trained to use the machine in a certain way, but had chosen on this particular occasion to use it in a way which was dangerous and this led to the accident occurring, different legal considerations will apply. In this situation the owner of the factory may wish to put forward legal argument based on facts surrounding the behaviour of the worker, and this will need to be investigated by the court in greater detail.

When reading a case, you will therefore find that questions of fact (that is, questions as to what actually happened) are intertwined with questions of law (that is, what legal rules apply) but you will need to try to disentangle the two so that you can make a satisfactory analysis of the case.

In *Cases and Materials* (8.2) you will find the report of *Clarke* v *Kato and Others, The Times*, 11 December 1996). Read the report through carefully, and then answer the following questions:

(a)   What issues of fact were important in this case? Were there some facts which the court considered to be less important than others, and why?

(b)   What questions of law did this case raise? Were some of the legal questions more important than others in helping the court to reach a decision in this case?

This is a case in which the facts found and legal questions raised in the court below were narrowed down by the Court of Appeal in order for it to reach its judgment. The county court had established the facts concerning the layout of the premises at which the accident took place, the availability of access, the design and negotiability of the area, and the type of use of the car park which actually occurred. It had been established that there was regular and unrestricted pedestrian user of the car park, and the Court of Appeal considered that this was sufficient ground on which to base the decision that the car park did come within the definition of a 'road'. As a result, it was unnecessary to make any specific finding of fact about the extent to which the area was used by prams and bicycles, because usage by prams and bicycles was not going to affect the decision on the legal issue. In answering question (a) it thus becomes apparent how the legal issues in the case can determine which of the factual issues are important.

A similar process can be seen at work in relation to the legal issues in question (b). Here, the central legal problem was that the Motor Insurers' Bureau would not compensate the victim of the uninsured driver unless it could be shown that the accident had occurred on a 'road', defined as 'any highway and any other road to which the public has access'. The county court had concentrated on the question as to whether the car park could be described as 'any other road to which the public has access'. The Court of Appeal pointed out that it was clear from the facts that the public did have access to the car park, so this meant that the legal argument could be narrowed down to the simple question of whether the car park came within the definition of the word 'road' at all. Question (b) thus shows how the identification of the relevant facts in a case can help to clarify the legal issues which must be decided.

In addition to the facts, the law and the evidence which you will be able to discern when you read a law report, if you study the legal arguments, you will notice that in some cases, the court reaches its judgment by making assumptions or inferences based on the facts and the evidence. This is an important area of legal reasoning which we need to explore.

8.6   Facts and Inferences

You will remember that when we discussed the distinction between fact and evidence, we noticed that when a legal dispute arises which leads to a court case, the parties will present the facts which they seek to prove as propositions, which they must then support with appropriate evidence. According to the theories of J. H. Wigmore, inferences are concerned with the process of thought by which pieces of evidence are linked together to arrive at proof. Inferential reasoning is a way of thinking which gives persuasive weight to each separate piece of evidence in order to prove the case as a whole.

For example, if we observe that there are tyre marks down the middle of the road, the inference is the process of thinking that a vehicle has come to an abrupt halt, and has perhaps skidded. If we then notice that there are fragments of broken glass and plastic in the road, the process of inferential reasoning may lead us to believe that a vehicle has collided with something, possibly after braking sharply. If we further observe that there is blood on the road, then we might infer that there has been an accident in which someone has been injured. In this way, the facts and the evidence which supports them give rise to a thought process which results in us becoming more and more convinced that there has been a road accident at this place. This process relies on the use of inference, and it is exactly this process which is used by opposing parties to a legal dispute, who wish to convince a court of the truth of their version of the facts.

SAQ 25

(Based on exercises in *Analysis of Evidence* by Anderson and Twining)

Set out below are a number of propositions in the form of statements of fact. What inferences would you draw from the facts if you wished to prove that Y had murdered X?

(a) Witness 1 (a doctor) examined Miss X at her farm at 11am on 1 February 1997. She was in a coma, and had severe head injuries consistent with having been hit repeatedly with an object such as a garden spade.

(b) Witness 1 says that when he arrived at the farm he saw Mr Y leaving the paddock where Miss X was lying. Mr Y was carrying a bloodstained garden spade, and had blood on his clothing.

(c) Witness 2 (a farmworker, who had summoned the doctor) says that only he, Mr Y and Miss X were present at the farm on the morning of 1 February 1997.

(d) Witness 2 further states that at about 10 am that morning he heard Miss X and Mr Y having a violent argument, and later saw Mr Y standing over the body of Miss X with the spade in his hand.

(e) Miss X died in hospital on 4 February 1997 without regaining consciousness.

(f) Forensic tests on the spade and on Mr Y's clothing indicated that the blood was of the same group as that of Miss X.

From these statements you will see that the evidence supplied does not by itself prove that Y murdered X. It is necessary to make a number of inferences in order to link the evidence together in such a way that a court might be persuaded that there is sufficient proof to reach the conclusion that Y murdered X.

The first inference that must be made (and you might not have thought of this) is a 'truth' inference, that is, that in the absence of any indication to the contrary, we infer that both of the witnesses are telling the truth. We might then infer that the bloodstained spade which Witness 1 saw Y carrying from the paddock has been in contact with an injured person or animal. Likewise, Y himself must have been in contact with blood in order for it to be present on his clothing. With the addition of the evidence that the blood was of the same group as that of X, we might infer that both the spade and Y himself had been in contact with X either before or after she sustained her injuries.

When the evidence of Witness 2 is then added to the picture, we can infer that X was murdered either by Witness 2 himself, or by Y. From the argument which Witness 2 overheard we can infer that Y had some reason to kill X, and his presence at the scene. observed by two witnesses, could lead to the conclusion that Y did kill X.

SAQ 26

The evidentiary facts set out above are capable of leading to the conclusion that Y did murder X, with the help of the inferences shown. But other questions remain to be taken into consideration.

(a) Are you convinced that Y did murder X? Could other inferences be drawn which would provide an alternative explanation of Y's behaviour?

(b) Is it possible to construct a case by way of inferential reasoning that Witness 2 was the murderer?

You may already have discerned that there is an element of speculation in this process of reasoning by inference. We have created some inferences which support the proposition that Y did kill X, but other inferences are of course possible. For example, we could infer from the facts presented that Y discovered X in a coma, after she had been attacked by some unknown person. Y picked up the spade which was lying by her body and thus became marked with her blood.

The fact that these alternative inferences are plausible raises questions about the adequacy of the proof that Y killed X. Remember that in a criminal trial, the jury must be satisfied beyond reasonable doubt that the accused has committed the crime. It is certainly true to say that it is possible that Y killed X, but it is not a foregone conclusion that a jury would be convinced that he had done so.

Once it has been established that there are alternative explanations for Y's behaviour, it is quite possible to use inferential reasoning to suggest that Witness 2 was in fact the killer, based on the evidence that only he and Y were present with X at the time. This illustrates three important points about this process of reasoning. First, where there are a number of rational inferences which are conceivable from the evidence, the greatest weight and value will be placed on the inference that is the most plausible and natural. If the lawyers for Y and Witness 2 were to construct an argument based on the inference that X had been killed by aliens, it is unlikely that this would convince a jury! The more natural the explanation given for a particular piece of evidence, the more highly probable this inference will seem to a court.

Secondly, notice the way in which the *standpoint* of the person analysing the evidence can influence the outcome of the exercise. If we were to take on the role of the lawyer acting for Y, and we attempted to analyse the evidence in such a way as to find a defence to the charge of murder, then we would draw different inferences from the material than would the lawyer acting for the prosecution in this case. It is therefore important to be aware of our role, and the purpose of our analysis, when we study factual material in this way, so that we are aware of the standpoint from which we view the case.

The third point to note is the way in which generalisations play a strong part in the process of inferential reasoning. As human beings, we all have a store of background knowledge which influences the way in which we see the world. In the example of the tyre marks on the road above, our inferences depended upon the generalisation that when motor vehicles are travelling at speed and the driver brakes sharply, skid marks are left on the road. Some generalisations are the result of observation and experience (as in the case of the tyre marks) but others can be the product of conditioning or prejudice (for example, the belief that women are not as good drivers as men). In studying the facts of cases, it is important to be aware of these generalisations, for they may prejudice the objectivity of our thinking about the factual material.

8.7 How to Organise Factual Information

It is now time to put together all the knowledge and skills which you have been acquiring in relation to the handling of factual information. Whether you are reading a law report in order to find the answer to an academic question, or whether you are acting in a professional capacity and assisting in the preparation of a case for court, you need to develop a system which enables you to organise factual information in a logical way. You need to be able to separate issues of fact from issues of law, and then bearing in mind your standpoint, you need to organise the evidentiary facts in such a way that they support the proposition which you are attempting to prove. In the course of this process you will need to make inferences, which will be influenced by your background knowledge and generalisations.

This logical process of taking individual facts and basing inferences upon them in order to prove a particular proposition is known as the 'inductive' process of reasoning.

ACTIVITY 30

In *Cases and Materials* (8.3) an extract from *Analysis of Evidence* by Twining and Anderson is set out. Read through this extract, and then consider the following questions.

(a) Why is it important for professionals such as lawyers and doctors to have high standards of reasoning?

(b) When dealing with clients, what sort of questions should lawyers be asking themselves as the case proceeds?

(c) Why is it necessary for lawyers to be skilled in using a number of different systems for organising and recording data?

As you will appreciate from reading the extract, because the work of professionals such as doctors and lawyers is so influential both for individuals and for society as a whole, it is vital that you develop the skills of reasoning and ordering factual material in a logical way. You will need to use your skills of analysis at every step of the way when you are advising clients. So you will constantly be reflecting on what you are doing and asking yourself questions concerning whether the client has provided enough information for you to work with, what more information might be needed from the client, and can this information be organised in such a way as to prove the client's case in a convincing fashion. As the extract indicates, for this data to be usable, you need to find ways of organising the material so that it can be analysed thoroughly. The way in which this is done will vary according to the purpose for which the analysis is being conducted.

J. H. Wigmore presented two methods of organisation and analysis of material, the chart method and the narrative method. The original chart method which he devised was exceedingly complex, and involved identifying the key facts and inferences needed to prove a particular proposition, and then presenting this 'key list' in a diagrammatic form. We are not going to attempt to recreate the diagrams which Wigmore developed, but we can use a modified form of his method for our own purposes. In fact you have already used some of the techniques which Wigmore developed when you practised making inferences from factual information earlier in the chapter.

8.7.1 ANALYSING FACTUAL INFORMATION USING INDUCTIVE REASONING: THE KEY LIST METHOD

Read *Cases and Materials* (8.3.1) and then follow the instructions below to produce an analysis of the information.

(a)   What is your standpoint whilst undertaking this exercise, and for what purpose are you making this analysis. What are the implications of your answers to these two questions?

(b)   What is the ultimate proposition which you are trying to prove?

(c)   From the possible theories which you could develop about the case, select and present as a logical statement one theory which sets out your argument concerning the case as a whole.

(d)   Make a list of the key evidentiary facts and the inferences based on the facts which you would combine in your attempt to prove the ultimate proposition.

This exercise demonstrates how to use many of the skills which you will have read about in this chapter. The whole process is one of inductive reasoning, using inferences based on generalisations to make the proof of certain propositions more or less likely. Your first task is to make yourself aware of the reason why you are doing this work and for whom, for these two factors will influence the outcome of your analysis. So it is important that you bear in mind that your standpoint is that of the organisation which will be responsible for prosecuting the person suspected of committing the crime. You are presenting the information in such a way that it will provide the basis of the prosecution case in court. The implication of these two points is that you will be concentrating on the evidentiary facts which will convince the court that your reasoning is correct, and that you have satisfactorily proved your case against the person who has been charged with the crime.

The ultimate proposition which you are trying to prove is simple enough – that is, that 'It was A who murdered B'. There will, however, be intermediate propositions which you will have to prove in order to arrive at this conclusion. In order to identify these intermediate propositions, it can help to develop a logical statement of the case as a whole which supports the conclusions which you have reached. This is known as the theory of the case. In this example, a logical theory might be that A had both the opportunity and the motive to murder B. Both the witness evidence and the forensic evidence support the theory that B was in A's car immediately prior to the incident, that A was seen in the vicinity of the crime at about the time it was committed, and that both A and A's car were contaminated by B's blood. Thus the evidence indicates that A murdered B.

In order to check that each stage of your theory is logically sound, it is helpful to draw up a list of the evidence itself and all the inferences which are based on the evidence and which lead to your ultimate proposition. There are a number of different ways of doing this, but your list might look something like the following:

(a) Witness 3 statement.

(b) Inference: A and B had a serious argument the day before the murder.

(c) Witness 1 statement.

(d) A owns a car which has the characteristics described by Witness 1.

(e) Inference: B was in A's car, which was going in the direction of the motorway, at 9.30 pm on 1 February.

(f) Witness 2 statement.

(g) A drove away from the vicinity of the crime shortly after it had been committed. A was under emotional or physical strain.

(h) B's body was found on the hard shoulder of the northbound carriage of the motorway at 10.30 pm on 1 February. He had bled to death as a result of several stab wounds to his back.

(i) A forensic report states that blood found on A's clothing and in A's car almost certainly belonged to B.

(j) Inference: A stabbed B to death.

Clearly there are a number of points in this argument where the lawyer defending A would draw different inferences, or point out gaps in the evidence. For example, no-one *saw* A murder B, so the defence may wish to argue that A's guilt has not been proved beyond reasonable doubt. But this exercise should help you to appreciate the way in which you can organise information in order to reach a particular conclusion.

8.7.2 ANALYSING FACTUAL INFORMATION USING INDUCTIVE REASONING: THE NARRATIVE METHOD

ACTIVITY 32

Turn to *Cases and Materials* (8.3.2) and read the extracts from *Analysis of Evidence* by *Anderson and Twining*. Now answer the following questions.

(a) According to A. M. Burrill, what difficulties face a jury which is required to make a decision based on the facts presented in court?

(b) What analogies does Burrill suggest to help us understand the way in which facts can be presented in order to prove a case?

(c) What are the different stages in the method which Wigmore suggests for making a narrative presentation of the facts?

You have now read about two different ways in which factual information can be ordered and presented with a view to proving a particular proposition. This logical process is important at all stages of a legal case, but as Burrill points out in the extract, is especially vital when presenting information to a jury. The members of the jury are expected to make their decision based on the facts of the case as a whole. This is difficult for them, because if the facts are viewed as a mass, they are likely to be confusing and overwhelming. This is compounded by the fact that the evidence presented by both sides of the argument may be finely balanced, and an incorrect theory of the case may have been chosen and the correct one overlooked.

To help the jury in this difficulty, the factual material needs to be arranged to provide a truthful representation of the case. Burrill likens this to arranging a *framework* of facts or constructing a *chain*, the links of which connect the crime committed with the individual charged. He also compares the evidentiary facts with *strands of rope or cable* which when woven together make a strong connection.

Wigmore builds on these ideas to provide a suggested method for analysing facts using the narrative method. He proposes four steps for this exercise. First, to set the scene with an introductory statement of the situation which has led to the court case. Secondly, arrangement of the evidence, both from the point of view of the prosecution and the defence, in such a way as to provide a logical scheme of proof. This arrangement should include the inferences made from the evidence and the provisional conclusions which can be drawn. Thirdly, the final conclusions from the analysis should be set out, and fourthly, when it is known, the actual decision of the jury in the case.

8.8   Conclusion

The ability to handle large quantities of factual information and to construct logical arguments from it is essential for both students and practitioners of the law. As you will appreciate, the **Learning Text** and the **Cases and Materials** are not designed to teach you everything which you need to know in this area. The work which you have done in the exercises and activities is only a simple introduction to what is a sophisticated skill which is acquired through practice. However, when you are next confronted with a mass of information which you have to analyse, you should be able to:

■   identify your standpoint and the purpose of your analysis, and the effect which these two factors will have on your work;

■   choose from a key list or narrative method of inductive reasoning for your method of analysis;

■   identify your ultimate proposition and arrange the factual material to make a logical proof;

■   appreciate the effect of generalisations and inferences upon your analysis.

At **8.10** you will find an exercise which you can use to test your knowledge and skill in some of these areas. From now on, when reading any law report or account of a case which contains a large amount of factual information, be aware of the methods of analysis which you have learned about in this chapter and try to apply them; it will change the way in which you think about case law!

8.9   Further Reading

Anderson T. and Twining W., *Analysis of Evidence*, London, Weidenfeld and Nicolson, 1991, Chapters 1–3 and 5–6.

8.10   End of Chapter Assessment Question

Read the case of *Bolitho (administratrix of the estate of Bolitho deceased)* v *City and Hackney Health Authority* [1997] 4 All ER 771, set out in *Cases and Materials* (8.3.2), noticing how the judge pays particular attention to the facts of the case. Then answer the following questions:

(a)   What do you think was the ultimate proposition which the appellant (i.e. Patrick's mother) wished to prove?

(b)   At the original hearing of the case in the High Court, what do you think were the propositions which the expert witness evidence for the appellant was intended to prove?

(c)   Lord Browne-Wilkinson identified two questions which the trial judge had to decide concerning causation. Were these questions of causation related to the legal or the factual aspects of the case?

(d)   If you had been acting for the defendants in this case (i.e. the Health Authority), what ultimate proposition would you have attempted to prove in this appeal, and what factual evidence and inferences would you have emphasised?

The answers to these questions can be found in *Cases and Materials* (8.5).

CHAPTER NINE

THE DOCTRINE OF PRECEDENT

9.1 Objectives

By the end of this chapter you should be able to:

■ define the doctrine of precedent;

■ describe its operation in different courts;

■ give reasons for and against its influence;

■ distinguish between *ratio decidendi* and *obiter dicta*;

■ describe how to ascertain the ratio of a case.

9.2 Introduction

Imagine that you have developed a mysterious illness and that you visit your general medical practitioner. The doctor has never encountered this illness before, but remembers that a partner in the practice described something similar a while ago. Your doctor consults the other partner to find out what was prescribed.

Next, imagine that you are a solicitor in private practice. A wealthy client has asked you to draw up his will which is to contain an extremely complex trust. You have not drafted such a clause before, but you know that one of the partners has previously prepared this sort of will. You go in search of the file containing the clauses which you need.

What is happening in both of the above cases is that the professional who is faced with an unfamiliar problem seeks a **precedent** to help him or her in arriving at the best solution to that problem. Using previous decisions to help resolve a current problem is a technique employed in all walks of life, but particularly in the courts of most legal systems.

In the English legal system this is referred to as the principle of *stare decisis* (which means 'stand by cases already decided') or the **doctrine of precedent** and it is a concept which has a vital part to play in the day to day decision-making which takes place in our courts.

In this chapter, the operation of the doctrine of precedent (*stare decisis*) in the courts of the English legal system will be examined. The knowledge which you acquire in this chapter will complete your understanding of the way in which the courts and the judges work, and enable you to make some evaluation of the importance of decisions made in different courts. *Cases and Materials* will help you to recognise and apply the principles which you will encounter both as a learner of the law in an academic context, and as a practitioner.

9.3   What is the Doctrine of Precedent?

In very simple terms, the doctrine means that a judge who is hearing a particular type of court case does not have to make a decision using simply his or her own knowledge of the relevant legal rules, but that similar previous decisions can be consulted to guide and justify the conclusion reached in the instant case. In fact, where a judge in a lower court is aware of a decision of a higher court which sets a precedent in an analogous case, then this previous decision **must** be followed, and it is this element of **binding** precedent which is distinctive within the English system.

So, for example, imagine that a new statute has been created by Parliament, which regulates the activities of estate agents. A dispute arises concerning the interpretation of one of the sections of the Act, and a court case ensues. The case reaches the Court of Appeal, which makes a decision about the definition of 'an estate agent'. In all future cases in which the definition of an estate agent is in issue, lower courts must observe this binding precedent, and apply the decision from the previous case in these situations.

Clearly, if this system is to operate effectively, then it is essential that there is an efficient and reliable system of reporting court cases. This is achieved through the work of the Incorporated Council of Law Reporting for England and Wales, which produces the authoritative version of case reports (known as The Law Reports) and through the publication of alternative series of reports by private publishers such as Butterworths. Because of the vast number of cases decided every year, not every case from every court is published in this way, but the system does provide judges with access to decisions of the superior courts which will assist them in reaching a conclusion.

By consulting both the official and the privately published law reports, members of the legal profession and the judiciary are able to obtain valuable information about the way in which cases involving particular facts and legal principles have been decided on previous occasions. Because these precedents are regarded as binding, solicitors and barristers are thus able to give more accurate advice to their clients, and the judges are able to follow the reasoning of previous courts.

There are, however, both advantages and disadvantages in the operation of a system of binding precedent.

From what you have learned of the operation of the doctrine of *stare decisis* so far, try to compile a list of advantages and disadvantages of the system of precedent as it is in England and Wales. Try to think of at least three points in favour of the doctrine and three against (although you may be able to think of more than this). Write them down below, and refer to them again when you have completed the work in this chapter. You may wish to add to or amend your list when you have learned more about the system.

At this stage, it is important to notice some of the basic arguments in favour of the doctrine as it is operated in the English legal system, and also to be aware of some of the drawbacks; not all lawyers (and not even all judges) agree with a strict application of the principle of *stare decisis*.

It is true that the doctrine enables judges to avoid having to solve the same legal problem more than once, and thus may save a considerable amount of judicial time and energy. A further advantage is that this system lends some degree of predictability to legal decision-making. This is of great importance to lawyers when attempting to advise their clients as to the likely outcome of litigation. When a particular fact situation or legal principle has featured in a previous court case, the lawyer is able to assess the case before him or her in the light of the previous decision, and guide the client according to whether the outcome is likely to be in the client's favour or not. Another argument in favour of a strict application of the doctrine is that use of previous precedents satisfies one of the requirements of justice, i.e., that people be treated alike in like circumstances. Thus, a case heard in the High Court in London, to which a precedent of the Court of Appeal is applicable, will, by the application of that precedent, be dealt with in the same way as a similar case being heard by the High Court in Nottingham.

There are however disadvantages, as well as advantages, in adhering to precedent in this way. Critics have argued that this system leads to judicial laziness, and discourages members of the judiciary from taking responsibility for thinking through solutions to legal problems. Certainly because the doctrine is essentially backward-looking, it may stifle creativity in decision-making, and may lead to stagnation in the law. Related to this latter point is the criticism that the law cannot develop and respond to changes in social circumstances, unless a case arises which allows a court the opportunity to amend a previous decision by not following the precedent. Legal change could therefore become dependent upon those who have the means to pursue litigation.

All in all, for every advantage provided by the doctrine of precedent, there appears to be a corresponding disadvantage. However, the operation of the doctrine is firmly embedded in the English legal system, and so the next step is to examine the way in which the doctrine is applied in individual courts.

9.4 How does the Doctrine Operate?

The hierarchy of the courts, about which you have learned in previous chapters, is an important factor in the operation of the doctrine in practice. A useful summary of this hierarchical approach has been made by the authors Twining and Miers in their book *How to do things with rules* (Weidenfeld and Nicholson, 1991) and it is worth learning these few simple principles, which apply whenever a court wishes to know whether or not to follow the decision of a previous case.

   (a)   If the precedent is a decision of a court superior to it in the hierarchy then it **must** follow that precedent in the present case. (i.e., it is **bound** by the precedent).

   (b)   If the precedent is one of the court's own previous decisions, then subject to certain exceptions, it **must** follow the precedent.

   (c)   If the precedent is a decision of a court inferior to it in the hierarchy, then it is **not** bound to follow the precedent, but may do so if it chooses.

These statements provide a good rule of thumb and are therefore worth memorising, but like all rules of thumb they do not tell the whole story, and in practice the situation is rather more complicated. In order to obtain the full picture, it is necessary to examine the position of each individual court in turn, and so details about the way in which precedent is applied in the different courts can be found in **9.5**. Before that, however, it is important to appreciate two of the technical aspects of the doctrine.

9.4.1 AVOIDING PRECEDENTS

First, it may be that although a judge is bound by a precedent in a particular case, there are good reasons why the judge may wish **not** to follow it. In these circumstances it is likely that the judge will try to **distinguish** the precedent, that is to find some significant difference between the facts of the two cases, so as to avoid having to follow the previous decision. If the court can find sufficient difference between the material facts of the two cases, then it may feel it is justified in departing from the precedent. This process of distinguishing cases is extremely important in practice, because it enables judges to develop the law, rather than being bound by precedent in every situation.

It is also open to the superior courts in the hierarchy to **reverse** the decision of a court lower down in the hierarchy during the course of the **same** case. This will occur if, for example, the High Court has reached a particular decision in a particular case, but then the Court of Appeal reaches the opposite conclusion in the ensuing appeal in that case.

The Court of Appeal and House of Lords also have the power to **overrule** the decision of a lower court, in a later, **different** case. For example, the High Court may reach a decision in case X, and that decision becomes a precedent for the future. Some time later, a similar case, case Y, is heard by the High Court. Case X is used as a precedent, but the losing party appeals to the Court of Appeal. The Court of Appeal finds the original decision in case X to have been erroneous, and overrules it.

SAQ 28

It is important that you feel confident about the terminology associated with the doctrine of precedent, and that you can use it correctly. Consider the following (fictitious) scenario, and fill in the missing words. You will find the answers at 9.8.

(a) In 1990, Betty Bloggs was convicted by the Crown Court of the murder of her husband Alf. In her defence, Betty claimed that Alf had treated her brutally throughout their 20 years of marriage, and that this constituted provocation, even though there had been no violence between them immediately prior to the murder. The Crown Court judge had been persuaded by this argument, and regarded Betty's defence as correct in law. On appeal by the prosecution, however, the Court of Appeal (Criminal Division) held that this extension of the defence of provocation was incorrect. The decision of the Crown Court on this point of law was . . . . by the Court of Appeal.

(b) In 1993, a similar case arose. Carrie Careful was charged with the murder of her husband Denis. She pleaded a similar defence to that of Betty Bloggs. The Crown Court regarded itself as bound by the previous decision in the Court of Appeal. However, in Carrie's case, the court found that Denis had been violent towards her within an hour of the murder taking place. Because of this difference in the facts, the Crown Court was able to . . . . the case of Betty Bloggs, and did not follow it.

(c) In 1994, Emily Earnest was charged with the murder of her husband Fred, in circumstances identical to those in the Betty Bloggs case. Both the Crown Court and the Court of Appeal followed the precedent set in the Betty Bloggs case, but on appeal to the House of Lords, it was decided that this interpretation of the law was completely incorrect, and the Betty Bloggs case was . . . .

9.4.2 *RATIO DECIDENDI* AND *OBITER DICTA*

Secondly, it is important to be aware of which part of the decision of a previous case is to be regarded as binding. The decision itself, i.e., who wins and who loses, is only really of interest to the parties in the case. What really matters, from the point of view of lawyers who wish to apply the doctrine of precedent, is the abstract principle which can be drawn from the case by combining the relevant legal principles with the essential facts on which the decision is based. This principle is known as the ***ratio decidendi*** (literally, the reason for deciding) and it is this part of the case which is absorbed into the general law, and which forms the basis of future legal reasoning. In discussion, lawyers generally abbreviate the term *ratio decidendi* to 'the *ratio*' (pronounced 'rayshio').

The *ratio decidendi* is often contrasted with other parts of the judgment which are said to be ***obiter dicta,*** (that is, sayings by the way). These are remarks made by a judge which are less central to the decision, for example, hypothetical examples, statements of law which support dissenting judgments, and remarks concerned with broader principles of law which may not be directly in issue in the instant case.

The ***ratio decidendi*** is therefore that part of a previously decided case which later judges regard as binding on them, because it embodies the legal rule which justifies a particular decision. But how is it identified in any particular case? Discerning the *ratio* of a case requires a close analysis of the judgment or judgments in the case, and is made more difficult by the fact that the judges do not identify it for the benefit of later readers.

Academic writers such as Professor A. Goodhart have attempted to formulate methods of discerning the *ratio*. Goodhart's theory is that the *ratio* can be found by taking account of the facts treated by the judge as material, and the judge's decision as based on them. But it should be noted that this is only a theory and finding the *ratio* tends to be an intuitive process. Some help may be derived from the headnote in a reported case, that is the summary of the facts and the decision in each case, inserted by the editor of the reports, but it is unwise to rely on these as a method of ascertaining the *ratio*. There is, unfortunately, no substitute for reading carefully through all the judgments of the case under discussion. In fact this can reveal that a case may have more than one *ratio*, either because a judge has identified several reasons for a decision, providing several *rationes decidendi*, or because several members of either the Court of Appeal of House of Lords have given separate judgments with slightly different *rationes*.

From now on, every time you read a reported case, you should study the judgments provided with a view to identifying the *ratio* of the case. You will then be able to compare your assessment of the case with that provided in the learning texts or other books. You will also have the opportunity to practise this skill at the end of this chapter.

9.5 The Doctrine as Applied in Individual Courts

9.5.1 THE COURT OF JUSTICE OF THE EUROPEAN COMMUNITIES

Decisions of this court are binding on all courts in the English legal system in matters of interpretation of legislation emanating from the institutions of the European Union. The European Court does not regard itself as bound by its own previous decisions.

9.5.2 THE HOUSE OF LORDS

Decisions of the House of Lords bind all inferior courts in this country.

From the beginning of this century until 1966, the House also regarded itself as bound by its own previous decisions. This was because it was felt that there had be an end to litigation, i.e., it had to be possible for people to see that once a case had been to the House of Lords, then there would be no further debate on that legal point.

However, this approach proved to be unduly restrictive, in that it effectively prohibited any development in the law. Therefore in 1966, Lord Gardiner LC on behalf of himself and the other Law Lords issued a Practice Statement which declared that the House would feel free to depart from its own previous decisions 'when it appears right to do so'. The Statement acknowledged that the House of Lords regarded the doctrine of precedent as an 'indispensable foundation' upon which to decide the law, but that 'too rigid adherence to precedent may lead to injustice in a particular case and also unduly restrict the proper development of the law'.

In *Cases and Materials* (9.1.1) you will find reproduced the text of the House of Lords Practice Statement. *(Practice Statement (Judicial Precedent)* [1966] 3 All ER 77). You will also see the text of the Press Release which was issued with the statement.

From reading these extracts, what do you learn about the circumstances in which the House of Lords would be prepared to depart from its own previous decisions, and the accompanying pitfalls which the House wished to avoid?

As you will see from the Practice Statement itself, the House of Lords was very conscious of the need for caution in the exercise of its new power. This was felt to be especially important in cases where contracts, settlements, and financial arrangements had been made in reliance on previous House of Lords decisions. The Law Lords also wished to avoid any reduction in the degree of certainty required for justice to be done in the sphere of criminal law. However, the House also recognised that there would be circumstances where modern conditions would require a change in the law, and that decisions which had been made in the past in response to factors which had since ceased to operate, could now be overruled by the use of the Practice Statement.

In practice, the Law Lords did indeed exercise caution in their use of this power, and following the publication of the Practice Statement in 1966, two years passed before the House of Lords departed from one of their own previous decisions. The first case in which the authority of the Statement was invoked was that of *Conway* v *Rimmer* [1968] AC 910 HL in which the case of *Duncan* v *Cammell Laird & Co.* [1942] AC 624 HL was overruled.

Both of these cases concerned the extent to which the Crown could claim the right not to disclose information during a court case. The earlier case of *Duncan* v *Cammell Laird & Co.* had been decided during the Second World War, and this had enabled the goverment to claim 'public interest immunity', and thus avoid the need to comply with an order of the court requiring disclosure of certain documents. The different circumstances under which the case of *Conway* v *Rimmer* arose meant that the House of Lords removed this immunity from the government. This case was therefore a good example of the way in which the Practice Statement could be used to adapt the law to changes in society.

This decision did not, however, mean that a judicial 'free-for-all' would ensue, and in the intervening years, the House of Lords has continued to use its power in a relatively small number of cases. For example, in *Herrington* v *British Railways Board* [1972] 1 All ER 749, a rule which had been propounded in the earlier House of Lords case of *Addie & Sons* v *Dumbreck* [1929] AC 358 HL *was* relaxed as a result of the Practice Statement. In *Addie,* the House had ruled that an occupier of property owed only a minimal duty of care to a trespasser, even though where that trespasser happened to be a child. However, changes in society's opinion as to the appropriate duty owed in these circumstances led the Law Lords to formulate a duty on the part of an occupier to act humanely towards trespassers.

Similarly, in *Miliangos* v *George Frank (Textiles) Ltd* [1975] 3 All ER 801, new developments in rules relating to the exchange rates for foreign currencies, and in particular the less favourable position of sterling, led the House of Lords to change its own earlier ruling in the case of *Re United Railways of Havana & Regla Warehouses Ltd* [1960] 2 All ER 332, that damages awarded by an English court could only be awarded in sterling. As a result of the *Miliangos* case, damages may be awarded by a court in England based on the currency specified in the contract which gave rise to the dispute.

Cases such as these, in which the Practice Statement has been used to positive effect, indicate that the House will expect to see that broad issues of justice and public policy are involved before altering a previous decision, and will not usually overturn a previous ruling simply because it is felt that the earlier decision was wrong. A good example of this line of reasoning can be seen in the case of *Jones* v *Secretary of State for Social Services* [1972] 1 All ER 145. This case concerned the interpretation of a statute, on which the House of Lords had previously given a ruling in the case of *Re Dowling* [1967] 1 AC 725. Despite the fact that four of the seven Law Lords who heard the *Jones* case felt that *Re Dowling* was wrongly decided, the House declined to depart from its earlier decision. Some of the reasons offered as justification for this decision were that no broad issues of justice or public policy or legal principle were involved, the case involved the interpretation of a statute and therefore any harmful consequences of the interpretation could be cured by further statutory provisions, and the need for finality in litigation.

The case of *R* v *Shivpuri* [1986] 2 All ER 334 proved to be an exception to the principles set out in the *Jones* case however. Here, the Lords took the unusual step of overruling a previous decision of their own which had only been made one year before. The case of *Anderton* v *Ryan* [1985] AC 560 was felt to have been wrongly decided, and to contain an error which distorted the law. The Law Lords felt that this situation needed to be remedied as quickly as possible by overruling the previous decision, despite the fact that this was a case which affected the criminal law and the interpretation of a statute, both factors which were thought to militate against the use of the Practice Statement. The Lords emphasised however that this was an exceptional case, and that use of the Practice Statement generally would remain a rare occurrence.

You may have noticed from examining the text of the Practice Statement in *Cases and Materials* that the House of Lords emphasised that this change in practice was not intended to affect the use of precedent in any other court. However, when you reach the section on precedent in the Court of Appeal, you will find that Lord Denning, a former, well-known Master of the Rolls, would have liked to extend the powers of the Court of Appeal in this direction, but was restrained by the House of Lords.

9.5.3   THE JUDICIAL COMMITTEE OF THE PRIVY COUNCIL

The Judicial Committee is not strictly bound by decisions of the House of Lords, nor does it regard itself as bound by its own previous decisions.

Decisions of the Committee are not viewed as binding on other courts, but its advice is regarded as being of the strongest persuasive value. This means that a court lower down the hierarchy is not strictly obliged to follow decisions of the Committee, but will give weight to its opinions which are treated as highly influential.

SAQ 29

Why does the composition of the Committee mean that its decisions are treated with such respect? (You may need to refresh your memory from earlier chapters to answer this question.)

For judicial sittings, the Privy Council will normally consist of the Lord Chancellor, and the Lords of Appeal in Ordinary. Thus the composition of the Council is usually the same as that of the House of Lords. This accounts for the respect with which its opinions are regarded, and explains its influence as part of the system of precedent.

9.5.4   THE COURT OF APPEAL (CIVIL DIVISION)

The Court of Appeal is bound by decisions of the House of Lords.

The decisions of the Court of Appeal itself are binding on the inferior courts in the hierarchy.

The Court of Appeal is **normally** bound by its own previous decisions. This is known as the 'self-binding rule', and means that unless one of the established exceptions to this rule applies, then the Court of Appeal will always follow its own previous precedents. The classic statement of the exceptions to the self-binding rule can be found in the case of *Young* v *Bristol Aeroplane Co. Ltd* [1944] 2 All ER 293. Here, Lord Greene MR identified three situations in which it would be possible for the Court of Appeal to depart from its own previous decisions:

   (a)   where previous decisions of the Court conflict with each other. In these circumstances the Court can decide which decision to follow and which to ignore;

   (b)   where a previous decision of the Court conflicts with a subsequent decision of the House of Lords. Here the Court of Appeal must follow the House of Lords ruling rather than its own even if it thinks the House of Lords ruling is wrong;

   (c)   where a previous precision of the Court appears to have been made **per incuriam**. This literally means 'through lack of care', which sounds as though it should enable later judges to ignore any previous precedent which seems to the later court to be wrong. The true position is not quite so simple however, as the technical application of the per incuriam rule is actually quite narrow.

According to the case of *Morelle* v *Wakeling* [1955] 1 All ER 708, a decision is regarded as having been made per incuriam if the Court of Appeal was in a state of ignorance or forgetfulness with regard to a relevant part of statute law or a binding precedent and, as a result, some part of the decision, or some step in the reasoning is found to be demonstrably wrong. The court did acknowledge the fact that in rare and exceptional cases, a decision might be held to be per incuriam where there was a 'manifest slip or error', and an illustration of this can be found in the case of *Williams* v *Fawcett* [1985] 1 All ER 787.

ACTIVITY 34

Read the extract from the case of *Williams* v *Fawcett* in *Cases and Materials* (9.1.2) and try to identify the reasons for the application of the per incuriam rule in this case. You should be able to find three different factors which led the Court of Appeal to choose not to follow a precedent established by two of its own previous decisions.

As you will see from the passage quoted, this was a case in which the Court of Appeal felt that there were special features justifying an extension of the traditionally accepted form of the per incuriam rule. Three of these features seem to be prominent in the judgment. They were first, the clarity with which the growth of the error could be detected if the previous decisions were read consecutively, secondly, the fact that the cases were concerned with the liberty of the subject, and thirdly, that the cases were most unlikely to reach the House of Lords, which meant that there would be no further opportunity to correct the error which had crept into the law.

The previous paragraphs describe the currently accepted understanding of the doctrine of precedent as it relates to the Court of Appeal. You should, however, be aware of the fact that during the 1970s, the then Master of the Rolls, Lord Denning, challenged this accepted view of the role of the Court of Appeal. In a number of controversial cases he led a campaign, first, to establish that the Court of Appeal was not always strictly bound by House of Lords decisions, and could even declare them to be wrongly decided using the doctrine of per incuriam, and secondly, to adopt the philosophy of the 1966 House of Lords Practice Statement in the Court of Appeal, so that the Court could choose not to follow its own previous decisions in circumstances where it felt that it was right to do so, without having to bring the case within the exceptions outlined in the case of *Young* v *Bristol Aeroplane Co. Ltd*.

Lord Denning received a great deal of criticism from the House of Lords as a result of expressing these revolutionary views. In the case of *Broome* v *Cassell & Co. Ltd* [1971] 1

All ER 801, he had led the Court of Appeal to reject an earlier House of Lords case concerning the award of exemplary damages (*Rookes* v *Barnard* [1964] 1 All ER 367) on the grounds that it had been decided per incuriam. When *Broome* v *Cassell & Co. Ltd* reached the House of Lords ([1972] 1 All ER 801) Lord Hailsham reminded Lord Denning that it was not open to the Court of Appeal 'to give gratuitous advice to judges of first instance to ignore decisions of the House of Lords in this way . . . it is necessary for each lower tier, including the Court of Appeal, to accept loyally the decisions of the higher tiers'.

Similarly, Lord Denning attacked the self-binding rule in the Court of Appeal in a number of cases, culminating in the case of *Davis* v *Johnson* [1978] 1 All ER 1132 which concerned the powers of the courts to provide protection to women who were subjected to violence by their cohabiting partners. Lord Denning had expressed the opinion that the Court of Appeal should be at liberty to depart from a previous decision of its own if convinced that the previous decision was wrong, in much the same way as the House of Lords had done since 1966. This view was again rejected by the House of Lords in no uncertain terms, and the principles set out in the case of *Young* v *Bristol Aeroplane Co. Ltd* were reafffirmed. It would seem therefore that the traditional view of precedent in the Court of Appeal now prevails.

The Court of Appeal is in the process of hearing appeals in the following three cases. Explain how the doctrine of precedent will apply in each case.

Case 1: There is a previous decision of the Court of Appeal (Case A) involving similar facts and legal issues, but the Court of Appeal hearing Case 1 thinks that whilst Case A was correctly decided, the decision is outdated in today's social climate.

Case 2: A previous case involving similar facts and legal issues was decided by the Court of Appeal in 1990 (Case B). The House of Lords has also made a ruling in a similar case (Case C) in 1993.

Case 3: There are two previous Court of Appeal precedents relevant to the point in issue. Both were decided on the same day, by differently constituted Courts of Appeal, and these two decisions conflict with each other.

In order to answer these questions, the traditional view of the doctrine of precedent must be adopted, Lord Denning's views having been rejected by the House of Lords.

In Case 1, the self-binding rule of the Court of Appeal is applicable. Where the facts and issues are covered by a previous precedent of the Court of Appeal, then unless one of the exceptions in *Young* v *Bristol Aeroplane Co. Ltd* applies, the Court is bound to follow it. The fact that it regards the previous precedent as outdated is irrelevant.

In Case 2, the self-binding rule would indicate that the Court should follow Case B. However, this is one of the exceptions from *Young's* case, i.e., that where there is a later

House of Lords decision which conflicts with the earlier Court of Appeal decision, then the House of Lords case (Case C) prevails and must be followed.

Case 3 again concerns the rule in *Young's* case. Because of the volume of cases conducted in the Court of Appeal, it is possible that similar cases could be heard by differently constituted courts on the same day, and different decisions reached. In such cases, a later Court of Appeal may choose which of these decisions to follow, and decline to follow the other.

9.5.5 THE COURT OF APPEAL (CRIMINAL DIVISION)

The rules of precedent are in theory identical in the two divisions of the Court of Appeal, i.e.., that the Court is bound by decisions of the House of Lords, and by its own previous decisions, subject to the exceptions outlined in the case of *Young v Bristol Aeroplane Co. Ltd*. Whilst the rule regarding House of Lords decisions remains the same, the self-binding rule is applied in a slightly different way in the criminal division. Case law indicates that the Court of Appeal (Criminal Division) may depart from its own previous decisions if it is satified that the law was misapplied or misunderstood, and that this power to deviate from the self-binding rule exists in addition to the exceptions set out in *Young's* case.

In *Cases and Materials* (9.1.3) there is a short extract from the case of *R v Taylor* [1950] 2 KB 368 which was decided by the Court of Criminal Appeal (which is the predecessor of the modern Court of Appeal (Criminal Division). What does this case reveal about the justification for applying the self-binding rule in a different way in criminal matters?

As you will appreciate, the liberty of the individual is at stake in cases which are heard by the Court of Appeal (Criminal Division), and this is felt to be a more important factor than the consistency which is produced by rigid adherence to precedent. The danger of a wrongful conviction outweighs the need to follow the doctrine in its strict form. A slightly different view of precedent is therefore taken in such cases.

9.5.6 THE DIVISIONAL COURTS OF THE HIGH COURT

Divisional Courts of the High Court are bound by decisions of the House of Lords and the Court of Appeal.

Decisions of the Divisional Courts are binding on inferior courts.

The Divisional Courts are normally bound by their own previous decisions, unless one or more of the three exceptions enunciated in the case of *Young v Bristol Aeroplane Co. Ltd*, applies. As in the Court of Appeal, there may be a greater degree of flexibility in this rule when the Divisional Court of the Queen's Bench considers criminal cases.

SAQ 31

You will notice that the rule of precedent which applies to the Divisional Courts is the same as that applied in the Court of Appeal. Can you think what the reason for this might be? (Hint: look back to the earlier chapters on the jurisdiction of the courts and the system of appeals for help with this point.)

The similarity of the rules concerning precedent in the Court of Appeal and the Divisional Courts of the High Court can be explained in terms of function. The Divisional Courts are not generally courts of first instance: as with the Court of Appeal, they are appellate courts, and in certain circumstances they replace the Court of Appeal as the appropriate forum for appeal. In such cases, the next avenue of appeal is the House of Lords, which means that the Divisional Courts enjoy a great degree of authority and seniority. It is therefore logical for the same rules of precedent to be adopted here.

9.5.7 THE HIGH COURT

The High Court is bound by decisions of those courts which are superior to it in the hierarchy.

Decisions of the High Court are binding on courts which are inferior to it in the hierarchy.

The High Court does not regard itself as strictly bound by its own previous decisions, but they are of strongest persuasive value. Where previous High Court decisions conflict therefore, the judge will generally follow the later case, but is not empowered to overrule the case which is not preferred.

9.5.8 THE CROWN COURT

The Crown Court is bound by decisions of superior courts.

Its decisions are binding on those courts which are inferior to it in the hierarchy.

Decisions of the Crown Court are of persuasive, but not binding, authority for other judges in the Crown Court.

9.5.9 COUNTY COURTS AND MAGISTRATES' COURTS

These courts are bound by all superior courts. Their own decisions are not binding on any courts, not even on other courts at the same level in the hierarchy.

9.6   Conclusion

The doctrine of judicial precedent, the canons of statutory interpretation, and the rules concerning the structure and functions of the courts, together provide a necessary foundation for your study of the substantive law. By working through the previous chapters, you should have acquired the basic skills which you will need in order to analyse the primary sources of law, and understand how legal issues are dealt with by the different courts.

In particular you should be able to:

■ describe the basic principles of the doctrine of *stare decisis*;

■ apply these principles to different courts in the English legal system;

■ discuss traditional and radical approaches to the doctrine;

■ appreciate the signifance of the doctrine for the development of the law.

At the end of this chapter you will find an exercise which will enable you to test your knowledge and skills in the areas covered by the learning text. You should then try to transfer these skills, and keep this knowledge in mind when you are analysing case and statute law in your further studies. I hope that you will want to return to this section of the textbook and *Cases and Materials* from time to time, so that you retain an interest in analysing the primary sources of law, and so that you do not forget the foundation principles which you will need as a lawyer.

9.7   Further Reading

Ingman, T., *The English Legal Process*, 6th edn, London: Blackstone Press, 1996, Chapter 9.

9.8   Answers to SAQ 28

(a) Reversed.

(b) Distinguished.

(c) Overruled.

9.9   End of Chapter Assessment Question

Read the extracts from the case of *Davis* v *Johnson* [1978] 1 All ER 1132, in *Cases and Materials* (**9.1.3**), or read the original report at the reference given, if you have access to a law library, and then answer the following questions. The answers can be found in *Cases and Materials* (**9.3**).

1.   What were the central factual issues in the case?

2.   What preliminary question of law had to be determined, and what was the question of statutory interpretation which had to be decided?

3.   Explain the route through the court system by which the case reached the House of Lords.

4.   Did the House of Lords as a whole favour the narrower or the broader view of construction of s. 1 of the Domestic Violence and Matrimonial Proceedings Act 1976? Did Lord Diplock agree with this?

5.   According to Lord Diplock, what is the rule which governs precedent in the Court of Appeal, when that court is reviewing one of its own previous decisions? How does that rule operate?

6.   What are the reasons for the rule mentioned in question 5?

7.   How did Lord Denning attempt to alter that rule? Did he succeed?

CASES AND MATERIALS

CHAPTER ONE

BASIC LEGAL SKILLS

1.1 Why Have You Chosen this Course?

MOTIVATING FACTORS FOR ACADEMIC STUDY

Ambition – the need to achieve
A career goal – promotion or a change of job
Curiosity or boredom
Intrinsic interest in the subject itself
External pressure – requirement of employer

1.2 How Do You Learn?

EXTRACT FROM STUDY DIARY

Monday
6.30 am to 7.30 am. Own study
Making notes on the civil court structure to use in an essay. Managed to select some useful information for the essay.

8.15 am to 8.30 am. On the bus
Refreshing memory on the separation of powers. Concentration not so good – perhaps learned one or two points.

1 pm to 1.30 pm. Lunch break at desk
Thought a bit more about the court essay and had one or two good ideas about how to structure the answer, but forgot to make a note of them and can't now remember what they were – must remember to keep a notebook handy for jotting down things like that.

8 pm to 9pm. Own study
Started to write essay. Interrupted three times by child wanting attention. Eventually managed to write about 500 words before concentration went completely.

1.3   How Do You Read?

1.3.1   READING TEXTBOOKS

Bailey, S.H. and Gunn M.J., *Smith and Bailey on the Modern English Legal System,*
3rd edn, London: Sweet and Maxwell, 1996, p. 39

C.   *TRIBUNALS*

1.   INTRODUCTION

The significant role played by administrative tribunals in the adjudication of legal disputes is a development of the present century, although it is possible to find examples of similar institutions in earlier centuries. For example, the General and Special Commissioners of Income Tax were established in 1799 and 1805 respectively, with both assessment and appellate functions. The Railway and Canal Commission was established in 1873, *inter alia*, to settle disputes between railway companies and between companies and their customers, and subsequently evolved into the Transport Tribunal.

The most important factors behind the expansion of the number of tribunals and the range of their work have been the advent of the welfare state and the development of state economic controls. The National Insurance Act 1911 set up the unemployment benefit scheme. All questions concerning claims to benefit were to be determined initially by an insurance officer. A workman dissatisfied with a determination could have it referred to a 'court of referees' consisting of a chairman appointed by the Board of Trade, one member from an 'employers' panel' and one from a 'workmens' panel.' A further right of appeal lay to an 'umpire' – a national appellate authority appointed by the Crown. This arrangement proved superior to alternative methods of adjudication used in legislation of the period, and was adopted as the general model for many of the new tribunals established in the following decades:

> The extension of governmental responsibility for welfare provision, regulation of the economy, employment policy and resource development has created new statutory rights, obligations and restraints. Consequently, new areas of potential dispute have opened up, the boundaries of which have been progressively extended, and which require legislative provision for adjudication. The tendency, for a variety of reasons, has been to use tribunals rather than ordinary courts for settling disputes of this kind.

This is not to say that there have been clear principles governing either the decision to allocate a particular decision to a tribunal or the details of the machinery established:

> Parliament's selection of subjects to be referred to tribunals and inquiries does not form a regular pattern. Certain basic guidelines can be detected, but the choice is influenced by the interplay of various factors – the nature of the decisions, accidents of history, departmental preferences and political considerations – rather than by the application of a set of coherent principles.

> These tribunals commonly determine disputes between the citizen and the state arising out of the administration of a statutory scheme. In addition, some determine disputes between citizens, normally arising out of protective legislation enacted for the benefit of one of the parties.

2.   THE FRANKS REPORT

A significant landmark in the development of tribunals was the 1957 report of the Committee on Administrative Tribunals and Enquiries chaired by Sir Oliver Franks. Part of the terms of reference required the Committee to review the constitution and working of tribunals other than the ordinary courts of law, constituted by a minister or for the purposes of a minister's functions. Among the general points made by the Committee were, first, that the special procedures within their terms of reference should be marked by the characteristics of 'openness, fairness and impartiality':

In the field of tribunals openness appears to us to require the publicity of proceedings and knowledge of the essential reasoning underlying the decisions; fairness to require the adoption of a clear procedure which enables parties to know their rights, to present their case fully and to know the case which they have to meet; and impartiality to require the freedom of tribunals from the influence, real or apparent, of Departments concerned with the subject matter of their decisions.

Secondly, the Committee noted that tribunals as a system for adjudication had come to stay, and indeed that the tendency to refer issues arising from legislative schemes to special tribunals was likely to grow rather than to diminish.

Thirdly, the Committee recommended the establishment of two permanent Councils on Tribunals, one for England and Wales and one for Scotland, to supervise tribunal and inquiry procedures.

In addition, the report made a whole series of detailed recommendations concerning both the constitution and procedures of tribunals generally and particular tribunals. Most of the proposals were implemented in the Tribunals and Inquiries Act 1958, subsequently consolidated in the Tribunals and Inquiries Acts 1971 and now 1992, and in changes of regulation and departmental practice.

3. THE COUNCIL ON TRIBUNALS

The 1958 Act established one Council on Tribunals, with a Scottish Committee. Its functions in respect of tribunals are:

(a) to keep under review the construction and working of the tribunals specified in Schedule 1 to the [1992] Act;

(b) to consider and report on particular matters referred to the Council by the Lord Chancellor and the Lord Advocate with respect to any tribunal other than a court of law whether or not specified in Schedule 1: . . .

Thus, its powers are consultative and advisory. It was not given the executive powers recommended by the Franks Report as to the appointment of tribunal members, the review of remuneration and the formulation of procedural codes. Certainly it has no power to reverse or require reconsideration of specific tribunal decisions. The Council has 15 members appointed by the Lord Chancellor and the Lord Advocate, and the Parliamentary Commissioner for Administration is a member *ex officio*. The membership comprises a mixture of lawyers, both practising and academic, and non-lawyers, with the latter predominating. The Council's requests for additional powers, put forward in its Special Report of 1980, were generally not accepted, although a code for consultation with government departments has been introduced. The Council has done much useful work in minor matters, securing, for example, many amendments to draft bills, rules and regulations, and some changes in tribunal practice. It has published a Report on Model Rules for Tribunals, a Code of Practice on Access for Disabled People using the Tribunal System and (with Property Holdings) a Register of Tribunal Hearing Accommodation. However, its political position is weak, its resources are inadequate and it 'remains an inconspicuous advisory committee.' It is still met from time to time by spurious arguments from Departments why a proposed new tribunal should not be placed under its jurisdiction; it sometimes, but not always, succeeds in overcoming them. Access to the deliberative stage of tribunal hearings is occasionally denied.

4. ADJUDICATION OR ADMINISTRATION

There has been some debate on whether tribunals are to be regarded as part of the machinery of justice or part of the machinery of administration. The Franks Committee stated:

Tribunals are not ordinary courts, but neither are they appendages of Government Departments. Much of the official evidence, including that of the Joint Permanent Secretary to the Treasury, appeared to reflect the view that tribunals should properly be regarded as part of the machinery of administration, for which the Government must retain a close and continuing responsibility. Thus, for example, tribunals in the social service field would be regarded as adjuncts to the administration of the services themselves. We do not accept this view. We consider that tribunals should properly be regarded as machinery provided by Parliament for adjudication rather than as part of the machinery of administration. The essential point is that in all these cases Parliament has deliberately provided for a decision outside and independent of the Department concerned, either at first instance (for example in the case of Rent Tribunals and the Licensing Authorities for Public Service and Goods Vehicles) or on appeal from a decision of a Minister or of an official in a special statutory position (for example a valuation officer or an insurance officer). Although the relevant statutes do not in all cases expressly enact that tribunals are to consist entirely of persons outside the Government service, the use of the term 'tribunal' in legislation undoubtedly bears this connotation, and the intention of Parliament to provide for the independence of tribunals is clear and unmistakable.

The supposed characteristic of independence cannot, however, be taken too far. Clearly it is desirable that the expression of the 'departmental view' in an individual case should be confined to the representations made at the hearing itself. However, in many respects the departments retain a general influence over tribunal decision-making. They are responsible for the formulation of the relevant primary legislation and procedural rules, albeit in consultation with the Council on Tribunals, and indeed for the 'detailed arrangements' for the working of the tribunals. There has, however, been a trend in recent years for the Lord Chancellor's Department to take over (or be given) responsibility for the operation of a growing list of tribunals. The Department is now responsible for the Land Tribunal, the Special and General Commissioners of Income Tax, VAT and Duties Tribunals, the Society Security and Child Support Commissioners, the Transport Tribunal, and the Immigration Adjudicators and administrative responsibility for the immigration appellate authorities. The Council on Tribunals has set out some broad guidelines as to the allocation of administrative responsibility for tribunals, suggesting that the main consideration should be the independence of the tribunal and the public perception of that independence. It was necessary to show that there was real independence, especially where the outcome of a tribunal's hearings would affect the public purse on a policy seen by the government or a department as vitally important. There could be a long term aim for the Lord Chancellor's Department to take over responsibility for all such tribunals, but this would not be realistic for the present. Other relevant factors were the tribunal's size and geographical spread, level and involvement with the law. The Council noted that most of the tribunals currently administered by the Department were relatively senior, relatively closely involved with specifically legal issues, and comparatively small, and only sat in a small number of places.

A further aspect of the role of the Lord Chancellor's Department is that it is involved in the consideration of proposals to create new tribunals and provides advice and guidance to other departments on tribunal matters when so requested.

The Franks view on this point has been criticised in two respects. First, it has been pointed out that some tribunals are 'policy-oriented' rather than 'court substitute':

For instance, where there is a dispute about social security entitlement, tribunals are basically used in place of the ordinary courts because the latter have become too expensive, formal and technical in their procedure. On the other hand, many matters of planning, whether in transport, land use, or industrial expertise, are given to tribunals because of the lack of expertise and doctrinal flexibility, or policy consciousness, on the part of the courts. Thus different weaknesses in the courts give rise to different types of tribunals.

Examples of policy-oriented tribunals include the Transport Tribunal and the Civil Aviation Authority.

Secondly, it has been argued that even court-substitute tribunals should be seen as hybrid in nature; not only machinery for adjudication but, as well, 'vital components of administration.'

5.   SUPPOSED ADVANTAGES OF TRIBUNALS AS COURT-SUBSTITUTES

The Franks Committee noted that tribunals have certain characteristics which often give them advantages over the courts: 'cheapness, accessibility, freedom from technicality, expedition and expert knowledge of their particular subject.' Generally, tribunal proceedings are cheaper, speedier, and more expert than courts of law. However, accessibility is hindered by the great complexity of the system of tribunals and the lack of publicity given to their work. Moreover, the Council on Tribunals has stated that:

Significant changes have . . . taken place in the general constitutional and administrative climate. There is, for example, a movement towards greater formalism in procedures for settling disputes. The process started with reforms following the Franks Report which, in general, made tribunals more like courts. . . . Since then the trend towards judicialisation has gathered momentum with the result that tribunals are becoming more formal, expensive and procedurally complex. Consequently they tend to become more difficult for an ordinary citizen to comprehend and cope with on his own.

Associated with this movement are the Council's arguments in favour of the extension of legal aid to tribunals, the appointment of lawyer chairmen and the extension of rights of appeal to the courts. It has also been pointed out that, despite declarations by tribunals that they are not bound by precedent, the requirements of consistency and predictability of decision lead to the development of general principles and an informal *de facto* system of precedent, especially as the decisions of certain tribunals are systematically reported.

Accordingly, it is perhaps more true today than ever that 'such differences as there are between [courts and tribunals] are not in any sense fundamental but at most differences in degree. . . .' In particular, it is not possible to argue that courts administer rules of law while tribunals administer both law and policy:

[N]o such clear line can or should be drawn. Indeed it was the evolution of this myth which helped establish the tribunal system by convincing the judges of the ordinary courts that they were concerned with legal but not with policy questions. . . . Properly understood, tribunals are a more modern form of court. In some cases they may have more discretion than the courts, and this is particularly true of the policy oriented tribunals. But certainly they have no more discretion than the Chancery Division has in handling trusts, wards or companies.

Other, more pragmatic, reasons for establishing tribunals rather than entrusting matters to courts include the need not to overburden the judiciary, the avoidance of Ministerial responsibility for sensitive decisions and the easing of the workload of government departments.

6.   THE TRIBUNALS AND INQUIRIES ACT 1992

Apart from establishing the Council on Tribunals, the 1992 Act makes provision for the selection of chairmen of certain tribunals, requires reasons to be given by Schedule 1 tribunals, provides in many cases for an appeal on a point of law to the High Court and renders inoperative most clauses in statutes passed before August 1, 1958 purporting to exclude judicial review.

1.3.2   READING CASES

R v COMERFORD [1998] 1 All ER 823 (CA)

COURT OF APPEAL, CRIMINAL DIVISION
LORD BINGHAM OF CORNHILL CJ, POTTS AND BUTTERFIELD JJ
14, 28 OCTOBER 1997

Jury – Protection of jury – Judge's discretion – Prosecution applying for jury protection without giving reasons or calling evidence – Judge granting application and ordering that jurors should be known by numbers instead of having their names read out – Whether judge right to do so – Whether defendant's conviction unsafe – Juries Act 1974, s. 12(3).

On the second day of the defendant's trial for attempting to possess cocaine with intent to supply, the judge, after hearing sworn evidence from a customs official in chambers on an ex parte application by the prosecution, discharged the jury. He gave no reasons for doing so to the defence, and the trial was rescheduled with a new jury. A few days before the second hearing, the prosecution applied for police protection of the second jury. Although the prosecution gave no reasons to support the application and called no evidence in support of it, the judge granted the application and also ordered that the jurors, instead of having their names read out in court in the ordinary way, should be known only by numbers. At the conclusion of the trial, the defendant was convicted. He appealed against his conviction, contending that it was unsafe because the judge had followed the incorrect procedure in relation to the jury, in particular in granting police protection without requiring the prosecution to give reasons or call evidence and in ordering the jury to be called and sworn in by numbers instead of names.

HELD – (1)   When applying for jury protection, the correct procedure for the prosecution to adopt was to make the application inter partes supported by reasons for doing so and evidence that protection was required. However if, because of the practicalities of the situation, that procedure could not be followed, it could be departed from provided that the judge was satisfied that any departure was necessary and would not render the trial process unfair. In the instant case, since the judge had been presented with apparently reliable sworn evidence which obliged him to discharge the first jury and justified his decision to order protection of the second jury, the procedure adopted had not rendered the conviction unsafe (see p. 829 *e* to *g*, p. 830 *b* to *d* and p. 832 *j*, post).

(2)   A departure from the standard procedure of empanelling a jury did not render a trial a nullity, unless it violated the legal right of the defendant or made the proceedings unfair to him. Moreover, on its true construction, s. 12(3) of the Juries Act 1974, which referred to the practice of calling out the name of each juror selected by ballot, did not require the public announcement of jurors' names, but merely defined the time at which a challenge to a juror could be made. Accordingly, although it was desirable that the usual procedure for empanelling a jury should be followed, in cases where there was a risk of interference with the jury, a judge would be justified in withholding the names of jurors if he reasonably thought it to be desirable, provided that the defendant's right of challenge was preserved. In the instant case, since it was clear that the judge had intended to preserve the defendant's right of challenge, and since the defendant had not contended that he would have exercised any right of challenge if the names of the jurors had been called out, no irregularity had taken place. The appeal would therefore be dismissed (see p. 830 *j*, p. 831 *j* to p. 832 *a d* to *j*, post).

Notes

For the discharge of the jury during trial, see 11(2) *Halsbury's Laws* (4th edn reissue) paras 1022, 1023.

For the Juries Act 1974, s 12, see 22 *Halsbury's Statutes* (4th edn) (1995 reissue) 616.

Cases referred to in judgment

R v Dodd (1981) 74 Cr App R 50, CA.
R v Felixstowe Justices, ex p Leigh [1987] 1 All ER 551, [1987] QB 582, [1987] 2 WLR 380, DC.
R v Gash [1967] 1 All ER 811, [1967] 1 WLR 454, CA.
R v Ling [1987] Crim LR 495, CA.

R v Mellor (1858) Dears & B 468, 169 ER 1084, CCR.
R v Williams (1925) 19 Cr App R 67, CA.

Cases also cited or referred to in skeleton arguments
R v Davis [1993] 2 All ER 643, [1993] 1 WLR 613, CA.
R v Harrington (1976) 64 Cr App R 1, CA.
R v Nicholson (1840) 4 Jur 558.
R v Putman (1991) 93 Cr App R 281, CA.
R v Pyle (April 1995, unreported), Crown Ct.
R v Raymond (November 1994, unreported), Crown Ct.
R v Rose [1982] 2 All ER 731, [1982] AC 822, HL.
R v Solomon [1957] 3 All ER 497, [1958] 1 QB 203, CCA.

Appeal against conviction
Thomas Anthony Comerford appealed against his conviction in the Crown Court at
Middlesex Guildhall on 26 November 1996 before Judge Blacksell QC and a jury of
attempting to possess cocaine with intent to supply. The facts are set out in the judgment
of the court.

Jonathan Goldberg QC and *Peter Lodder* (assigned by the *Register of Criminal Appeals*) for
the appellant.
Simon Draycott (instructed by the *Solicitor for the Customs and Excise*) for the Crown.
                                                                              Cur adv vult

28 October 1997. The following judgment of the court was delivered.

LORD BINGHAM OF CORNHILL CJ: On 26 November 1996 the appellant was
convicted following a trial in the Crown Court at Middlesex Guildhall of attempting to
possess cocaine with intent to supply. The quantity of the cocaine was large and the
value high. He was sentenced to ten years' imprisonment. He appeals against conviction
by leave of the single judge.

The grounds of appeal relate to an order made and a procedure adopted in relation to
the jury at the outset of the trial. This makes it unnecessary to rehearse the underlying
facts in detail. The charge related to a large-scale operation to import cocaine into the
United Kingdom from Ecuador. The operation was monitored by undercover officers of
the Ecuador police and HM Customs and Excise. The appellant's participation took place
at a late stage of the importation process. The main issue at the trial was whether he
knew what was being imported. By their verdict the jury resolved this issue against him.

The trial of the appellant first began on 12 November 1996. The prosecution made a
public interest immunity application to the judge ex parte, but that was unrelated to the
matters now in issue. A jury was sworn, and the prosecution case was opened. On the
following day, before the hearing began, the Crown made a further public interest
immunity application to the judge. The defence were given no indication of the subject
matter of this application, which was heard in chambers. Present when the application
was made were the trial judge, prosecuting counsel and two senior officers of HM
Customs and Excise. Neither the defendant nor anyone on his behalf was present. There
was no court clerk or shorthand writer. But a tape was running. We have this tape. We
also have, and have read, a transcript of the exchanges recorded on the tape. The judge
heard sworn evidence from one customs official. There was discussion between him and
prosecuting counsel. The application occupied the morning, and the court did not sit
until after the short adjournment. Defence counsel asked counsel for the Crown to tell
him what was to happen, but prosecuting counsel felt unable to say. The judge was
asked the same question in the absence of the jury, but also felt unable to say. The jury
were, however, asked to return into court, and when they did so the judge at once told
them that they were discharged from returning a verdict in the case. He declined to give
any reasons to the defence for this decision.

It was arranged that a fresh trial of the appellant would begin on Monday, 18
November in front of the same judge but with a new jury. It was also arranged that on
14 and 15 November there should be legal argument on the agreed basis that rulings

given would be binding even before the swearing of the fresh jury. On 14 November the Crown applied for police protection of the second jury, giving no reasons to support this application and calling no evidence in support of it. The defence opposed this application, submitting (1) that to order jury protection was a drastic step, not to be taken lightly; (2) that the consequences for the appellant were serious because the jury might infer that the court considered the defendant or his associates to be likely to interfere with them; (3) that following *R* v *Ling* [1987] Crim LR 495 reasons for the application should be given, and evidence called to support it; (4) that the case was not of a type which showed an increased risk of jury interference by its very nature (such as a case involving terrorism or Mafia-type organised crime); and (5) that, if necessary, reasons could be given and/or evidence called in chambers or even in the absence of the appellant, so that cross-examination might take place and reasoned objections advanced by the defence.

The judge did not accede to these arguments. The Crown declined to give reasons, and no evidence was called. The judge, however, agreed that this was not a case of a kind which showed an increased risk of jury interference by its very nature. On 15 November the judge ruled that the jury should be protected. His decision was that protection should be given at level 3, the highest level. He was invited by the defence to deliver a private reasoned judgment, which he did and which was made available to the Registrar of Criminal Appeals but to no other party. We have seen and read a written judgment dated 18 November 1996 signed by the judge referring to the application made to him on 13 November 1996. We have also seen and read a written judgment dated 19 November 1996 confirming the judge's decision that protection should be at the highest of the three conventional levels, based on the advice given by the police.

Before the fresh jury were sworn on 18 November, the judge ruled that the names of the jurors should not be read in open court in the ordinary way but that the jurors should be called by numbers allocated to each one of them individually. He said:

> Now the next matter is that the logistics of jury protection, it having been determined it's appropriate in this case, are as follows; I would say it to you and defence counsel that a panel has been obviously acquired properly in the normal way. They are, at the moment, being held in the library as I have been informed and there are 23 and each one has been allocated a number – 1 to 23 – and the clerk of the court will summon from that panel a number at random from the list that he has or holds and when they come into the jury box, there having been selected, obviously they are available to you, for the defendant and anybody else. And if [sic] a proper challenge can then be made. If not, they will then be sworn by a new number that will be placed in front of them in the jury box. When they come into this room, having been selected at random, they acquire the number in front of them and it's by that number that the individual juror will be known. The clerk of the court in this case, who will be of assistance throughout, is the only person who will have the details of identification.

Defending counsel, who had had no time to consider this procedure, raised no objection. From a later observation of the judge, it appears that the appellant may have been specifically asked whether he proposed to challenge any jurors and have indicated that he did not. Following the judge's ruling, jurors were called into court and took their places in the jury box. Their names were not announced in open court. No challenges were made and the jury were sworn.

With the benefit of a short opportunity to consider the matter, during the opening of the case by the Crown, defending counsel submitted to the judge that the procedure adopted for the swearing of the jury was unlawful. He described the objection as a technicality (a description which he now withdraws), but submitted that the traditional procedure for swearing the jury was a matter to be followed to the letter, and that the failure to name the jurors in open court was a departure from that procedure. He accepted that there would not necessarily have been any challenge for cause had the names been announced publicly, but suggested that a name may ring a bell when a face does not. The judge gave a short ruling in which he expressed satisfaction that the requirements of the Juries Act 1974 had been fulfilled, and that the jury had been properly sworn.

Counsel for the appellant now submits that the judge was wrong to make an order for the protection of the jury, and wrong in particular to do so without requiring the Crown to give reasons which would enable the defence to present reasoned argument and without calling evidence which the defence could test in cross-examination. Counsel also submits that the judge was wrong to permit the jury to be called and sworn by numbers rather than by name.

It is a truism that the jury is the lynch-pin of trial on indictment. The proper functioning of the jury is crucial to the fair and effective conduct of the trial. To that end statute regulates the composition of juries, the selection of jurors and the challenging of jurors. To that end also, almost infinite care is taken in directing the jury on the proper approach to their task, on the relevant law and on the facts. But all these rules and procedures are rendered of little effect if the integrity of an individual juror, and thus of the jury as a whole, is compromised. Such a compromise occurs when any juror, whether because of intimidation, bribery or any other reason, dishonours or becomes liable to dishonour his or her oath as a juror by allowing anything to undermine or qualify the juror's duty to give a true verdict according to the evidence.

Intimidation or bribery of jurors is fortunately unusual. But cases do arise in which a defendant, or friends or associates of a defendant, or others with an interest in the outcome of a defendant's trial, seek to influence the jury's verdict by unlawful means. Indeed, such activities have become sufficiently familiar to earn the colloquial description of 'jury nobbling' by which they are generally known. Where an attempt to nobble a jury is apprehended, one possible response would be to dispense with a jury altogether in such a case, on the ground that any attempt to nobble a judge sitting alone would be bound to fail. But that is not the response which we have adopted. Instead, where an attempt to nobble a trial jury is apprehended, the response has been to afford the individual jurors such level of protection as is judged necessary to protect them against any unlawful approach or communication, whether intimidatory or corrupt. The affording of such protection, however, when it comes to the knowledge of the jurors concerned (as with other than minimal protection it will), carries its own dangers. Despite judicial warnings that the affording of protection must not cause jurors to draw any inference adverse to the defendant, the defendant may fear that some jurors may be tempted to view with disfavour an accused person whose friends or associates are themselves thought likely to act in a criminal way. Alternatively, a juror who appreciates that protection has been given for his own safety may be inclined to acquit to reduce any risk of personal mischief to himself. These dangers will deter a judge from ordering high level protection of a jury unless the judge is convinced that there is a real and present danger of nobbling if protection is not given. But where such a real and present danger is perceived to exist, the judge is likely, in pursuance of his duty to ensure a just and effective trial, and in the exercise of his discretion, to order such protection. He will not knowingly accept a significant risk that the interests of justice may be defeated by a nobbling of the jury.

Some, but not very much, guidance on this problem is to be found in the authorities. In *R v Dodd* (1981) 74 Cr App R 50 at 53–54 the Court of Appeal said:

> At the start of the trial, on the application of the prosecution, the learned judge ordered jury protection; that is, that while away from the court each member of the jury should have police protection. All three applicants submit that the learned judge ought not to have made the order. They submit, rightly, that it is exceptional to order jury protection. They submit that it is prejudicial to the defendants and particularly so in a case where the real contest to be raised by the defendants is the honesty of the police officers giving evidence at the trial. They submit that jury protection ought not to be ordered unless there is evidence that the defendants or one of them has, in a previous trial, sought to interfere with the jury, or alternatively that there is evidence that in the present trial there is some proper evidence that such an attempt is to be made. In the present case the information which the police placed before the learned trial judge was that there was a sum of £30,000 on offer to try and deter Young and/or Simpson from giving evidence. In our judgment this question is one for the judge to decide, and it is his discretion which matters. A suitable formula was worked out for what the jury were to be told and again we can find no grounds for saying that the judge was wrong to exercise his discretion as he did.

We have read the transcript of the judgment of the court given by O'Connor LJ on 9 December 1986 in *R v Ling* [1987] Crim LR 495. He said:

Two matters arise on this appeal. First, before the trial started counsel for the prosecution made a submission to the learned judge that he should authorise that the jury should be protected. Argument and evidence on that topic was heard and the judge ruled that the jury should be protected. The first ground of appeal is that he was wrong so to do; that it was prejudicial to the appellants and that that in itself is a ground for allowing this appeal . . .

The court then made reference to *R* v *Dodd* and continued:

Before we look at the short facts in this case we think it necessary to state how this matter should be approached. Trial by jury inevitably carries with it the risk that an attempt may be made to pervert the course of justice by trying to influence jurors, be it by bribery, intimidation or otherwise. There are some cases where this risk is increased to such an extent that the proper administration of justice requires that the jury be protected from possible interference. In these cases two questions arise: (1) on what material is the judge to make the decision to authorise protection?; (2) what are the jurors to be told? The first question raises a number of problems. When the application is made counsel for the prosecution will state his reasons for making the request. Sometimes the nature of the case may be enough to show that the necessary increase of risk is present. For example, where the offences charged arise out of terrorist bomb attacks or protection racketeering. In contrast, we have cases like the present where the three appellants were charged with theft of valuable goods from a vehicle or vehicles in the loser's vehicle compound. The grounds for the application were that the prosecution believed that the appellants were associated with a much larger body of men engaged in similar thefts in the same part of London and that when any group were brought to trial, associates came to court to interfere with witnesses and the jury. Are the defendants entitled to require the prosecution to establish their contention by calling evidence or does the judge have a discretion to act on counsel's submissions? In our judgment the judge has a discretion as to whether the prosecution should be required to call evidence in support of the application. It is of course open to the defence to submit that the judge should not authorise protection without hearing evidence. If the judge does require evidence it is open to the defence to cross-examine the witnesses. If the judge concludes that the risk of interference has been substantially increased he may authorise protection. We do not think that burden of proof or standard of proof have any bearing on this exercise. It is enough to say that if there is material from which the judge can fairly infer that the risk of interference is substantially increased then he can authorise protection. As to the second question, we do not think that there is any need for the jury to be told the reasons for authorising protection. It might be very prejudicial to the defendants. See the reasons referred to in *R* v *Dodd*. The practice has been for counsel to agree a formula with the judge and we see nothing wrong with this procedure. If counsel choose not to co-operate the judge must decide. In this case the judge did decide what to tell the jury and he said: 'What I was proposing to say was this: during the course of this trial you will be under the surveillance of police officers when you are not in court. These officers have no connection with this trial. This is just a precaution. You should not be alarmed. It is a precaution that is taken from time to time and by no means does it follow that anything untoward will happen to any of you. Most importantly, you must not allow this fact in any way to influence your decision in the trial, which decision you will take upon the evidence and upon nothing else. In particular, do not allow yourselves to be prejudiced in any way against any of these three defendants by reason of the precautions that are being taken. And then I was proposing to tell the jury that further details of procedure would be given to them in due course.' So long as the jury are told that the fact of protection is not to be used by them in any way adverse to the defendants, just how it is put is not important. What the judge said in this case was short, simple and sufficient, and not open to any possible objection.

The court outlined the basis upon which the Crown had made its application in that case, and summarised the evidence. It reached the conclusion that the trial judge had had material to justify making the order he did, that it was a matter for his discretion and that there were no grounds for interfering with his decision.

This last decision touches on the procedural problems which are likely to arise when an application is made for an order that the jury be protected. Such application will be made by the prosecutor. Since the granting of the application may potentially have an adverse effect on the defence, it is obviously necessary that the prosecutor should, whenever possible, make his application in the presence of the defence and give reasons for making it and call evidence (open to cross-examination by the defence) in support of the application. That represents the ideal. It is an ideal which cannot always be achieved in practice. But it is necessary that any departure from the ideal should be fully considered and that no departure should be sanctioned unless the trial judge is satisfied that the departure is necessary, and that the departure will not render the trial process itself other than completely fair to the defendant. It is axiomatic that no matter what the exigencies of any case, no procedural application should be granted which might in any way jeopardise the fairness of the outcome of the trial. That consideration is paramount. If a defendant cannot be fairly tried he must not be tried at all.

Our practice has, however, sanctioned measures for the protection of juries in appropriate cases. The practice is to warn the jury in very clear terms that they must not in any way hold it against the defendant that such measures have been taken. Such a warning was given in this case, and no complaint is made that it was in any way inadequate. As in any other case the jury must decide the case on the evidence they hear in court and nothing else. We have no reason to doubt that the jury paid proper attention to the warning given.

The question we must answer is whether we consider this conviction unsafe because the trial judge made an order for the protection of the jury; without requiring the Crown to give reasons to the defence and without requiring it to call evidence in the presence of the appellant or his counsel. The defence have now been informed, which they were not informed at the trial, that there was apparently compelling evidence before the trial judge that an attempt had been made or would be made to nobble the first jury, and, that a person had been observed during the swearing of the first jury, in the public gallery, making a written note of the jurors' names. There were further disclosures, made to the judge on oath, and known to us, which remain secret and unknown to the defence. Both prosecuting counsel and the judge felt constrained at the trial to withhold these disclosures from the defence, and the Crown remain concerned that no disclosure should be made, even now, beyond those which have been made.

It is plainly highly desirable that all possible information should be disclosed to the defence, and that all exchanges with the judge should so far as possible take place openly in the presence of the defendant or his representatives. Any ex parte communication between the Crown and the trial judge gives rise to a feeling of unease. Such communications should be kept to a minimum. On the facts of this case, however, we are satisfied that the trial judge was presented with apparently reliable sworn evidence which obliged him to discharge the first jury, and fully justified his discretionary decision to order a high level of protection for the fresh jury when empanelled. Even if the defence had been told a little more than they were, the judge would have been bound to make these orders, and the defence must surely have inferred that the first jury were thought likely to have been nobbled, even if they knew nothing of the grounds for such belief. While we can understand the concern of the appellant and his advisers, there is nothing in the procedure adopted in relation to jury protection which causes us to consider this conviction unsafe.

It was argued for the appellant that if and when jury protection orders are judged necessary, the practical implementation of such orders should be under the control and supervision of the court; and that the practical effect of such orders should be made clear to all parties. We do not accept the first of these points. It would seem to us inappropriate that the court should interfere with the conduct of a police operation. The only legitimate concern of the court, once the order is made, is to ensure that there is no improper communication between any police officer and a juror. We have reservations about the second point also — given that such orders will only be made where nobbling is apprehended, it may well undermine the effectiveness of the protection to communicate precise details of how the protection will be afforded. Subject to that important qualification, however, it is desirable that the defence should, so far as possible, be informed how the protection will be given.

Counsel for the appellant also makes a second and more fundamental submission: that the omission to name the jurors who were empanelled to try the appellant, in open court, rendered the trial a nullity, leaving this court no choice but to quash the conviction and (if so advised) order a venire de novo. This result, it is argued, is dictated by long-standing practice, authority and statute.

A standard procedure has for very many years been followed when empanelling a jury. The clerk of the court invites the members of the jury in waiting to answer to their names, and then calls out the name of each juror selected by ballot. He then explains the means of making a challenge to the defendant, stating that the challenge is to be made after the names of the jurors who are to try him have been called. The form of words used is set out in *Archbold's Criminal Pleading, Evidence and Practice* (1997 edn) p. 405 and is very familiar. Plainly the procedure adopted here was a departure from this standard practice. We do not, however, consider that the mere fact of this departure renders the trial a nullity, unless it violated the legal right of the appellant or made the proceedings unfair to him.

In *R v Williams* (1925) 19 Cr App R 67 a conviction was quashed and a venire de novo ordered when a lawful challenge to a juror, properly made, was ignored. The same result would probably have followed in *R v Gash* [1967] 1 All ER 811, [1967] 1 WLR 454, where a defendant was effectively denied a right to challenge five biased jurors, had the defendant not served most of his sentence by the time of the appeal; as it was, the conviction was quashed. It is not, however, every irregularity in the empanelling of a jury which renders the trial a nullity. In *R v Mellor* (1858) Dears & B 468, 169 ER 1084 the name of juror A was called but by mistake juror B answered, entered the jury box, was sworn and was a member of the jury which returned the verdict. There was a sharp division of judicial opinion whether a mistrial had occurred, but a narrow majority considered that it had not.

Reliance was placed on an observation of Watkins LJ in *R v Felixstowe Justices, ex p Leigh* [1987] 1 All ER 551 at 560–561, [1987] QB 582 at 595, where he said:

> Consider too the position of jurors, interference with whom is unhappily not un-known, especially these days. They are known persons. Their names are announced in open court before they take the oath.

The case, however, concerned the lawfulness of a practice adopted by a local bench of magistrates of withholding the names of those who sat in court to hear cases. There was no issue before the court concerning security, and no issue concerning juries. It is plain that this observation, although of course commanding respect, is not authority on the present question.

We were referred to the most relevant provisions of the Juries Act 1974, s. 5(1) governs the preparation of panels of jurors. Section 5(2) entitles a defendant to reasonable facilities for inspecting the panel from which the jurors who try him are or will be drawn. Section 11(1) provides that the jury to try an issue before a court shall be selected by ballot in open court from the panel of summoned jurors. In this case, we understand that jurors were duly selected by ballot, although it appears that numbers and not names were drawn. Section 12 of the 1974 Act provides, so far as relevant:

> (1)   In proceedings for the trial of any person for an offence on indictment – (a) that person may challenge . . . all or any of the jurors for cause, and (b) any challenge for cause shall be tried by the judge before whom that person is to be tried . . .
>
> (3)   A challenge to a juror in any court shall be made after his name has been drawn by ballot (unless the court, pursuant to section 11(2) of this Act, has dispensed with balloting for him) and before he is sworn.
>
> (4)   The fact that a person summoned to serve on a jury is not qualified to serve shall be a ground of challenge for cause; but subject to that, and to the foregoing provisions of this section, nothing in this Act affects the law relating to challenge of jurors . . .
>
> (6)   Without prejudice to subsection (4) above, the right of challenge to the array, that is to say the right of challenge on the ground that the person responsible for

summoning the jurors in question is biased or has acted improperly, shall continue to be unaffected by the fact that, since the coming into operation of section 31 of the Courts Act 1971 (which is replaced by this Act), the responsibility for summoning jurors for service in the Crown Court, the High Court and county courts has lain with the Lord Chancellor.

It was argued, with particular reference to sub-s (3), that this section contained a mandatory requirement that names be called. We do not so read it. No doubt the draftsman assumed that the ordinary practice would be followed, and that names would be called. The purpose of sub-s (3) is, however, in our judgment to define the time at which the challenge is to be made rather than to require the public announcement of jurors' names. We accept that s. 12(6) preserves a defendant's right to challenge the array, but we cannot see that this right was in any way infringed. We assume that an effective challenge to the array would require exercise of the facilities guaranteed by s. 5(2). Section 18 of the 1974 Act provides:

(1)   No judgment after verdict in any trial by jury in any court shall be stayed or reversed by reason – (a) that the provisions of this Act about the summoning or empanelling of jurors, or the selection of jurors by ballot, have not been complied with, or (b) that a juror was not qualified in accordance with section 1 of this Act, or (c) that any juror was misnamed or misdescribed, or (d) that any juror was unfit to serve.

(2)   Subsection (1)(a) above shall not apply to any irregularity if objection is taken at, or as soon as practicable after, the time it occurs, and the irregularity is not corrected.

(3)   Nothing in subsection (1) above shall apply to any objection to a verdict on the ground of personation.

We would accept that counsel for the appellant objected to the procedure for empanelling the jury as soon as practicable after the procedure was implemented. But we are not persuaded that any irregularity was involved. If the appellant had been denied an effective opportunity to exercise his right of challenge, he would on the authorities be entitled to an order that the conviction be quashed and a venire de novo ordered. It is, however, quite clear that the trial judge intended to preserve the appellant's right of challenge. It may be that he was told that no such right would be exercised. But even if he was not so informed, it is not and never has been the appellant's contention that any right of challenge would have been exercised had the names of the jurors been called aloud in open court. Had the appellant's decision to exercise his right of challenge depended on knowing the names of the jurors, he could have exercised his right to ascertain the names of all the jurors forming the relevant panel, and we have no doubt that the judge would have been willing to hear, and if necessary rule on, any challenge made after inspecting the names of the panel, even if the challenge was (of necessity in the circumstances) made late. There is nothing whatever to suggest that the appellant had any right to challenge any of the members of the jury which convicted him, and there was in our view no violation of his common law or statutory rights.

It is highly desirable that in normal circumstances the usual procedure for empanelling a jury, should be followed. But if, to thwart the nefarious designs of those suspected of seeking to nobble a jury, it is reasonably thought to be desirable to withhold jurors' names, we can see no objection to that course provided the defendant's right of challenge is preserved.

For these reasons we dismiss this appeal.

Appeal dismissed. The court refused leave to appeal to the House of Lords but certified, under s. 33(2) of the Criminal Appeal Act 1968, that the following point of law, of general public importance was involved in the decision: whether a trial on indictment is necessarily rendered a nullity if the names of the jurors empanelled to serve are not called aloud in open court.

N P Metcalf Esq Barrister.

ANSWERS TO ACTIVITY 3: *COMERFORD* CASE

(a)   Thomas Anthony Comerford

(b)   Defendant; Appellant. The term defendant is used of a person who has been charged with a criminal offence, and appears in court to answer that charge. If the defendant disputes the outcome of the prosecution and appeals against the court's decision, then he or she becomes the appellant.

(c)   26 November 1996.
Crown Court – Middlesex Guildhall.
Judge Blacksell QC.

(d)   Court of Appeal, Criminal Division.
Lord Bingham of Cornhill CJ and Potts and Butterfield JJ.
(Do not worry if you do not at present understand about the different types of judges mentioned here. You will learn more about this in **Chapters 3 and 4**.)

(e)   14 and 28 October 1997 – that is the date on which the case was heard, and the date on which judgment was given.

(f)   This is the name of the barrister who took notes on the case in court for the law report.

(g)   Standard procedures with regard to the calling out of names of jurors and the arrangement of protection for jurors can be departed from provided that this does not violate the defendant's rights.

1.3.3   READING STATUTES

CONFISCATION OF ALCOHOL (YOUNG PERSONS) ACT 1997
(1997, c. 33)

An Act to permit the confiscation of intoxicating liquor held by or for use by young persons in public and certain other places; and for connected purposes.

[21st March 1997]

1.   Confiscation of intoxicating liquor
   (1)   Where a constable reasonably suspects that a person in a relevant place is in possession of intoxicating liquor and that either—
      (a)   he is under the age of 18; or
      (b)   he intends that any of the liquor should be consumed by a person under the age of 18 in that or any other relevant place; or
      (c)   a person under the age of 18 who is, or has recently been, with him has recently consumed intoxicating liquor in that or any other relevant place,
the constable may require him to surrender anything in his possession which is, or which the constable reasonably believes to be, intoxicating liquor and to state his name and address.
   (2)   A constable may dispose of anything surrendered to him under sub-section (1) in such manner as he considers appropriate.
   (3)   A person who fails without reasonable excuse to comply with a requirement imposed on him under subsection (1) commits an offence and is liable on summary conviction to a fine not exceeding level 2 on the standard scale.
   (4)   A constable who imposes a requirement on a person under subsection (1) shall inform him of his suspicion and that failing without reasonable excuse to comply with a requirement imposed under that subsection is an offence.
   (5)   A constable may arrest without warrant a person who fails to comply with a requirement imposed on him under subsection (1).

(6) In subsection (1) 'relevant place', in relation to a person, means—

(a) any public place, other than licensed premises; or

(b) any place, other than a public place, to which the person has unlawfully gained access;

and for this purpose a place is a public place if at the material time the public or any section of the public has access to it, on payment or otherwise, as of right or by virtue of express or implied permission.

(7) In this section 'intoxicating liquor' and 'licensed premises', in relation to England and Wales, have the same meanings as in the Licensing Act 1964 and, in relation to Northern Ireland, have the same meanings as in the Licensing (Northern Ireland) Order 1996.

2. Short title, commencement and extent

(1) This Act may be cited as the Confiscation of Alcohol (Young Persons) Act 1997.

(2) Section 1 shall not come into force until such day as the Secretary of State may by order made by statutory instrument appoint.

(3) This Act extends to England and Wales and Northern Ireland.

CHAPTER TWO

INTRODUCTION TO THE LAW

2.1 Classification of the Law

RULES OF THE SUPREME COURT

ORDER 3

Time

1. 'Month' means calendar month

Without prejudice to section 5 of the Interpretation Act 1978, in its application to these rules, the word 'month', where it occurs in any judgment, order, direction or other document forming part of any proceedings in the Supreme Court, means a calendar month unless the context otherwise requires.

2. Reckoning periods of time

(1) Any period of time fixed by these rules or by any judgment, order or direction for doing any act shall be reckoned in accordance with the following provisions of this rule.

(2) Where the act is required to be done within a specified period after or from a specified date, the period begins immediately after that date.

(3) Where the act is required to be done within or not less than a specified period before a specified date, the period ends immediately before that date.

(4) Where the act is required to be done a specified number of clear days before or after a specified date, at least that number of days must intervene between the day on which the act is done and that date.

(5) Where, apart from this paragraph, the period in question, being a period of 7 days or less, would include a Saturday, Sunday or bank holiday, Christmas Day or Good Friday, that day shall be excluded.

In this paragraph 'bank holiday' means a day which is, or is to be observed as, a bank holiday, or a holiday, under the Banking and Financial Dealings Act 1971, in England and Wales.

4. Time expires on Sunday, etc.

Where the time prescribed by these rules, or by any judgment, order or direction, for doing any act at an office of the Supreme Court expires on a Sunday or other day on which that office is closed, and by reason thereof that act cannot be done on that day, the act shall be in time if done on the next day on which that office is open.

5. Extension, etc, of time

(1) The Court may, on such terms as it thinks just, by order extend or abridge the period within which a person is required or authorised by these rules, or by any judgment, order or direction, to do any act in any proceedings.

(2) The Court may extend any such period as is referred to in paragraph (1) although the application for extension is not made until after the expiration of that period.

(3)   The period within which a person is required by these rules, or by any order or direction, to serve, file or amend any pleading or other document may be extended by consent (given in writing) without an order of the Court being made for that purpose.

(4)   In this rule references to the Court shall be construed as including references to the Court of Appeal, a single judge of that Court and the registrar of civil appeals.

6.   Notice of intention to proceed after year's delay

Where a year or more has elapsed since the last proceeding in a cause or matter, the party who desires to proceed must give to every other party not less than one month's notice of his intention to proceed.

A summons on which no order was made is not a proceeding for the purpose of this rule.

ORDER 10

Service of Originating Process: General Provisions

1.   General provisions

(1)   A writ must be served personally on each defendant by the plaintiff or his agent.

(2)   A writ for service on a defendant within the jurisdiction may, instead of being served personally on him, be served —

(a)   by sending a copy of the writ by ordinary first-class post to the defendant at his usual or last known address, or

(b)   if there is a letter box for that address, by inserting through the letter box a copy of the writ enclosed in a sealed envelope addressed to the defendant.

In sub-paragraph (a) 'first-class post' means first-class post which has been pre-paid or in respect of which prepayment is not required.

(3)   Where a writ is served in accordance with paragraph (2) —

(a)   the date of service shall, unless the contrary is shown be deemed to be the seventh day (ignoring Order 3, rule 2 (5)) after the date on which the copy was sent to or, as the case may be, inserted through the letter box for the address in question;

(b)   any affidavit proving due service of the writ must contain a statement to the effect that —

(i)   in the opinion of the deponent (or, if the deponent is the plaintiff's solicitor or an employee of that solicitor, in the opinion of the plaintiff) the copy of the writ, if sent to, or, as the case may be inserted through the letter box for, the address in question, will have come to the knowledge of the defendant within 7 days thereafter; and

(ii)   in the case of service by post, the copy of the writ has not been returned to the plaintiff through the post undelivered to the addressee.

(4)   Where a defendant's solicitor indorses on the writ a statement that he accepts service of the writ on behalf of that defendant, the writ shall be deemed to have been duly served on that defendant and to have been so served on the date on which the indorsement was made.

(5)   Subject to Order 12, rule 7, where a writ is not duly served on a defendant but he acknowledges service of it, the writ shall be deemed, unless the contrary is shown, to have been duly served on him and to have been so served on the date on which he acknowledges service.

(6)   Every copy of a writ for service on a defendant shall be sealed with the seal of the office of the Supreme Court out of which the writ was issued and shall be accompanied by a form of acknowledgment of service in Form No. 14 in Appendix A in which the title of the Action and its number have been entered.

(7)   This rule shall have effect subject to the provision of any Act and these rules and in particular to any enactment which provides for the manner in which documents may be served on bodies coporate.

ORDER 12

Acknowledgment of Service to Writ or Originating Summons

1.   Mode of acknowledging service

(1)   Subject to paragraph (2) and to Order 80, rule 2, a defendant to an action begun by writ may (whether or not he is sued as a trustee or personal representative or in any

other representative capacity) acknowledge service of the writ and defend the action by a solicitor or in person.

(2) The defendant to such an action who is a body corporate may acknowledge service of the writ and give notice of intention to defend the action either by a solicitor or by a person duly authorised to act on the defendant's behalf but, except as aforesaid or as expressly provided by any enactment, such a defendant may not take steps in the action otherwise than by a solicitor.

(3) Service of a writ may be acknowledged by properly completing an acknowledgment of service, as defined by rule 3, and handing it in at, or sending it by post to, the appropriate office, that is to say, if the writ was issued out of an office of the Supreme Court at the Royal Courts of Justice, that office, or if the writ was issued out of a district registry that registry.

(4) If two or more defendants to an action acknowledge service by the same solicitor and at the same time, only one acknowledgment of service need by completed and delivered for those defendants.

(5) The date on which service is acknowledged is the date on which the acknowledgment of service is received at the appropriate office.

BAIL ACT 1976
(1976, c. 63)

An Act to make provision in relation to bail in or in connection with criminal proceedings in England and Wales, to make it an offence to agree to indemnify sureties in criminal proceedings, to make provision for legal aid limited to questions of bail in certain cases and for legal aid for persons kept in custody for inquiries or reports, to extend the powers of coroners to grant bail and for connected purposes.

[15th November 1976]

3. General provisions

(1) A person granted bail in criminal proceedings shall be under a duty to surrender to custody, and that duty is enforceable in accordance with section 6 of this Act.

(2) No recognizance for his surrender to custody shall be taken from him.

(3) Except as provided by this section—

(a) no security for his surrender to custody shall be taken from him,

(b) he shall not be required to provide a surety or sureties for his surrender to custody, and

(c) no other requirements shall be imposed on him as a condition of bail.

(4) He may be required, before release on bail, to provide a surety or sureties to secure his surrender to custody.

(5) If it appears that he is unlikely to remain in Great Britain until the time appointed for him to surrender to custody, he may be required, before release on bail, to give security for his surrender to custody.

The security may be given by him or on his behalf.

(6) He may be required (but only by a court) to comply, before release on bail or later, with such requirements as appear to the court to be necessary to secure that—

(a) he surrenders to custody,

(b) he does not commit an offence while on bail,

(c) he does not interfere with witnesses or otherwise obstruct the course of justice whether in relation to himself or any other person,

(d) he makes himself available for the purpose of enabling inquiries or a report to be made to assist the court in dealing with him for the offence.

[(6ZA) Where he is required under subsection (6) above to reside in a bail hostel or probation hostel, he may also be required to comply with the rules of the hostel.]

[(6A) In the case of a person accused of murder the court granting bail shall, unless it considers that satisfactory reports on his mental condition have already been obtained, impose as conditions of bail—

(a)   a requirement that the accused shall undergo examination by two medical practitioners for the purpose of enabling such reports to be prepared; and

(b)   a requirement that he shall for that purpose attend such an institution or place as the court directs and comply with any other directions which may be given to him for that purpose by either of those practitioners.

(6B)   Of the medical practitioners referred to in subsection (6A) above at least one shall be a practitioner approved for the purposes of [section 12 of the Mental Health Act 1983].]

(7)   If a parent or guardian of a child or young person consents to be surety for the child or young person for the purposes of this subsection, the parent or guardian may be required to secure that the child or young person complies with any requirement imposed on him by virtue of [subsection (6) or (6A) above] but—

(a)   no requirement shall be imposed on the parent or the guardian of a young person by virtue of this subsection where it appears that the young person will attain the age of seventeen before the time to be appointed for him to surrender to custody; and

(b)   the parent or guardian shall not be required to secure compliance with any requirement to which his consent does not extend and shall not, in respect of those requirements to which his consent does extend, be bound in a sum greater than £50.

(8)   Where a court has granted bail in criminal proceedings [that court or, where that court has committed a person on bail to the Crown Court for trial or to be sentenced or otherwise dealt with, that court or the Crown Court may] on application—

(a)   by or on behalf of the person to whom [bail was] granted, or

(b)   by the prosecutor or a constable,

vary the conditions of bail or impose conditions in respect of bail which [has been] granted unconditionally.

[(8A)   Where a notice of transfer is given under section 4 of the Criminal Justice Act 1987, subsection (8) above shall have effect in relation to a person in relation to whose case the notice is given as if he had been committed on bail to the Crown Court for trial.]

(9)   This section is subject to [subsection (2) of section 30 of the Magistrates' Courts Act 1980] (conditions of bail on remand for medical examination).

4.   General right to bail of accused persons and others

(1)   A person to whom this section applies shall be granted bail except as provided in Schedule 1 to this Act.

(2)   This section applies to a person who is accused of an offence when—

(a)   he appears or is brought before a magistrates' court or the Crown Court in the course of or in connection with proceedings for the offence, or

(b)   he applies to a court for bail in connection with the proceedings.

This subsection does not apply as respects proceedings on or after a person's conviction of the offence or proceedings against a fugitive offender for the offence.

(3)   This section also applies to a person who, having been convicted of an offence, appears or is brought before a magistrates' court to be dealt with under [Part II of Schedule 2 to the Criminal Justice Act 1991 (breach of requirement of probation, community service, combination or curfew order)].

(4)   This section also applies to a person who has been convicted of an offence and whose case is adjourned by the court for the purpose of enabling inquiries or a report to be made to assist the court in dealing with him for the offence.

(5)   Schedule 1 to this Act also has effect as respects conditions of bail for a person to whom this section applies.

(6)   In Schedule 1 to this Act 'the defendant' means a person to whom this section applies and any reference to a defendant whose case is adjourned for inquiries or a report is a reference to a person to whom this section applies by virtue of subsection (4) above.

(7)   This section is subject to [section 41 of the Magistrates' Courts Act 1980] (restriction of bail by magistrates' court in cases of treason).

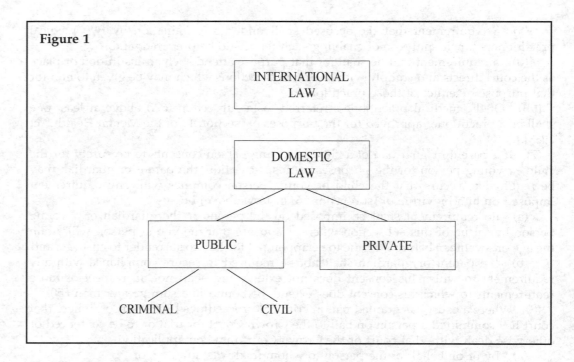

Figure 1

2.2   Sources of Law

2.2.1   PARLIAMENT

LAW OF PROPERTY (MISCELLANEOUS PROVISIONS) ACT 1989

(1989, c. 34)

Arrangement of Sections

Sect.
1.   Deeds and their execution.
2.   Contracts for sale etc. of land to be made by signed writing.
3.   Abolition of rule in Bain v. Fothergill.
4.   Repeals.
5.   Commencement.
6.   Citation.
       Schedules:
          Schedule 1—Consequential amendments relating to deeds.
          Schedule 2—Repeals.

An Act to make new provision with respect to deeds and their execution and contracts for the sale or other disposition of interests in land; and to abolish the rule of law known as the rule in Bain v Fothergill.

[27th July 1989]

1.   Deeds and their execution
   (1)   Any rule of law which—
     (a)   restricts the substances on which a deed may be written;
     (b)   requires a seal for the valid execution of an instrument as a deed by an individual; or
     (c)   requires authority by one person to another to deliver an instrument as a deed on his behalf to be given by deed,
is abolished.
   (2)   An instrument shall not be a deed unless—

(a) it makes it clear on its face that it is intended to be a deed by the person making it or, as the case may be, by the parties to it (whether by describing itself as a deed or expressing itself to be executed or signed as a deed or otherwise); and

(b) it is validly executed as a deed by that person or, as the case may be, one or more of those parties.

(3) An instrument is validly executed as a deed by an individual if, and only if—

(a) it is signed—

(i) by him in the presence of a witness who attests the signature; or

(ii) at his direction and in his presence and the presence of two witnesses who each attest the signature; and

(b) it is delivered as a deed by him or a person authorised to do so on his behalf.

(4) In subsections (2) and (3) above 'sign', in relation to an instrument, includes making one's mark on the instrument and 'signature' is to be construed accordingly.

(5) Where a solicitor or licensed conveyancer, or an agent or employee of a solicitor or licensed conveyancer, in the course of or in connection with a transaction involving the disposition or creation of an interest in land, purports to deliver an instrument as a deed on behalf of a party to the instrument, it shall be conclusively presumed in favour of a purchaser that he is authorised so to deliver the instrument.

(6) In subsection (5) above—

'disposition' and 'purchaser' have the same meanings as in the Law of Property Act 1925; and

'interest in land' means any estate, interest or charge in or over land or in or over the proceeds of sale of land.

(7) Where an instrument under seal that constitutes a deed is required for the purposes of an Act passed before this section comes into force, this section shall have effect as to signing, sealing or delivery of an instrument by an individual in place of any provision of that Act as to signing, sealing or delivery.

(8) The enactments mentioned in Schedule 1 to this Act (which in consequence of this section require amendments other than those provided by subsection (7) above) shall have effect with the amendments specified in that Schedule.

(9) Nothing in subsection (1)(b), (2), (3), (7) or (8) above applies in relation to deeds required or authorised to be made under—

(a) the seal of the county palatine of Lancaster;

(b) the seal of the Duchy of Lancaster; or

(c) the seal of the Duchy of Cornwall.

(10) The references in this section to the execution of a deed by an individual do not include execution by a corporation sole and the reference in subsection (7) above to signing, sealing or delivery by an individual does not include signing, sealing or delivery by such a corporation.

(11) Nothing in this section applies in relation to instruments delivered as deeds before this section comes into force.

2. Contracts for sale etc. of land to be made by signed writing

(1) A contract for the sale or other disposition of an interest in land can only be made in writing and only by incorporating all the terms which the parties have expressly agreed in one document or, where contracts are exchanged, in each.

(2) The terms may be incorporated in a document either by being set out in it or by reference to some other document.

(3) The document incorporating the terms or, where contracts are exchanged, one of the documents incorporating them (but not necessarily the same one) must be signed by or on behalf of each party to the contract.

(4) Where a contract for the sale or other disposition of an interest in land satisfies the conditions of this section by reason only of the rectification of one or more documents in pursuance of an order of a court, the contract shall come into being, or be deemed to have come into being, at such time as may be specified in the order.

(5) This section does not apply in relation to—

(a) a contract to grant such a lease as is mentioned in section 54(2) of the Law of Property Act 1925 (short leases);

(b) a contract made in the course of a public auction; or

(c)   a contract regulated under the Financial Services Act 1986; and nothing in this section affects the creation or operation of resulting, implied or constructive trusts.

(6)   In this section—

'disposition' has the same meaning as in the Law of Property Act 1925;

'interest in land' means any estate, interest or charge in or over land or in or over the proceeds of sale of land.

(7)   Nothing in this section shall apply in relation to contracts made before this section comes into force.

(8)   Section 40 of the Law of Property Act 1925 (which is superseded by this section) shall cease to have effect.

3.   Abolition of rule in *Bain* v *Fothergill*

The rule of law known as the rule in *Bain* v *Fothergill* is abolished in relation to contracts made after this section comes into force.

4.   Repeals

The enactments mentioned in Schedule 2 to this Act are repealed to the extent specified in the third column of that Schedule.

5.   Commencement

(1)   The provisions of this Act to which this subsection applies shall come into force on such day as the Lord Chancellor may by order made by statutory instrument appoint.

(2)   The provisions to which subsection (1) above applies are—

(a)   section 1 above; and

(b)   section 4 above; except so far as it relates to section 40 of the Law of Property Act 1925.

(3)   The provisions of this Act to which this subsection applies shall come into force at the end of the period of two months beginning with the day on which this Act is passed.

(4)   The provisions of this Act to which subsection (3) above applies are—

(a)   sections 2 and 3 above; and

(b)   section 4 above, so far as it relates to section 40 of the Law of Property Act 1925.

6.   Citation

(1)   This Act may be cited as the Law of Property (Miscellaneous Provisions) Act 1989.

(2)   This Act extends to England and Wales only.

SCHEDULES

Section 1   SCHEDULE 1

CONSEQUENTIAL AMENDMENTS RELATING TO DEEDS

The Law of Property Act 1925

1.   The Law of Property Act 1925 shall be amended as follows.

2.   In section 52(2)(e) for the words 'not required by law to be under seal' there shall be substituted the words 'other than those falling within section 115 below'.

3.   In section 74(2) for the words 'not under seal' there shall be substituted the words 'which is not a deed'.

4.   In section 80(1) for the words from 'under' to 'eighty-one' there shall be substituted the words 'made under seal after 31st December 1881 but before the coming into force of section 1 of the Law of Property (Miscellaneous Provisions) Act 1989 or executed as a deed in accordance with that section after its coming into force'.

5.   The following subsection shall be added at the end of section 81—

'(5)   In its application to instruments made after the coming into force of section 1 of the Law of Property (Miscellaneous Provisions) Act 1989 subsection (1) above shall have effect as if for the words 'under seal, and a bond or obligation under seal,' there were substituted the words 'bond or obligation executed as a deed in accordance with section 1 of the Law of Property (Miscellaneous Provisions) Act 1989'.

The Powers of Attorney Act 1971

6.   In section 1 of the Powers of Attorney Act 1971—
   (a)   in subsection (1), for the words 'signed and sealed by, or by direction and in the presence of', there shall be substituted the words 'executed as a deed by'; and
   (b)   subsection (2) shall cease to have effect.
7.—(1)   The following words shall be substituted for the words from the beginning of subsection (1) of section 7 of that Act to the end of paragraph (a)—
   '7.—(1)   If the donee of power of attorney is an individual, he may, if he thinks fit—
      (a)   execute any instrument with his own signature, and'.
   (2)   In subsection (2) of that section—
      (a)   the words 'or (4)' shall cease to have effect; and
      (b)   for the words 'those subsections' there shall be substituted the words 'that subsection'.

The Solicitors Act 1974

8.   In section 22(3)(b) of the Solicitors Act 1974 for the words 'under seal' there shall be substituted the words 'intended to be executed as a deed'.

Section 4   SCHEDULE 2

                                         REPEALS

Chapter	Short title	Extent of repeal
15 & 16 Geo. 5 c.20.	The Law of Property Act 1925.	Section 40. Section 73. In section 74(3), the words 'and in the case of a deed by affixing his own seal,'.
1971 c.27	The Powers of Attorney Act 1971.	Section 1(2) In section 7, subsection (1), the words 'and seal' and in subsection (2), the words 'or (4)'.

2.3 End of Chapter Assessment Question

Read carefully through the following story and then identify the different types of legal action which may result from it.

Albert is riding his pedal cycle along a country lane, when a car driven by Brenda hurtles past him and knocks him off his bike. Brenda has for many years harboured a grudge against Albert. Albert sustains serious injuries and is hospitalised for several months.

When he emerges from hospital, he discovers that the landlord of the flat which he was occupying before the accident has let the flat to another tenant. Albert applies to the local authority for accommodation, but he is told that he does not come within the statutory definition of 'homelessness'. Albert wishes to challenge the decision of the local authority.

2.4 End of Chapter Assessment Outline Answer

One of the vital skills which you must acquire in order to tackle legal problems, is that of identifying the legal issues to which the facts of any particular case give rise. Whether you are attempting to answer a coursework or examination question, or whether you are considering a case history in legal practice, you will need to ask yourself certain questions about the type of law with which you are dealing, before you can start to apply it. This will be the case regardless of the subject area concerned, so whether you are dealing with land law or contract law, you will need to go through this process of identifying the issues and legal concepts involved, before you begin to answer the question in earnest. This does not mean to say that you will necessarily include these intitial deliberations in your answer to a coursework or exam question. Rather, this process will form the background to your efforts to arrive at a solution to the problem. The first end of chapter assessment question illustrates this progression of thought.

Initially you will need to consider whether the problem with which you are faced concerns domestic law alone, or whether there are elements of European law or international law within the scenario. You will then identify whether you are dealing with public or private law issues, based on the identity of the parties involved in the story. You will then be in a position to isolate the areas of substantive law which are relevant to the question, and the details of the principles, cases and statutes which will bring you to some conclusions concerning the issues raised by the question. At this stage, depending upon the wording of the question, you may also need to consider which courts would have jurisdiction in respect of the issues raised, and how any legal action might be pursued. The paragraphs which follow illustrate this process as it would take place for the End of Chapter Assessment Question.

This case history concerns issues of domestic law. Both public and private law issues are raised, and a number of different courts may be involved in the resolution of the disputes to which the facts give rise.

The police may prosecute Brenda for committing one of the statutory driving offences and this obviously falls in the category of criminal law, part of the public law.

If Brenda intended to injure Albert, as opposed to driving badly, then she might also be charged with one of the more serious criminal offences of assault. The Crown Prosecution Service would decide whether to proceed with prosecution, and which offence or offences Brenda should be charged with.

Albert may also sue Brenda in the tort of negligence. (Albert would thus be the plaintiff and Brenda the defendant.) She may also be held liable for the head injuries she has caused because of her negligent driving and may be required to compensate Albert by paying damages to him. This is a civil law matter and comes in the category of private law.

A further civil, private law matter which Albert may wish to pursue concerns the tenancy of the flat which he was occupying before the accident. If the landlord has let the flat to another tenant before the expiry of Albert's tenancy agreement, then the landlord will be in breach of contract and Albert may claim damages from the landlord.

Finally, with regard to Albert's dispute with the local authority, if he wishes to challenge the decision concerning the definition of 'homelessness', then this is a civil, public law matter, and Albert will wish to seek a judicial review of the decision.

CHAPTER THREE

THE STRUCTURE AND JURISDICTION OF THE COURTS: CIVIL CASES

3.1 Terms and Definitions

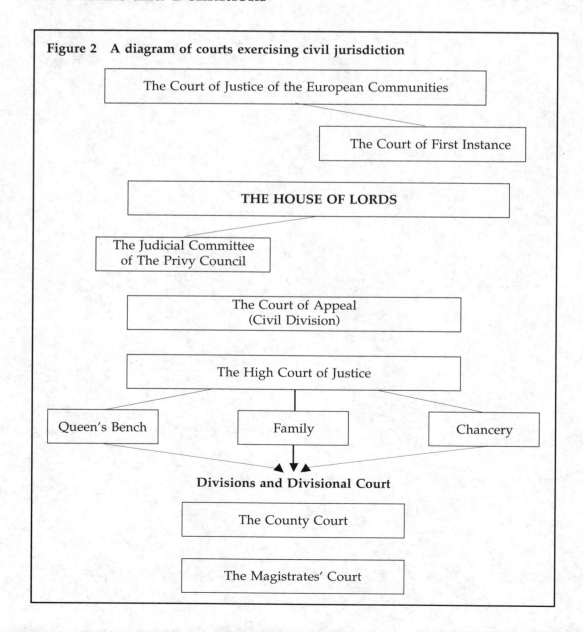

Figure 2 A diagram of courts exercising civil jurisdiction

The Court of Justice of the European Communities

The Court of First Instance

THE HOUSE OF LORDS

The Judicial Committee of The Privy Council

The Court of Appeal (Civil Division)

The High Court of Justice

Queen's Bench   Family   Chancery

Divisions and Divisional Court

The County Court

The Magistrates' Court

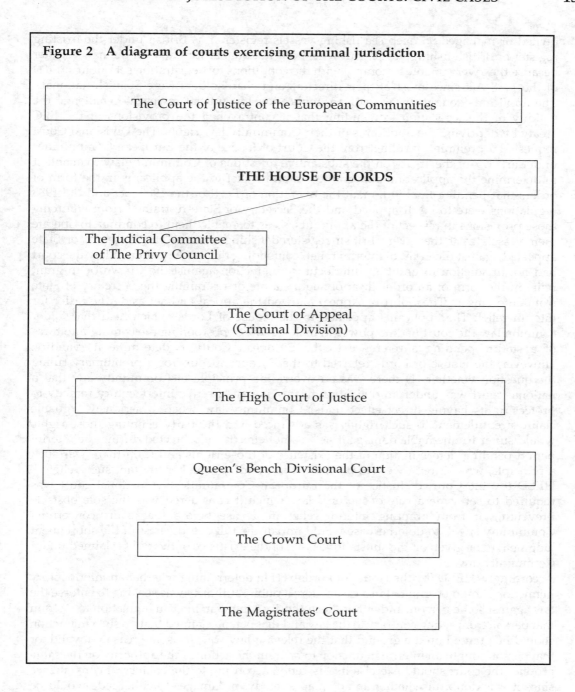

Figure 2   A diagram of courts exercising criminal jurisdiction

The Court of Justice of the European Communities

THE HOUSE OF LORDS

The Judicial Committee
of The Privy Council

The Court of Appeal
(Criminal Division)

The High Court of Justice

Queen's Bench Divisional Court

The Crown Court

The Magistrates' Court

3.2 The Courts which Exercise Civil Jurisdiction

3.2.1 THE COURT OF JUSTICE OF THE EUROPEAN COMMUNITIES
(COMMONLY KNOWN AS THE EUROPEAN COURT OF JUSTICE)

FACTORTAME LTD AND OTHERS v SECRETARY OF STATE FOR TRANSPORT
(No. 2) **(Case C–213/89) [1991] 1 All ER 70 (ECJ, HL)**

The Secretary of State was empowered under the Merchant Shipping Act 1988 to make
regulations for a new register of British fishing vessels. In the exercise of those powers
he promulgated the Merchant Shipping (Registration of Fishing Vessels) Regulations
1988 under which a fishing vessel could only qualify for entry on the new register if,
inter alia, the whole of its legal title and at least 75% of its beneficial ownership was
vested in British citizens or companies. The applicants were English companies which

owned or managed 95 deep sea fishing vessels registered as British under the existing register of British fishing vessels but which did not qualify for entry on the new register because they were unable to comply with the conditions for registration set out in s. 14(1) of the 1988 Act since most of their directors and shareholders were Spanish nationals. The applicants sought, by way of an application for judicial review, to challenge the validity of the legislation, contending that it contravened the provisions of the EEC Treaty by depriving the applicants of their Community law rights. The Divisional Court requested a preliminary ruling from the Court of Justice of the European Communities under art. 177 of the Treaty on the substantive questions of Community law to enable it to determine the application and granted interim relief to the applicants in the form of orders that pending final judgment the operation of Pt. II of the 1988 Act and the 1988 regulations were to be disapplied and the Secretary of State restrained from enforcing those provisions in respect of the applicants, so as to enable them to continue to operate their vessels as if they were British registered fishing vessels. The Secretary of State appealed against the grant of interim relief, contending that under common law the court had no jurisdiction to grant an interlocutory injunction against the Crown or to grant relief in the form of an order disapplying a statute or restraining the Secretary of State from enforcing it. The Court of Appeal allowed the appeal and set aside the order for interim relief. The applicants appealed to the House of Lords, which held that under common law the court had no power to make an order postponing the coming into force of a statute pending a reference to the European Court to determine its validity. However, the House of Lords referred to the European Court for a preliminary ruling the question whether (1) there was an overriding principle of Community law that a national court was under an obligation to provide an effective interlocutory remedy to protect rights having direct effect under Community law where a seriously arguable claim of entitlement to such rights was advanced and the party claiming those rights would suffer irremediable damage if he was not effectively protected during the interim period pending determination of the existence of those rights and (2) if there was such a principle, what criteria were to be applied in deciding whether to grant such relief.

HELD (by the Court of Justice of the European Communities): A national court was required to set aside a rule of national law which it considered was the sole obstacle preventing it from granting interim relief in a case before that court concerning Community law, if to do otherwise would impair the full effectiveness of the subsequent judgment to be given on the substantive issue of the existence of the rights claimed under Community law. . .

Accordingly, HELD (by the House of Lords): (1) In determining whether an interlocutory injunction should be granted in a case where a public authority was seeking to enforce the law against some person, and either the authority sought an interim injunction to restrain that person from acting contrary to the law and that person claimed that no such injunction should be granted on the ground that the relevant law was, for some reason, invalid, or that person sought an interim injunction to restrain the action of the authority on the same ground, the court should exercise its discretion according to the balance of convenience since it was doubtful whether an adequate remedy in damages to either side would be available. In doing so, the court should take into account, in particular, the importance of upholding the law of the land in the public interest, bearing in mind the need for stability in society and the duty placed on certain authorities to enforce the law in the public interest. However, the court should not restrain an apparently authentic law unless it was satisfied, having regard to all the circumstances, that the challenge to its validity was prima facie so firmly based as to justify such an exceptional course being taken. . .

(2) Applying those principles, the applicants had a strong case to present to the European Court that the evidence presented by the Secretary of State was not sufficient to outweigh obvious and immediate damage which would continue to be caused to them if they were to be granted no interim relief, and therefore the balance of convenience favoured the granting of interim relief to the applicants. The appeals would therefore be allowed. . .

Reference

By a judgment dated 18 May 1989 (see *Factortame Ltd* v *Secretary of State for Transport* [1989] 2 All ER 692, [1990] 2 AC 85) the House of Lords referred to the Court of Justice of the European Communities for a preliminary ruling under art. 177 of the EEC Treaty two questions . . . on the interpretation of Community law with regard to the extent of the power of national courts to grant interim relief where rights claimed under Community law were at issue. The questions were raised in the course of an appeal to the House of Lords by Factortame Ltd and other companies incorporated under the laws of the United Kingdom and the directors and shareholders of those companies (the applicants) against the decision of the Court of Appeal (Lord Donaldson MR, Bingham and Mann LJJ) on 16 March 1989 allowing an appeal by the Secretary of State for Transport against the decision of the Divisional Court of the Queen's Bench Division (Neill LJ and Hodgson J) on 10 March 1989 granting the applicants interim relief until final judgment was given on their applications for judicial review of the decision of the Secretary of State regarding their continued eligibility to register their vessels as British fishing vessels. Written observations were submitted to the court by the United Kingdom, Ireland, the applicants and the Commission of the European Communities. The language of the case was English. The facts are set out in the report for the hearing presented by the Judge Rapporteur.

THE JUDGE RAPPORTEUR (C N KAKOURIS) presented the following report for the hearing.

1—BACKGROUND TO THE DISPUTE

1. The appellants in the main proceedings, including Factortame Ltd (the applicants), are a number of companies incorporated under the laws of the United Kingdom and also the directors and shareholders of those companies, most of whom are Spanish nationals. Those companies between them own or manage 95 fishing vessels which were until 31 March 1989 registered as British fishing vessels under the Merchant Shipping Act 1894. 53 of those vessels were originally registered in Spain and flew the Spanish flag. Those 53 vessels were registered under the 1894 Act at various dates from 1980 onwards. The remaining 42 vessels had always been British. They were purchased by the applicants at various dates, mainly since 1983.

2. The statutory system governing the registration of British fishing vessels was radically altered by Pt. II of the Merchant Shipping Act 1988 and the Merchant Shipping (Registration of Fishing Vessels) Regulations 1988, SI 1988/1926. It is common ground that the United Kingdom amended the previous legislation in order to put a stop to the practice known as 'quota hopping', whereby, according to that state, its fishing quotas are 'plundered' by fishing vessels flying the British flag but lacking any genuine link with the United Kingdom.

3. The 1988 Act provided for the establishment of a new register of all British fishing vessels, including those registered in the old register maintained under the 1894 Act. However, only fishing vessels fulfilling the conditions laid down in s. 14 of the 1988 Act may be registered in the new register.

4. Briefly, the conditions laid down in s. 14 of the new Act, which must be fulfilled cumulatively, are as follows.

(a) *Nationality* The legal title to the vessel must be vested wholly in qualified British citizens or companies. At least 75% of the beneficial ownership of the vessel must be vested in qualified British citizens or companies. A company is 'qualified' if it is incorporated in the United Kingdom and has its principal place of business there, and if at least 75% of its shares are held by legal owners and beneficial owners who are British citizens. Furthermore, at least 75% of its directors must be British citizens. The figure of 75% may be raised provisionally to 100%, pursuant to regulations adopted under the 1988 Act. The United Kingdom has not yet availed itself of this possibility. That nationality requirement also applies to a charterer or operator of the vessel, whether he be a natural person or a company.

(b) *Residence and domicile* This is a further requirement along with nationality.

(c) *Direction and control* The vessel must be managed, and its operations directed and controlled, from the United Kingdom.

5. The 1988 Act and the 1988 regulations came into force on 1 December 1988. However, under s. 13 of the 1988 Act, the validity of registrations made under the previous Act has been extended for a transitional period until 31 March 1989.

6.   At the time of the institution of the proceedings in which the appeal arises, the 95 fishing vessels of the applicants failed to satisfy one or more of the conditions for registration under s. 14(1) of the 1988 Act and thus failed to qualify for registration. Since those vessels could no longer engage in fishing as from 1 April 1989, the companies in question sought by means of an application for judicial review to challenge the compatibility of Pt. II of the 1988 Act with Community law.

7.   In particular, in their application of 16 December 1988 to the High Court of Justice, Queen's Bench Division, the applicants sought: (i) a declaration that the provisions of Pt. II of the 1988 Act should not apply to them on the grounds that such application would be contrary to Community law, in particular arts. 7, 52, 58 and 221 of the EEC Treaty; (ii) an order prohibiting the Secretary of State from treating the existing registration of their vessels (under the 1894 Act) as having ceased from 1 April 1989; (iii) damages; (iv) interim relief pending final determination of the issues.

8.   The Divisional Court of the Queen's Bench Division gave judgment on 10 March 1989, in which it: (i) decided that it was unable to determine the issues of Community law raised in the proceedings without making a reference under art. 177 of the EEC Treaty (now Case 221/89, currently pending before the court); and (ii) ordered that, pending final judgment or further order by the court, the operation of Pt. II of the 1988 Act and of the 1988 regulations be disapplied and the Secretary of State be restrained from enforcing it in respect of any of the applicants and any vessel owned (in whole or in part), managed, operated or chartered by any of them so as to enable registration of any such vessel under the 1894 Act to continue in being.

9.   On 13 March 1989 the Secretary of State appealed against the Divisional Court's order for interim relief. By judgment of 22 March 1989 the Court of Appeal held unanimously that under the British constitution the courts had no power to disapply Acts of Parliament on a temporary basis. It therefore set aside the Divisional Court's order and granted leave to appeal to the House of Lords.

II—THE HOUSE OF LORDS JUDGMENT OF 18 MAY 1989

10.   In its judgment of 18 May 1989 in *Factortame Ltd* v *Secretary of State for Transport* [1989] 2 All ER 692, [1990] 2 AC 85 the House of Lords finds in the first place that the applicants' claims that they will suffer irreparable damage if the interim relief which they seek is not granted and they are successful in the main proceedings are well founded.

11.   With regard to the question whether the British courts are empowered to suspend on a temporary basis the operation of an Act and to issue an interim injunction to that effect against the Secretary of State so as to protect the rights claimed by a party under directly enforceable provisions of Community law, the House of Lords finds in the first place that under national law, the British courts have no power to grant interim relief in a case such as this. The considerations on which that finding of the House of Lords is based may be summarised as follows.

12.   In the first place, the presumption that an Act of Parliament is compatible with Community law unless and until declared to be incompatible does not permit the British courts to grant interim relief which consists in suspending the operation of the Act in question. In this connection the House of Lords points out that an order granting the appellants the interim relief which they seek will only serve their purpose if it declares that which Parliament has enacted to be the law not to be the law until some uncertain future date. Any such order would irreversibly determine in the applicants' favour for a period of some two years rights which are necessarily uncertain until a preliminary ruling has been given by the Court of Justice.

13.   Second, the old common law rule that a court has no jurisdiction to grant an interlocutory injunction against the Crown, that is to say against the government, also precludes the grant of interim relief in the main proceedings. The House of Lords points out in that connection that in *R* v *Secretary of State for the Home Dept, ex p Herbage* [1986] 3 All ER 209, [1987] QB 782 the Queen's Bench Division took the view that s. 31 of the Supreme Court Act 1981 (which provides that the High Court of Justice may grant interim relief, where it would be just and convenient to do so, in all cases in which an application for judicial review has been made) had removed the Crown's immunity from interim relief and this was subsequently affirmed by the Court of Appeal in *R* v *Licensing Authority, ex p Smith Kline & French Laboratories Ltd* (*Generics (UK) Ltd intervening*) (*No 2*)

[1989] 2 All ER 113, [1990] 1 QB 574. According to the House of Lords, however, those judgments were based on an erroneous construction of the Supreme Court Act 1981. It therefore overruled them in its judgment in the present case and came to the conclusion that, as a matter of English law, the courts have no jurisdiction to grant interim injunctions against the Crown.

14. Next, the House of Lords turns to the question whether Community law empowers the national courts to grant interim relief of the kind forming the subject matter of the main proceedings, regardless of what is laid down by national law, in order to protect rights which are indeed defensible on serious grounds but whose existence has yet to be established and which are claimed by a party under Community law.

15. After setting out the position of the parties on that point, the House of Lords points out that 'Community law embodies a principle which appears closely analogous to the principle of English law that delegated legislation must be presumed to be valid unless and until declared invalid' (see [1989] 2 All ER 692 at 709, [1990] 2 AC 85 at 151) and refers to the court's judgment in *Granaria BV* v *Hoofdproduktschap voor Akkerbouw-produkten* Case 101/78 [1979] ECR 623. Next, it refers to *Foto-Frost* v *Hauptzollamt Lübeck-Ost* Case 314/85 [1987] ECR 4199 at 4232 (para. 19), in which the court stated:

> . . . the rule that national courts may not themselves declare Community acts invalid may have to be qualified in certain circumstances in the case of proceedings relating to an application for interim measures . . .

16. In those circumstances, the House of Lords considered that the dispute raised an issue concerning the interpretation of Community law and it therefore decided, pursuant to art. 177 of the EEC Treaty, to stay the proceedings until the Court of Justice had given a preliminary ruling on the following questions:

> 1. Where: (i) a party before the national court claims to be entitled to rights under Community law having direct effect in national law ('the rights claimed'), (ii) a national measure in clear terms will, if applied, automatically deprive that party of the rights claimed, (iii) there are serious arguments both for and against the existence of the rights claimed and the national court has sought a preliminary ruling under Article 177 as to whether or not the rights claimed exist, (iv) the national law presumes the national measure in question to be compatible with Community law unless and until it is declared incompatible, (v) the national court has no power to give interim protection to the rights claimed by suspending the application of the national measure pending the preliminary ruling, (vi) if the preliminary ruling is in the event in favour of the rights claimed, the party entitled to those rights is likely to have suffered irremediable damage unless given such interim protection, does Community law either (a) oblige the national court to grant such interim protection of the rights claimed; or (b) give the court power to grant such interim protection of the rights claimed?
>
> 2. If question 1(a) is answered in the negative and question 1(b) in the affirmative, what are the criteria to be applied in deciding whether or not to grant such interim protection of the rights claimed?

ANSWERS TO ACTIVITY 11: *FACTORTAME* CASE

1. This case was referred to the European Court first by the Divisional Court of the Queen's Bench Division, and then secondly by the House of Lords on a different point.

2. The procedure used to obtain a ruling from the European Court was that set out in Article 177 of the Treaty of Rome (the EC Treaty).

3. The ruling of the European Court established the principle that rules of national law may be set aside by member states where those rules conflict with principles of Community Law.

3.2.2 THE HOUSE OF LORDS

DAVIS v JOHNSON [1978] 1 All ER 1132 (HL)

HOUSE OF LORDS
LORD DIPLOCK, VISCOUNT DILHORNE, LORD KILBRANDON, LORD SALMON AND LORD SCARMAN
16th, 17th JANUARY, 9th MARCH 1978

The appellant and the respondent were joint tenants of a council flat. Although they were not married, they lived together as man and wife. The appellant was the father of the respondent's baby girl who lived with them in the flat. Their relationship was, however, marred by violence. The respondent was frequently beaten by the appellant and subjected in at least two instances to extreme violence of a horrifying nature. As a result she fled with the child, then aged $2\frac{1}{2}$, to a refuge for 'battered wives' and subsequently applied to a county court, under s. 1 of the Domestic Violence and Matrimonial Proceedings Act 1976, for an injunction restraining the appellant from assaulting or molesting her or the child and ordering him to vacate the flat and not return. The injunction was granted. On 26 October, on the appellant's application, another county court judge rescinded so much of the order as required the appellant to leave the flat. The respondent appealed to the Court of Appeal which, having held, by a majority, that the court was not bound by its earlier decisions in *B* v *B* [[1978] 1 All ER 821] and *Cantliff* v *Jenkins* [[1978] 1 All ER 836], allowed the appeal and restored the order requiring the appellant to vacate the flat. The appellant appealed to the House of Lords, contending, inter alia, that s. 1 of the 1976 Act did not confer on a county court jurisdiction to exclude a person from premises in which he had a proprietary interest.
HELD: Section 1 did not affect property rights but it could affect the enjoyment of those rights and, having regard to the clear and unambiguous language of s. 1 and the intention of Parliament in enacting it, i.e. to protect a party to a marriage or a relationship akin to a marriage from domestic violence and conduct by the other party which put at risk the first party's security or sense of security in the home, s. 1(1)(c) was to be construed as investing a county court, when dealing with an originating application alleging domestic violence, with power to grant the applicant an injunction excluding the respondent from the premises in which the parties had been living, irrespective of the respondent's proprietary rights in the premises. The appeal would therefore be dismissed . . . *B* v *B* . . ., and *Cantliff* v *Jenkins* . . ., overruled.

PER CURIAM: (i) Because of the position of the Court of Appeal as an intermediate appellate court, with an increasing membership and number of divisions in which it sits, and the consequent need for the legal certainty resulting from the binding effect of previous decisions, the rule that, subject to certain clearly defined exceptions, the Court of Appeal is bound by its previous decisions should be re-affirmed expressly and unequivocally . . .; *Young* v *Bristol Aeroplane Co. Ltd* [1944] 2 All ER 293 approved.
   (ii)   It has always been a well-established and salutary rule that Hansard can never be relied on by counsel in court and therefore can never be relied on by the court in construing a statute or for any other purpose . . .; dictum of Lord Reid in *Beswick* v *Beswick* [1967] 2 All ER at 1202 applied.
   Decision of the Court of Appeal [[1978] 1 All ER 841], affirmed.

Appeal
On 11 October 1977 the respondent, Jennifer Therese Davis, applied to the Brentford County Court for an injunction under s. 1 of the Domestic Violence and Matrimonial Proceedings Act 1976 containing the following provisions: (i) that the appellant, Nehemiah Johnson, should not assault, threaten, molest or otherwise interfere with the respondent, and (ii) that the appellant should vacate the flat at 13 Nisbet House, Homerton Road, Hackney, London E9 ('the premises') of which the parties were joint tenants and not return thereto. On 11 October his Honour Judge Barr made the order for non-molestation but adjourned the application for the order excluding the appellant from the premises. On 18 October Mr J G Paulusz, sitting as a deputy circuit judge, made an order that the appellant should vacate the premises and not return thereto, and attached

a power of arrest to the order. On 24 October, following the decision of the Court of Appeal in *Cantliff* v *Jenkins*, the appellant applied for an order that the order of 18 October excluding him from the premises be suspended and that he be permitted to re-enter. On 26 October his Honour Judge Bernard Lewis rescinded so much of the order of 18 October as required the appellant to vacate the premises and not return thereto. The respondent appealed to the Court of Appeal against the order of 26 October on the ground, inter alia, that the judge had been wrong in law in ruling that the 1976 Act did not give him power to exclude a party from premises of which he was a joint tenant. The appellant filed a cross-notice of appeal against the order of 18 October on the ground that the deputy circuit judge had misdirected himself in holding that he had power to exclude the appellant from the premises notwithstanding that the appellant and the respondent were joint tenants of the premises. On 28 November 1977 the Court of Appeal (Lord Denning MR, Sir George Baker P and Shaw LJ, Goff and Cumming-Bruce LJJ dissenting) allowed the appeal and restored the order of the deputy circuit judge. The appellant appealed to the House of Lords. The facts are set out in the opinion of Lord Diplock.

Their Lordships took time for consideration.

3.2.3 THE HIGH COURT OF JUSTICE

3.2.3.1 Queen's Bench Division

TUCKER v *DIRECTOR OF PUBLIC PROSECUTIONS* [1992] 4 All ER 901 (QBD)

Any challenge made to a sentence imposed by magistrates should be to the Crown Court by way of an appeal rather than to the Divisional Court of the Queen's Bench Division by way of a case stated in all but the most exceptional cases where the harshness of the sentence amounts to an excess of jurisdiction. . .

R v *Crown Court at St Albans, ex p Cinnamond* [1981] 1 All ER 802 and *R* v *Crown Court at Croydon, ex p Miller* (1986) 85 Cr App R 152 followed.

Case stated
Andrew Philip Tucker appealed by way of a case stated by the magistrates for the Middlesex commission area sitting at Ealing in respect of their adjudication on 6 April 1990 whereby they disqualified the appellant for 18 months and endorsed his licence following his plea of guilty to a charge of failing without reasonable cause to provide a specimen of blood, contrary to s. 7(6) of the Road Traffic Act 1988. The facts are set out in the judgment of Pill J.

PILL J (delivering the first judgment at the invitation of Woolf LJ): This is an appeal by way of case stated from the justices for the Middlesex commission area sitting at Ealing in respect of their adjudication. The facts stated in the case are that on 18 November 1989 the appellant was charged that on that day, being a person who was required in pursuance of s. 7 of the Road Traffic Act 1988 to provide a specimen, did, without reasonable cause, fail to provide such a specimen contrary to s. 7(6) of the Road Traffic Act 1988 and Sch. 2 to the Road Traffic Offenders Act 1988.

On 10 January 1990 the appellant pleaded guilty to that offence. He was sentenced on 6 April 1990. He was disqualified from driving for a period of 18 months. The facts found by the justices were that on 18 November 1989 the appellant met friends at a wine bar. In the course of about one and a half hours he drank a glass of white wine as well as soft drinks. He left the wine bar at about 10.15 pm and drove towards his home via Western Avenue. In the course of that journey he had a puncture and called into a petrol station. Whilst he was there he had an argument with two youths who then ran off when they heard that the appellant was a martial arts instructor. The appellant then drank a can of Special Brew beer which had been left in the car. The police were called. The appellant went back to the car and drank another can of beer. When the police arrived the appellant was given a breath test. He was then taken to the Southall police station and required to provide a specimen of blood, since the breath machine was not working, and he had failed to give the sample.

The question arose as to whether the appellant should be disqualified. It was submitted on his behalf that the specimen had not been required to ascertain ability to drive or the proportion of alcohol in the blood at the time he had been driving or attempting to drive. That submission was accepted by the justices and the question of disqualification became discretionary. It was also submitted that even if the justices were against the appellant on that point there were special reasons for not ordering disqualification.

At para. 6 of the case the justices state:

We were of the opinion that as we found that the specimen was not required to ascertain the Appellant's ability to drive or the proportion of alcohol at the time the Appellant was driving or attempting to drive that the issue of disqualification was a matter for our discretion. We imposed a fine of £350.00. We considered on the facts found as shown in paragraph 2 above to exercise our discretion to disqualify the Appellant for a period of 18 months and ordered that his licence be endorsed.

The question which the justices posed for the opinion of this court is whether on the facts before the court the justices were correct in their decision to exercise their discretion to order disqualification in the manner they determined.

It has to be underlined that this is an appeal by way of case stated. The appellant had a right of appeal to the Crown Court which was not exercised. It is also provided that any person who was a party to any proceedings before a magistrates' court or is aggrieved by the conviction, order, determination or other proceedings of the court may question the proceeding on the ground that it is wrong in law or is in excess of jurisdiction by applying to the justices composing the court to state a case for the opinion of the High Court. However, as stated in *Stone's Justices' Manual 1991* vol 1, para 1–765, if a defendant is aggrieved by a decision of justices on matters of fact, the proper remedy is by appeal to the Crown Court.

R v *GENERAL COUNCIL OF THE BAR, EX PARTE PERCIVAL* [1990] 3 All ER 137 (QBD)

The applicant, who was the head of a set of a barristers' chambers, accused another member, who was the financial and general administrator of the chambers, of mishandling chambers money and reported him to the Bar Council as being in breach of para. 6 of the Code of Conduct for the Bar of England and Wales [3rd edn], which provided that a barrister should not engage in conduct which was, inter alia, dishonest or which would bring the profession into disrepute. A serious breach of para. 6 amounting to professional misconduct could result in disbarment under para. 7, while the lesser offence of breach of proper professional standards could render the barrister liable under para. 8 to an admonishment. The applicant's complaint was referred to the Professional Conduct Committee of the Bar Council, to which, pursuant to r. 2 of its rules, was delegated the power 'to investigate and sift complaints . . . to prefer charges . . . and be responsible for prosecuting any such charges' before a disciplinary tribunal. The committee decided that the barrister should be charged with a breach of proper professional standards under para. 8. The applicant, who considered that the barrister should have been charged with the more serious charge of professional misconduct under para. 7, applied for judicial review of the committee's decision, seeking (i) a declaration that the committee was required by r. 3(e)(viii) of its rules to prefer a charge of professional misconduct against the barrister because a prima facie case of professional misconduct had been disclosed by the complaint and (ii) an order that the committee prefer a charge of professional misconduct against the barrister rather than a charge of breach of proper professional standards. The questions arose (i) whether the applicant had locus standi to make the application, (ii) whether the Divisional Court had jurisdiction to hear and determine the application or whether the application fell within the exclusive jurisdiction of the judges, as visitors of the Inns of Court, to discipline members of the Bar, (iii) whether a prosecuting authority's decision to prosecute or not was reviewable at all, (iv) whether public policy prevented the court considering the application and (v) whether the committee's decision was unreasonable or tainted by procedural irregularity.

HELD: (1) The applicant had sufficient interest in the Professional Conduct Committee's decision by reason of the fact that as the head of chambers of the barrister against whom the complaint had been made he had a responsibility to ensure that any lapse from proper professional conduct or the observance of proper professional standards by a member of his chambers was properly investigated and if necessary referred to a disciplinary tribunal. Moreover, as the complainant, he was the only person in a position to challenge a decision by the committee not to investigate a complaint or not to initiate a prosection of a complaint . . .; *O'Reilly* v *Mackman* [1982] 3 All ER 1124, *R* v *Metropolitan Police Comr, ex p Blackburn* [1968] 1 All ER 763 and *Public Disclosure Commission* v *Isaacs* [1989] 1 All ER 137 considered.

(2) The acts and omissions of the Professional Conduct Committee were susceptible to judicial review because, as the body to whom the Bar Council's prosecuting functions of sifting and assessing complaints and prosecuting complaints before the disciplinary tribunal had been delegated, the committee was required to carry out those functions in accordance with its own rules and was subject to judicial review if it did not. Furthermore, there were no public policy reasons which prevented the court considering the application. However, since the committee had acted within the limits of its discretion and had not acted unreasonably, perversely or with any procedural irregularity the application would be dismissed . . .; *R* v *Benchers of Gray's Inn* (1780) 1 Doug 353 and *Lincoln* v *Daniels* [1961] 3 All ER 740 considered.

PER CURIAM: A prosecuting authority's discretion whether to prosecute or not is plainly reviewable but given the fact that there is potentially an almost infinite variety of circumstances in which that discretion may be exercised it would not be right to set strictly defined limits to the judicial review of a prosecuting authority. Each case is to be considered with due regard to the powers, functions and procedures of the authority and the manner in which it has dealt with the particular complaint . . .; *R* v *Metropolitan Police Comr, ex p Blackburn* [1968] 1 All ER 763, *Selvarajan* v *Race Relations Board* [1976] 1 All ER 12 and *R* v *Police Complaints Board, ex p Madden* [1983] 2 All ER 353 considered.

Application for judicial review

The Rt Hon Sir Walter Ian Percival QC, the complainant in proceedings before the Professional Conduct Committee of the Bar Council concerning a member of his chambers, John Samuels QC, applied with the leave of McCowan J given on 5 May 1989 for judicial review of a decision of the committee contained in a letter dated 16 January 1989 not to prefer charges of professional misconduct against Mr Samuels. The relief sought was (1) a declaration that the committee was obliged pursuant to r. 3(e)(viii) of its rules to prefer charges of profesional misconduct against Mr Samuels arising out of the applicant's complaint alleging serious breaches by Mr Samuels of his duties under para. 6 of the Code of Conduct for the Bar and (2) an order that the committee should forthwith prefer such charges. The facts are set out in the judgment of the court.

3.2.3.2 Queen's Bench Division

ANSWERS TO ACTIVITY 13

1(a) Jurisdiction of the Divisional Court of the Queen's Bench Division in cases concerning appeal against sentence.

(b) Breach of proper professional standards giving rise to dispute over conduct and powers of Professional Conduct Committee of Bar Council.

2(a) Magistrates' court, Middlesex Commission area.

(b) Divisional Court of the Queen's Bench Division. (This is the strictly accurate answer to this question, but of course the dispute had already been heard before the Professional Conduct Committee of the Bar Council, and leave to plead the case before the full court had been granted in a preliminary hearing before McCowan J.)

3(a) Appellate.

(b) Supervisory.

3.2.4   COUNTY COURTS

HIGH COURT AND COUNTY COURTS JURISDICTION ORDER 1991

2. Jurisdiction

(1)   A county court shall have jurisdiction under—

(a)   sections 30, 146 and 147 of the Law of Property Act 1925,

(b)   section 58C of the Trade Marks Act 1938,

(c)   section 26 of the Arbitration Act 1950,

(d)   section 63 (2) of the Landlord and Tenant Act 1954,

(e)   section 28 (3) of the Mines and Quarries (Tips) Act 1969,

(f)   section 66 of the Taxes Management Act 1970,

(g)   section 41 of the Administration of Justice Act 1970,

(h)   section 139 (5) (*b*) of the Consumer Credit Act 1974,

(i)   section 13 of the Torts (Interference with Goods) Act 1977,

(j)   section 87 of the Magistrates' Courts Act 1980,

(k)   sections 19 and 20 of the Local Government Finance Act 1982,

(l)   sections 15, 16, 21, 24 and 139 of the County Courts Act 1984,

(m)   section 39 (4) of, and paragraph 3 (1) of Schedule 3 to, the Legal Aid Act 1988,

(n)   sections 99, 102 (5), 114, 195, 204, 230, 231 and 235 (5) of the Copyright, Designs and Patents Act 1988, and

(o)   section 40 of the Housing Act 1988,

whatever the amount involved in the proceeding and whatever the value of any fund or asset connected with the proceedings.

(2)   A county court shall have jurisdiction under—

(a)   section 10 of the Local Land Charges Act 1975, and

(b)   section 10(4) of the Rentcharges Act 1977,

where the sum concerned or amount claimed does not exceed £5,000.

(3)   A county court shall have jurisdiction under the following provisions of the Law of Property Act 1925 where the capital value of the land or interest in land which is to be dealt with does not exceed £30,000:

(a)   sections 3, 49, 66, 181, and 188;

(b)   proviso (iii) to paragraph 3 of Part III of Schedule 1;

(c)   proviso (v) to paragraph 1 (3) of Part IV of Schedule 1;

(d)   provisos (iii) and (iv) to paragraph 1 (4) of Part IV of Schedule 1.

(4)   A county court shall have jurisdiction under sections 89, 90, 91 and 92 of the Law of Property Act 1925 where the amount owing in respect of the mortgage or charge at the commencement of the proceedings does not exceed £30,000.

(5)   A county court shall have jurisdiction under the proviso to section 136 (1) of the Law of Property Act 1925 where the amount or value of the debt or thing in action does not exceed £30,000.

(6)   A county court shall have jurisdiction under section 1 (6) of the Land Charges Act 1972—

(a)   in the case of a land charge of Class C(i), C(ii) or D(i), if the amount does not exceed £30,000;

(b)   in the case of a land charge of Class C(iii), if it is for a specified capital sum of money not exceeding £30,000 or, where it is not for a specified capital sum, if the capital value of the land affected does not exceed £30,000;

(c)   in the case of a land charge of Class A, Class B, Class C(iv), Class D(ii), Class D(iii) or Class E, if the capital value of the land affected does not exceed £30,000;

(d)   in the case of a land charge of Class F, if the land affected by it is the subject of an order made by the court under section 1 of the Matrimonial Homes Act 1983 or an application for an order under that section relating to that land has been made to the court;

(e)   in a case where an application under section 23 of the Deeds of Arrangement Act 1914 could be entertained by the court.

(7)   A county court shall have jurisdiction under sections 69, 70 and 71 of the Solicitors Act 1974 where a bill of costs relates wholly or partly to contentious business done in a county court and the amount of the bill does not exceed £5,000.

(8)   The enactments and statutory instruments listed in the Schedule to this Order are amended as specified therein, being amendments which are consequential on the provisions of this article.

3. Injunctions

The High Court shall have jurisdiction to hear an application for an injunction made in the course of or in anticipation of proceedings in a county court where a county court may not, by virtue of regulations under section 38 (3) (b) of the County Courts Act 1984 or otherwise, grant such an injunction.

4. Allocation—Commencement of proceedings

Subject to articles 5 and 6, proceedings in which both the county courts and the High Court have jurisdiction may be commenced either in a county court or in the High Court.

5.—(1)   Proceedings in which county courts have jurisdiction and which include a claim for damages in respect of personal injuries shall be commenced in a county court, unless the value of the action is £50,000 or more.

(2)   In this article 'personal injuries' means personal injuries to the plaintiff or any other person, and includes disease, impairment of physical or mental condition, and death.

6.   Applications under section 19 of the Local Government Finance Act 1982 and appeals under section 20 of that Act shall be commenced in the High Court.

7. Allocation—Trial

(1)   Subject to the following provisions of this article, proceeding in which both the High Court and the county courts have jurisdiction may be tried in the High Court or in a county court.

(2)   The following provisions of this article apply to proceedings in which both the High Court and the county courts have jurisdiction, other than proceedings mentioned in section 23, 24 or 32 of the County Courts Act 1984, save that paragraphs (3) and (4) do not apply to proceedings which have no quantifiable value.

(3)   An action of which the value is less than £25,000 shall be tried in a county court unless—

(a)   a county court, having regard to the criteria set out in sub-paragraphs (a) to (d) of paragraph (5), considers that it ought to transfer the action to the High Court for trial and the High Court considers that it ought to try the action; or

(b)   it is commenced in the High Court and the High Court, having regard to the said criteria, considers that it ought to try the action.

(4)   An action of which the value is £50,000 or more shall be tried in the High Court unless—

(a)   it is commenced in a county court and the county court does not, having regard to the criteria set out in sub-paragraphs (a) to (d) of paragraph (5), consider that the action ought to be transferred to the High Court for trial; or

(b)   the High Court, having regard to the said criteria, considers that it ought to transfer the case to a county court for trial.

(5)   The High Court and the county courts, when considering whether to exercise their powers under section 40 (2), 41 (1) or 42 (2) of the County Courts Act 1984 (Transfer) shall have regard to the following criteria—

(a)   the financial substance of the action, including the value of any counterclaim,

(b)   whether the action is otherwise important and, in particular, whether it raises questions of importance to persons who are not parties or questions of general public interest,

(c)   the complexity of the facts, legal issues, remedies or procedures involved, and

(d)   whether transfer is likely to result in a more speedy trial of the action, but no transfer shall be made on the grounds of sub-paragraph (d) alone.

8. Enforcement

(1)   A judgment or order of a county court for the payment of a sum of money which it is sought to enforce wholly or partially by execution against goods—

(a)   shall be enforced only in the High Court where the sum which it is sought to enforce is £5,000 or more and the proceedings in which the judgment or order was obtained did not arise out of an agreement regulated by the Consumer Credit Act 1974;

(b)   shall be enforced only in a county court where the sum which it is sought to enforce is less than £2,000;

(c)   in any other case may be enforced in either the High Court or a county court.

(2)   Section 85 (1) of the County Court Act 1984 is amended by the insertion, at the beginning of the subsection, of the words 'Subject to article 8 of the High Court and County Courts Jurisdiction Order 1991,'.

9.   Definition of value of action

(1)   For the purposes of articles 5 and 7—

(a)   the value of an action for a sum of money, whether specified or not, is the amount which the plaintiff or applicant reasonably expects to recover;

(b)   an action for specified relief other than a sum of money —

(i)   has a value equal to the amount of money which the plaintiff or applicant could reasonably state to be the financial worth of the claim to him, or

(ii)   where there is no such amount, has no quantifiable value;

(c)   an action which includes more than one claim—

(i)   if one or more of the claims is of a kind specified in paragraph (b) (ii), has no quantifiable value;

(ii)   in any other case, has a value which is the aggregate of the value of the claims as determined in accordance with paragraphs (a) and (b) (i).

(2)   In determining the value of an action under paragraph (1), claims for —

(a)   unspecified further or other relief,

(b)   interest other than interest pursuant to a contract, and

(c)   costs,

shall be disregarded.

(3)   In determining the value, under paragraph (1), of an action which is brought by more than one plaintiff or applicant regard shall be had to the aggregate of the expectations or interests of all the plaintiffs or applicants.

(4)   In determining the value of an action under paragraph (1) (a) —

(a)   the sum which the plaintiff or applicant reasonably expects to recover shall be reduced by the amount of any debt which he admits that he owes to a defendant in that action and which arises from the circumstances which give rise to the action;

(b)   no account shall be taken of a possible finding of contributory negligence, except to the extent, if any, that such negligence is admitted;

(c)   where the plaintiff seeks an award of provisional damages as described in section 32A (2) (a) of the Supreme Court Act 1981, no account shall be taken of the possibility of a future application for further damages;

(d)   the value shall be taken to include sums which, by virtue of section 22 of the Social Security Act 1989, are required to be paid to the Secretary of State.

10.   The value of an action shall be determined —

(a)   for the purposes of article 5, as at the time when the action is commenced, and

(b)   for the purposes of article 7, as at the time when the value is declared in accordance with rules of court.

11.   Crown proceedings — transitional provisions

For a period of two years from the date upon which this Order comes into force no order shall be made transferring proceedings in the High Court to which the Crown is a party to a county court, except —

(a)   when the proceedings are set down to be tried or heard ; or

(b)   with the consent of the Crown.

12.   Savings

This Order shall not apply to:

(a)   family proceedings within the meaning of Part V of the Matrimonial and Family Proceedings Act 1984;

(b)   proceedings to which section 27 (1) of the County Courts Act 1984 (Admiralty jurisdiction) applies.

3.3 End of Chapter Assessment Question

It has been said that the organisation of business between the High Court, county courts and magistrates' courts creates anomalies, inefficiencies, and confusion.

Critically examine this statement and consider whether amalgamation of the three courts to create a single civil court would remove these difficulties.

3.4 End of Chapter Assessment Outline Answer

For many years there has been a considerable degree of overlap in the type of jurisdiction exercised by the High Court, the county courts and the magistates' courts in civil cases and this has certainly been seen in some quarters as a cause of anomalies, inefficiences and confusion.

The Queen's Bench Division of the High Court and the county courts share jurisdiction in respect of the commonest types of civil litigation, i.e. contract (including debt) and tort cases. A would-be litigant who wishes to dispute the terms of a contract, the breach of a contract, supply of goods and services etc., or who alleges that a tort e.g. nuisance, trespass, or more commonly a personal injury has been committed, is faced with a choice of venue, and is expected to commence proceedings in the appropriate court, despite the fact that it is not immediately apparent to a lay-person which court this might be. This means that in most cases, professional legal help will have to be sought in order to determine which court to use, which might be regarded as an example of the inefficiency of the system.

Decisions as to where to commence proceedings are based on the provisions of the Courts and Legal Services Act 1990, and the High Court and County Court Jurisdiction Order 1991, together with the 1991 Practice Direction on this matter. According to these rules, in all cases it is advisable to commence proceedings in the court in which it is likely that they will be heard, and to determine this, the first criterion to be applied is the value of the case. Thus contract and tort cases where the amount of money in issue is worth less than £25,000 are to be tried in the county courts unless there are reasons why the case should be tried in the High Court. Similarly cases in which the amount in issue is more than £50,000, are to be tried in the High Court, unless that Court considers that the case is suitable to be heard in the county courts.

This rule immediately raises the question as to whether it is anomalous that the value of a case should be the primary determining factor in deciding the forum for trial, or whether other aspects of the case, for example complexity of the legal issues involved, are more important criteria. Using the value of the case to choose the venue for trial does at least have the advantage that in many cases the sum of money in dispute may be known from the outset, whereas any legal difficulties may only emerge as the case progresses to trial. The complexity of the facts, legal issues, remedies or procedures involved are therefore factors which are taken into account once the action has been commenced, and will be used by either the High Court or county court judge to assist in any decision to transfer a case from one court to another. So, for example, a case may begin in the county courts on the basis that the amount of money in dispute is less than £25,000. It may then become apparent that the case involves complex legal issues, or that the action is important because it raises questions of general public interest. The county court judge may then transfer the case to the Queen's Bench Division of the High Court. This can of course be justified on the grounds that the judges of the High Court are more highly qualified and more experienced in complex cases than the judges of the county courts, but it may also be a cause of the confusion complained of in the premise to this question.

Another major area of overlap in the jurisdiction of the Family Division of the High Court, the county courts and the magistrates' courts is in the law relating to family matters. The Family Division has the greatest degree of power in this sphere, having jurisdiction in all types of matrimonial matters both original and appellate, as well as matters of legitimacy, adoption and proceedings under the Children Act 1989, and the Domestic Violence and Matrimonial Proceedings Act 1976. Certain county courts are designated as divorce county courts, and can deal with undefended divorce cases, applications for injunctions to prevent molestation, and certain matters relating to children under the Children Act 1989. Similarly, magistrates' courts, when constituted as 'Family Proceedings Courts', may hear cases concerning financial provision for a spouse or children, personal protection or exclusion orders and adoption, residence and contact matters.

The fact that such apparently similar types of cases can be heard in any one of three different courts may indeed by another anomaly and source of confusion for those who have to use the services of the courts. This is particularly so in relation to cases arising under the provisions of the Children Act 1989, as for the purposes of this Act, the three courts are regarded as one unified court, and cases may be transferred between the three courts, as the complexity of the case and the interests of the child require. Such transfers may be necessary in order to achieve the best legal outcome in any particular case, but may also add to the stress suffered by participants in what will already be emotionally charged situations.

It might also be assumed that the existence of three different courts with jurisdiction in these areas would be an inefficient arrangement. Closer examination reveals however that there are significant and important differences in the powers of the three courts. It must never be forgotten, for example, that the magistrates' courts have no power to grant a divorce, undefended or otherwise!

The suggestion of amalgamation of the three courts to create a single civil court has been put forward by various different interested groups over the years, in the hope that this would eliminate some of the problems referred to above. The wholesale restructuring of the courts has been avoided however, perhaps because of the potential cost and difficulty involved in deciding how rules of procedure, personnel and jurisdiction would be amended to accommodate this change. The nearest we have come to achieving a unified court is in the transfer provisions which govern cases involving children in the three courts, and also the transfer rules allowing contract and tort cases to be switched from High Court to county courts and vice versa. A wholesale reform of the civil courts seems only a distant possibility.

CHAPTER FOUR

THE STRUCTURE AND JURISDICTION OF THE COURTS: CRIMINAL CASES

4.1   The Judicial Committee of the Privy Council

PRATT AND ANOTHER v ATTORNEY GENERAL FOR JAMAICA AND ANOTHER
[1993] 4 All ER 769 (PC)

PRIVY COUNCIL
LORD GRIFFITHS, LORD LANE, LORD ACKNER, LORD GOFF OR CHIEVELEY, LORD LOWRY, LORD SLYNN OF HADLEY AND LORD WOOLF
28–30 JUNE, 1, 5–6, 8, 12–14 JULY, 2 NOVEMBER 1993

On 15 January 1979 the two appellants were convicted in Jamaica on a charge of murder and sentenced to death. Within three days they applied for leave to appeal. There was then a delay of almost two years before a hearing by the Court of Appeal of Jamaica of the application for leave could be arranged, part of that delay being attributable to delay in obtaining legal aid. On 5 December 1980 the Court of Appeal announced that the application for leave to appeal would be dismissed for reasons to be given later. No date was set for the execution. The rules and practice in force in Jamaica laid down a strict timetable for appeals to the Judicial Committee of the Privy Council and further provided that execution would only be stayed so long as that timetable was adhered to. Furthermore, under ss. 90 and 91 of the Jamaican Constitution a written report of the case from the trial judge and the case record were required to be submitted to the Jamaican Privy Council, which then advised the Governor General whether the sentence should be commuted. However, in practice a case was not referred to the Jamaican Privy Council and the Governor General until after any appeal to the Judicial Committee had been decided. On 16 August 1984 the first appellant wrote to the Registrar of the Court of Appeal asking for the reasons why his application for leave to appeal was dismissed. It then transpired that no reasons had been prepared because the papers had been misfiled and forgotten. Reasons were then prepared and handed down on 24 September 1984. In the meantime the first appellant petitioned the Inter-American Commission on Human Rights, which on 3 October 1984 rejected his submission that his trial had been unfair but recommended that his sentence be commuted for humanitarian reasons. On 28 January 1986 he petitioned the United Nations Human Rights Committee under the International Covenant on Civil and Political Rights and on 13 March the appellants lodged notice of intention to petition for special leave to appeal to the Judicial Committee, but leave was refused on 17 July. On 21 July the United Nations Committee requested Jamaica not to carry out the death sentence on the appellants before the committee had had an opportunity to consider the complaint but the Jamaican Privy Council, having considered the appellants' case for the first time, recommended that the state not accede to the request and a warrant of execution was issued on 13 February 1987 for the death penalty to be carried out on 24 February. On 23 February the Governor General issued a stay of execution pending consideration by the Inter-American Commission and the United Nations Committee. On 9 July the Inter-American Commission requested that the appellants' execution be commuted for humanitarian reasons but following further consideration of the appellants' case by the Jamaican Privy Council a second warrant of execution was issued on 23 February 1988 for execution on 1 March. On 29 February a second stay of execution was issued by the Governor General pending the United Nations Committee's review of the case. On 6 April 1989 the committee held that the failure of the Court of Appeal to deliver reasons for 45 months was a violation of the appellants' human rights and recommended that the death sentence imposed on the appellants be commuted. After a further delay of 18 months the Jamaican Privy Council reconsidered the appellants' case on 17 September 1990 and rejected the recommendations made by the United Nations Committee. On 21 February 1991, after further delay while the Governor General obtained legal advice on the legal status of decisions of human rights bodies, a third warrant of execution was issued for execution on 7 March. On 28 February 1991 the appellants commenced proceedings in the Supreme Court for constitutional redress under s. 25(1) of the Constitution claiming that their execution after such a prolonged delay of some 12 years since they were sentenced to death would be 'inhuman . . . punishment or other treatment' and thus in breach of s. 17(1) of the Constitution. On 14 June their application was dismissed and on 8 June 1992 the Court of Appeal dismissed their appeal. The appellants appealed to the Judicial Committee. The Crown contended that the death penalty for murder did not contravene s. 17(1) no matter how long the delay between the passing of sentence and execution since under s. 17(2) 'the infliction of any . . . punishment which was lawful in Jamaica' could not be held to contravene s. 17(1).

HELD: (1) Section 17 (2) of the Jamaican Constitution authorised the passing of a judicial sentence of a description of punishment lawful in Jamaica before independence and was not concerned with the act of the Executive in carrying out the punishment. The section, while preserving all descriptions of punishment lawful immediately before independence and preventing them from being attacked under s. 17(1) as inhuman or degrading forms of punishment or treatment, did not have any relevance to the question of delay and the problem that arose from delay in carrying out a sentence . . .; *Riley* v *A-G of Jamaica* [1982] 3 All ER 469 not followed.

(2) Prolonged delay in carrying out a sentence of death after that sentence had been passed could amount to 'inhuman . . . punishment or other treatment' contrary to s. 17(1) of the Jamaican Constitution irrespective of whether the delay was caused by the shortcomings of the state or the legitimate resort of the accused to all available appellate procedures. A state that wished to retain capital punishment had to accept the responsibility of ensuring that execution followed as swiftly as practicable after sentence, allowing a reasonable time for appeal and consideration of reprieve and, if the appellate procedure enabled the prisoner to prolong the appellate hearings over a period of years, the fault was to be attributed to the appellate system that permitted such delay and not to the prisoner who took advantage of it. However, if the delay was due entirely to the fault of the accused, such as an escape from custody or frivolous and time wasting resort to legal procedures which amounted to an abuse of process, the accused could not be allowed to take advantage of that delay, since to do so would be to permit the accused to use illegitimate means to escape the punishment lawfully inflicted upon him. Having regard to unacceptable delay since the appellants had been sentenced to death and the fact that their petitions to the Inter-American and United Nations human rights bodies did not fall within the category of frivolous procedures disentitling them to ask the Board to look at the whole period of delay, the execution of the appellants would be an infringement of s. 17(1) of the Constitution. The appeal would therefore be allowed and the sentences of the appellants commuted to life imprisonment . . .; *Abbott* v *A-G of Trinidad and Tobago* [1979] 1 WLR 1342 and *Riley* v *A-G of Jamaica* [1982] 3 All ER 469 not followed.

PER CURIAM: (1) If capital punishment is to be retained in Jamaica it must be carried out with all possible expedition. In any case in which execution is to take place more than five years after sentence there will be strong grounds for believing that the delay is such as to constitute 'inhuman or degrading punishment or other treatment' for the purposes of s. 17(1) of the Constitution . . .

(2)   Sections 90 and 91 of the Constitution are to be construed as imposing a duty on the Governor General to refer cases where a sentence of death has been passed to the Jamaican Privy Council and on the council to give their advice as soon as practical. The procedure contained in the Instructions approved by the Governor General in Privy Council dated 14 August 1962 for dealing with applications from or on behalf of prisoners under sentence of death should be reinstated. In the absence of special circumstances the Governor General should ordinarily refer a capital case to the council immediately after the appeal is dismissed by the Court of Appeal. Capital appeals must be expedited and the aim should be to hear a capital appeal within a year of conviction. It should be possible to complete the entire domestic appeal process within approximately two years. . .

Appeal

Earl Pratt and Ivan Morgan appealed with special leave from the judgment of the Court of Appeal of Jamaica (Rowe P, Forte and Gordon JJA) dated 8 June 1992 dismissing their appeal from the judgment of the Full Court (Wolfe, Patterson and Harrison JJ) delivered on 14 June 1991 dismissing the actions brought by the appellants for constitutional redress under s. 25 of the Constitution in which the appellants sought declarations, inter alia, that they had been subjected to inhuman or degrading punishment and treatment and would be subjected to such punishment and treatment if the sentence of death passed by Parnell J on 15 January 1979 following their conviction for murder was carried out. The appellants had also sought an injunction restraining the second respondent, the superintendent of St Catherine District Prison from carrying out the execution of the appellants. The first respondent to the appeal was the Attorney General of Jamaica. The facts are set out in the opinion of the Board.

2 November 1993. The following opinion of the Board was delivered.

LORD GRIFFITHS: The appellants, Earl Pratt and Ivan Morgan, were arrested 16 years ago for a murder committed on 6 October 1977 and have been held in custody ever since. On 15 January 1979 they were convicted of murder and sentenced to death. Since that date they have been in prison in that part of Saint Catherine's prison set aside to hold prisoners under sentence of death and commonly known as death row. On three occasions the death warrant has been read to them and they have been removed to the condemned cells immediately adjacent to the gallows. The last occasion was in February 1991 for execution on 7 March; a stay was granted on 6 March consequent upon the commencement of these proceedings. The statement of these bare facts is sufficient to bring home to the mind of any person of normal sensitivity and compassion the agony of mind that these men must have suffered as they have alternated between hope and despair in the 14 years that they have been in prison facing the gallows. It is unnecessary to refer to the evidence describing the restrictive conditions of imprisonment and the emotional and psychological impact of this experience, for it only reveals that which it is to be expected. These men are not alone in their suffering for there are now 23 prisoners in death row who have been awaiting execution for more than ten years and 82 prisoners who have been awaiting execution for more than five years. It is against this disturbing background that their Lordships must now determine this constitutional appeal and must in particular re-examine the correctness of the majority decision in *Riley* v *A-G of Jamaica* [1982] 3 All ER 469, [1983] 1 AC 719.

The death penalty

The death penalty in the United Kingdom has always been carried out expeditiously after sentence, within a matter of weeks or in the event of an appeal even to the House of Lords within a matter of months. Delays in terms of years are unheard of.

In earlier times execution for murder, as opposed to other capital offences, followed immediately after conviction. In 1751 an Act 'for better preventing the horrid Crime of Murder' (the Murder Act 1751) provided that all persons convicted of murder should be executed on the next day but one after sentence, unless convicted on Friday in which case they were to be executed on Monday and kept in solitary confinement upon bread and water until executed. The extreme rigour of the regime of immediate execution for murder was re-enacted in the Act 9 Geo 4 c 31 (offences against the person (1828)) but was repealed by the Act 6 & 7 Will 4 c 30 (execution for murder (1836)) 'more effectually to preserve from an irrecoverable Punishment any Persons who may hereafter be convicted upon erroneous or perjured Evidence' and it was enacted that henceforth sentence of death in murder cases should be pronounced in the same manner and the judge should have the same powers as after convictions for other capital offences.

In England the practice in capital cases, henceforth including murder, was for the sheriff to fix a date of execution in the fourth week after the death sentence was passed. In Scotland, the date of execution was fixed by the court under s. 2 of the Criminal Law (Scotland) Act 1830: if sentence was pronounced south of the Forth, it was fixed between 15 and 21 days hence, and if north of the Forth, between 20 and 27 days hence. In both England and Scotland the Court of Appeal heard an appeal in a capital case within three weeks of verdict. If the appeal was unsuccessful a revised execution date was set not less than 14 or more than 18 days after the day when the appeal was dismissed, in order to allow the Secretary of State time to decide whether the sentence should be commuted. The *Report of the Royal Commission on Capital Punishment 1949–1953* (Cmd 8932) gave the average delay in 1950 as six weeks if there was an appeal and three weeks if there was not.

In 1947 there was great public disquiet that men convicted of a murder on the Gold Coast had been under sentence of death for two years. The matter was debated in Parliament and the Colonial Secretary gave an assurance to the House that the rules and practice to be adopted in the colonies should be quite sufficient to prevent a repetition of the happenings in the Gold Coast. The concern expressed by members of Parliament in the course of the debate reflected the expectation that the colonies would follow the long-established practice in this country that execution would not be long delayed after sentence. Mr Winston Churchill MP expressed the sentiment of the House when he said: 'People ought not to be brought up to execution, or believe that they are to be executed, time after time whether innocent or guilty, however it may be, whatever their crime. That is a wrong thing.'

The rules and practice referred to by the Colonial Secretary were those that laid down a strict timetable for appeals to the Judicial Committee of the Privy Council and provided that execution would only be stayed so long as the timetable was adhered to. Such rules were in force in Jamaica before independence and were adopted after independence by the Governor General in Privy Council on 14 August 1962; it will in due course be necessary to consider why they were not followed in this case.

Delay of the character which has occurred in this case had never happened in Jamaica before independence. The appellants' case contains a schedule showing the time that elapsed between the date of conviction, appeal and execution in 40 capital cases immediately after independence between the years 1962 and 1970. The time is never more than 18 months and usually considerably shorter. The Solicitor General felt unable to accept the accuracy of this schedule, but no figures were submitted to contradict it, and their Lordships accept it as showing that the delays that are now being encountered in the execution of the death penalty are of fairly recent origin.

It is difficult to envisage any circumstances in which in England a condemned man would have been kept in prison for years awaiting execution. But if such a situation had been brought to the attention of the court their Lordships do not doubt that the judges would have stayed the execution to enable the prerogative of mercy to be exercised and the sentence commuted to one of life imprisonment. Prior to independence, applying the English common law, judges in Jamaica would have had the like power to stay a long delayed execution, as foreshadowed by Lord Diplock in *Abbott* v *A-G of Trinidad and Tobago* [1979] 1 WLR 1342 at 1348 when he said:

> In such a case, which is without precedent and, in their Lordships' view, would involve delay measured in years, rather than in months, it might be argued that the taking of the condemned man's life was not 'by due process of law'.

And as was asserted by Lord Templeman in *Bell* v *DPP of Jamaica* [1985] 2 All ER 585 at 589, [1985] AC 937 at 950 where he said:

> Their Lordships do not in any event accept the submission that prior to the Constitution the law of Jamaica, applying the common law of England, was powerless to provide a remedy against unreasonable delay . . .

4.2   The High Court of Justice

4.2.1   THE DIVISIONAL COURT OF THE QUEEN'S BENCH DIVISION

GRIFFITH v JENKINS AND ANOTHER [1992] 1 All ER 65 (HL)

The two respondents were charged with a number of offences of alleged illegal fishing for trout in a stream which was private property and theft of three trout. The respondents appeared before justices, who held that the respondents had no case to answer and dismissed the informations at the close of the prosecution case. The prosecutor appealed by way of a case stated pursuant to s. 111 of the Magistrates' Courts Act 1980 to the Divisional Court of the Queen's Bench Division, which allowed the appeal on the ground that the justices' decision was vitiated by errors of law. The court would have remitted the case to the justices under s. 6 of the Summary Jurisdiction Act 1857 with the court's opinion on the questions of law raised and with a direction to continue the hearing but for the fact that two of the three justices who were party to the decision had since retired. The court was invited by the prosecutor to remit the case for rehearing before a freshly constituted bench, but it held that it had no power to do so. The prosecutor appealed to the House of Lords on the question whether on the proper construction of s. 6 of the 1857 Act, which gave the court power to 'make such . . . order in relation to the matter . . . as to the Court may seem fit', the High Court had power to order a rehearing by different justices on determining questions of law arising on a case stated by justices pursuant to s. 111 of the 1980 Act.

HELD: The High Court had power on hearing an appeal from justices by a case stated under s. 6 of the 1857 Act to order a rehearing before the same or a different bench of justices if a rehearing appeared to be an appropriate course. In the circumstances, however, it would not be appropriate to order a rehearing of the charges against the respondents having regard to the fact that three years had elapsed since the offences, which were of a relatively trivial character, and the errors of law which vitiated the acquittals had not been prompted by submissions advanced by the defence but arose from points which the justices took of their own motion. Accordingly, the appeal would be dismissed . . .

Dictum of Lord Goddard CJ in *Rigby* v *Woodward* [1957] 1 All ER 391 at 393 disapproved.

PER CURIAM: A rehearing ought only to be ordered in circumstances where a fair trial is still possible. A rehearing will normally be ordered where errors of law by justices have led to an acquittal which is successfully challenged and a rehearing is the only way in which the matter can be put right. However, whether a rehearing should be ordered following a successful appeal against conviction by the defendant in circumstances where the error in the proceedings which vitiated the conviction has left the issue of the defendant's guilt or innocence unresolved and a rehearing may appear to be inappropriate or oppressive must depend on how the proceedings were conducted, the nature of the error vitiating the conviction, the gravity of the offence and any other relevant considerations . . .; dictum of Lord Alverstone CJ in *Taylor* v *Wilson* (1911) 22 Cox CC 647 at 652 disapproved.

Appeal

Gail Ann Griffith (the prosecutor) appealed with the leave of the Appeal Committee of the House of Lords given on 5 June 1991 from the decision of the Divisional Court of the Queen's Bench Division (Bingham LJ and McCullough J) on 10 April 1991 whereby the court, having allowed the prosecutor's appeal by way of a case stated by justices for the county of Avon, sitting at Keynsham Magistrates' Court in Bristol and quashed the justices order dated 30 August 1989 dismissing summonses against the respondents, Lee Hanson and Graham Anthony Jenkins, for illegal trout fishing and theft of fish on 9 January 1989 contrary to various provisions of the Salmon and Freshwater Fisheries Act 1975 and the Theft Act 1968, ruled that it had no jurisdiction to remit the case for rehearing before a freshly constituted bench in circumstances where two of the three justices who had heard the decision had in the meantime retired. On 16 April 1991 the court refused leave to appeal to the House of Lords but certified under s. 1 of the Administration of Justice Act 1960 that a point of law of general public importance . . . was involved in the decision. The facts are set out in the opinion of Lord Bridge. Their Lordships took time for consideration.

12 December 1991. The following opinions were delivered.

LORD BRIDGE OF HARWICH: My Lords, this appeal arises out of a summary trial of relatively trivial offences but raises an important question as to the powers of the High Court hearing an appeal by case stated from a magistrates' court.

The two respondents appeared before the Avon justices at Keynsham Magistrates' Court on informations charging them with a number of offences under the Salmon and Freshwater Fisheries Act 1975 and the Theft Act 1968 arising out of an incident on 9 January 1989 in which it was alleged that they were illegally fishing for trout in a stream which is the private property of the Bristol Water Co. At the close of the case for the prosecution the justices held that the respondents had no case to answer and dismissed the informations. In due course they stated a case for the opinion of the High Court, to whom the prosecutor appealed. The Divisional Court of the Queen's Bench Division (Bingham LJ and McCullough J) held that the justices' decision was vitiated by errors of law and would in the ordinary way have remitted the case to the justices with the court's opinion on the questions of law raised and with a direction to continue the hearing. But this course was not possible since two of the three justices who were party to the decision had since retired. The court was invited by the prosecutor to remit the case for rehearing before a freshly constituted bench, but held, with evident reluctance, that it had no power to do so. Pursuant to s. 1(2) of the Administration of Justice Act 1960 the court certified that the following question of law was involved in the decision:

> Whether on a proper construction of s. 6 of the Summary Jurisdiction Act 1857 the High Court has power to order a re-hearing by different Justices on determining questions of law arising on a case stated by Justices pursuant to s. 111 of the Magistrates' Courts Act 1980.

The prosecutor now appeals by leave of your Lordships' House.

Section 111(1) of the Magistrates' Courts Act 1980 provides:

> Any person who was a party to any proceedings before a magistrates' court or is aggrieved by the conviction, order, determination or other proceeding of the court may question the proceeding on the ground that it is wrong in law or is in excess of jurisdiction by applying to the justices composing the court to state a case for the opinion of the High Court on the question of law or jurisdiction involved . . .

Section 6 of the Summary Jurisdiction Act 1857, as amended, provides:

> The Court to which a case is transmitted under the Magistrates' Courts Act 1980 shall hear and determine the question or questions of law arising thereon, and shall thereupon reverse, affirm, or amend the determination in respect of which the case has been stated, or remit the matter to the justice or justices, with the opinion of the court thereon, or may make such other order in relation to the matter, and may make such orders as to costs, as to the Court may seem fit . . .

Both Bingham LJ and McCullough J commented on the width of the language used in this section and were, I think, surprised to find, as they held, that judicial authority restricted the scope of the court's power in such a way as to preclude them from taking the obvious course of ordering a rehearing. I agree with them. Nothing could be wider than the words empowering the court to 'make such other order in relation to the matter . . . as to the Court may seem fit'. In a section which provides an appellate procedure designed to correct errors of law in summary trials which have resulted in wrongful acquittals as well as wrongful convictions, nothing less than clear and cogent authority will persuade me that those words do not authorise the court to order a rehearing when that is the appropriate remedy to meet the justice of the case.

Taylor v *Wilson* (1911) 22 Cox CC 647 was a case where the defendant appealed by case stated against his conviction by justices on the ground that it was based on inadmissible evidence. Counsel for the respondent prosecutor accepted that he could not support the justices' decision, but invited the court to remit the case for rehearing. Lord Alverstone CJ, after giving his reasons for holding that the conviction could not stand, said (at 652):

> Then the question has been raised by counsel for the respondent as to what we ought to do in the circumstances. I do not desire to express any opinion as to what power we have got beyond saying that I think it would require a very strong argument to convince me that where there has been a conviction on matters which were gone into by the justices on a wrong ruling of law, we ought to order the case to be tried again, unless the justices have done what they not infrequently do—namely, ask for directions and adjourn the proceedings, so that they may act upon our decision . . . For the reasons I have given I think that, in the view the magistrates took in allowing this evidence to be given, the conviction was wrong, and that we ought not to grant a new trial, even if we have the power to do so, in this case.

This authority was not cited to the Divisional Court in the instant case and does not bear directly on the point at issue, since it addresses only the question of the exercise of discretion to order a rehearing, assuming that the power to do so exists.

The earliest case directly in point is *Rigby* v *Woodward* [1957] 1 All ER 391, [1957] 1 WLR 250. This was another successful defendant's appeal against conviction. The appellant was the second of two defendants jointly charged with unlawful wounding. The first defendant gave evidence that it was the second defendant, not he, who had attacked the victim. The justices, inexplicably, refused to allow the solicitor who appeared for the second defendant to cross-examine the first defendant on his evidence, but proceeded in the event to acquit the first defendant and to convict the second. Lord Goddard CJ, after stating the reasons why the conviction could not stand and reading s. 6 of the 1857 Act, said ([1957] 1 WLR 250 at 254, cf [1957] 1 All ER 391 at 393):

> Sometimes justices who before they have decided a case have some question of law arising before them state a case for the opinion of the court and ask their opinion on it. There are other cases in which justices dismiss the information and the prosecutor brings the case up saying that there has been a mistake of law, or that on the facts proved the only proper decision could have been a conviction; or again the defendant may bring up the case claiming that on the facts found by the justices he was entitled to be acquitted. But there is no power to order a re-trial in the ordinary sense of that expression. If this court holds that on a submission of no case to answer justices were wrong in stopping it they can be ordered to resume the hearing of the case because they very likely have not heard the defence. If we sent this case back, I do not see how it could be dealt with. The co-defendant who gave evidence and was acquitted and was not cross-examined might possibly not be found. We do not know where he is or whether he can be called. We cannot make the prosecution call him. It seems to me that there has been an unfortunate departure from the ordinary principles of justice. It has resulted in a conviction, and although it may be that the appellant is guilty and that the justices were right in the opinion they formed, we cannot allow a proceeding of this sort to stand. We must decide the question of law that is raised here in favour of the appellant and, having done so, as it seems to me that it is impossible for us to order a re-trial, which I do not think we have power to do, it follows that the conviction must be quashed. I regret it, but that is the only decision we can give.

Lynskey J said ([1957] 1 WLR 250 at 254–255, cf [1957] 1 All ER 391 at 394):

> I agree with great reluctance, but it seems to me here that the justices have clearly gone wrong. They have deprived the appellant of the right of obtaining certain evidence from the co-defendant. That co-defendant has now been acquitted, and we cannot remit the case to the justices with the opinion of the court thereon as the justices could not act on this opinion because the co-defendant cannot be brought back. The result is that the justices made an error which we cannot put right and that being so there is no course open to us except to quash the conviction.

In *Maydew* v *Flint* (1984) 80 Cr App R 49 the defendant was charged with an offence under s. 6(1) of the Road Traffic Act 1972 of driving with alcohol in the blood in excess of the statutory limit. He had been involved in an accident. Under the statute as originally enacted a defendant could not be convicted of the offence under s. 6(1) if he had consumed alcohol after ceasing to drive and before giving a blood sample. But the law was amended by the Transport Act 1981, which introduced a new s. 10(2) into the 1972 Act which puts the onus on the defendant to prove that he consumed alcohol after ceasing to drive and that, if he had not done so, the proportion of alcohol in the sample would not have exceeded the limit. The appellant Maydew's offence was alleged to have been committed before, but his trial took place after, the new provisions came into force. He appeared in person before the justices and gave evidence that he had consumed alcohol after the accident, but the justices unfortunately applied the new law and held that he had not discharged the onus placed on him by s. 10(2) of the 1972 Act as amended. On appeal by case stated the only issue was whether the court could and should order a rehearing. Counsel for the prosecutor relied on an early case, *Shackell* v *West* (1859) 2 E & E 326, 121 ER 123, as authority contradicting the view expressed by Lord Goddard CJ in *Rigby* v *Woodward* that there is no power under s. 6 of the 1857 Act to order a rehearing. The judgment of Robert Goff LJ analysed *Shackell* v *West* and concluded, rightly in my opinion, that it was not authority establishing positively the proposition that there is such a power. He added (at 54):

> That being so, we are faced simply with a decision of this Court, presided over by the Lord Chief Justice, in which a clear view was expressed as to the powers of this Court under s. 6 of the Act of 1857. In those circumstances, it would, in my judgment, be quite wrong for us to depart from that statement of the law, especially as it has been accepted as correct since 1957 and has, I understand, never been challenged or departed from, and indeed has been followed.

In the instant case both Bingham LJ and McCullough J considered that it would be wrong to depart from the view of the law expressed in *Rigby* v *Woodward* and *Maydew* v *Flint*.

McCullough J, delivering the first judgment, indicated that such researches as he, the Crown Office and counsel for the appellants had been able to undertake in the time available had not discovered any confirmation of Robert Goff LJ's understanding that Lord Goddard CJ's dictum in *Rigby* v *Woodward* had since been followed. Counsel's further researches, of which your Lordships have had the benefit, so far from confirming that understanding show that it was mistaken. Whilst no other case before *Maydew* v *Flint* has been found in which the court declined jurisdiction to order a rehearing, three unreported cases and two reported cases have been brought to our attention in which the court, disposing of an appeal by case stated under s. 6 of the 1857 Act, assumed without question that it had power to order a rehearing before a different bench and did so. I summarise these cases briefly in chronological order.

In *Stivadoros* v *Evans* (16 June 1975, unreported) the defendant appearing in person before the justices failed to cross-examine the principal witness for the prosecution, but her own evidence when it came to be given flatly contradicted what the prosecution witness had said. The justices refused an application by the prosecutor to allow the prosecution witness to be recalled and proceeded to acquit the defendant. On the prosecutor's appeal, Lord Widgery CJ, delivering a judgment with which Waller and Kilner Brown JJ agreed, said:

> I think [the justices] were wrong in the exercise of their discretion. There are two courses open to us. One is that we should allow the appeal and have this case tried again by a fresh bench, and the other is that we should invite the bench who decided this matter last July to make certain findings of fact and to hear [the prosecution witness] for that purpose. It seems quite clear that the more convenient course of the two is the former, so I would allow this appeal and I would direct that the matter be reheard ab initio before a wholly different bench.

In *Williams* v *Mohamed* [1976] Crim LR 577 justices had dismissed a prosecution without finding the facts on the basis of a misconceived preliminary point of law. Here again it was Lord Widgery CJ who delivered the judgment allowing the prosecutor's appeal and ordering a rehearing before a different bench. The judges agreeing with him were Melford Stevenson and Wien JJ.

In *Shorrocks* v *Riley* (20 January 1981, unreported) the case stated by justices revealed manifest inconsistencies in their findings of fact leading to their decision to acquit the defendant. On the prosecutor's appeal Donaldson LJ, delivering a judgment with which Forbes J agreed, said:

> It seems to me that the findings of fact are so inconsistent with the conclusion . . . that the right course is to quash this decision and send it back to the magistrates with the direction that the matter be reheard before a different bench of magistrates.

In *Jeffrey* v *Black* [1978] 1 All ER 555, [1978] QB 490 the Divisional Court (Lord Widgery CJ, Forbes and Croom-Johnson JJ) held, on a prosecutor's appeal, that justices had acquitted after erroneously refusing to receive admissible evidence tendered by the prosecutor. Here again the order made by the court was that the case be sent back for rehearing by a different bench.

Finally, *Vines* v *Cameron* (25 November 1985, unreported) is one more decision, later in date than *Maydew* v *Flint*, where, on a prosecutor's appeal against acquittal, the Divisional Court (Mustill LJ and McCullough J), allowing the appeal, ordered rehearing before a different bench.

Now it is true that in none of these five cases was *Rigby* v *Woodward* referred to nor was any issue raised as to the power of the court under s. 6 of the 1857 Act to order a rehearing. But this, it seems to me, must have been because it never occurred to any of the judges concerned or to counsel appearing before them to doubt that the court had such a power. It is true also that all those five cases were prosecutors' appeals against acquittals resulting from errors of law made by justices, whereas in *Taylor* v *Wilson*, *Rigby* v *Woodward* and *Maydew* v *Flint* the question whether a rehearing could or should be ordered arose in the context of a successful defendant's appeal against conviction. But the question whether the court has power under s. 6 of the 1857 Act to order a rehearing before either the same or a different bench cannot receive different answers according to whether it is the prosecutor or the defendant who is appealing. I cannot resist the conclusion that Lord Goddard CJ was in error when he asserted that the court had no such power. His judgment in *Rigby* v *Woodward* was extemporary and gave no reasons in support of his opinion to that effect. Even the respect due to Lord Goddard CJ's great learning does not, I think, constrain us to treat this dictum as sacrosanct. I do not for a moment question the correctness of the decision in the case. Quite apart from any question of vires the acquittal of the co-defendant made a rehearing of the case against the appellant a practical impossibility.

My conclusion is that there is always power in the court on hearing an appeal by case stated under s. 6 of the Summary Jurisdiction Act 1857 to order a rehearing before either the same or a different bench when that appears to be an appropriate course and the court, in its discretion, decides to take it. It is axiomatic, of course, that a rehearing will only be ordered in circumstances where a fair trial is still possible. But where errors of law by justices have led to an acquittal which is successfully challenged and where the circumstances of the case are such that a rehearing is the only way in which the matter can be put right, I apprehend that the court will normally, though not necessarily, exercise its discretion in favour of that course. I recognise that very different considerations may apply to the exercise of discretion to order a rehearing following a successful appeal against conviction by the defendant in circumstances where the error in the proceedings which vitiated the conviction has left the issue of the defendant's guilt or innocence unresolved. In some such cases to order a rehearing may appear inappropriate or oppressive. But this must depend on how the proceedings have been conducted, the nature of the error vitiating the conviction, the gravity of the offence and any other relevant considerations. It would be most unwise to attempt to lay down guidelines for the exercise of such a discretion and I have no intention of doing so. But I would not regard the strong opinion expressed by Lord Alverstone CJ in *Taylor* v *Wilson* (1911) 22 Cox CC 647 at 652 against the exercise of discretion to order a retrial following a conviction based on a wrong ruling in law as any longer appropriate in the 1990s.

Unfortunately any rehearing of the present case, if the House were to order one, would take place more than three years after the date when the offences were alleged to have been committed. As I have said, they were of a relatively trivial character; the evidence for the prosecution suggested an illegal catch by the respondents of three trout. Moreover, the errors of law which vitiated the acquittals were not prompted by submissions advanced on behalf of the defence, but arose from points which the justices took of their own motion. In these circumstances I would not think it appropriate now to order a rehearing. The effect of this, if your Lordships agree, is that the order of the Divisional Court will stand and the appeal, therefore, will technically fall to be dismissed. But in substance, of course, the appellant has succeeded on the important issue of law in the appeal and I would both answer the certified question in the affirmative and order the appellant's costs before the House to be paid out of central funds.

4.3   The Crown Court

JURIES ACT 1974

(1974, c. 23)

An Act to consolidate certain enactments relating to juries, jurors and jury service with corrections and improvements made under the Consolidation of Enactments (Procedure) Act 1949.
[9th July 1974]

1.   Qualification for jury service
Subject to the provisions of this Act, every person shall be qualified to serve as a juror in the Crown Court, the High Court and county courts and be liable accordingly to attend for jury service when summoned under this Act, if—
    (a)   he is for the time being registered as a parliamentary or local government elector and is not less than eighteen nor more than sixty-five years of age; and
    (b)   he has been ordinarily resident in the United Kingdom, the Channel Islands or the Isle of Man for any period of at least five years since attaining the age of thirteen,
but not if he is for the time being ineligible or disqualified for jury service; and the persons who are ineligible, and those who are disqualified, are those respectively listed in Parts I and II of Schedule 1 to this Act.

8.   Excusal for previous jury service
    (1)   If a person summoned under this Act shows to the satisfaction of the appropriate officer, or of the court (or any of the courts) to which he is summoned—
    (a)   that he has served on a jury, or duly attended to serve on a jury, in the prescribed period ending with the service of the summons on him, or
    (b)   that the Crown Court or any other court has excused him from jury service for a period which has not terminated,
the officer or court shall excuse him from attending, or further attending, in pursuance of the summons.
    (2)   In subsection (1) above 'the prescribed period' means two years or such longer period as the Lord Chancellor may prescribe by order made by statutory instrument subject to annulment in pursuance of a resolution of either House of Parliament, and any such order may be varied or revoked by subsequent order under this subsection.
    (3)   Records of persons summoned under this Act, and of persons included in panels, shall be kept in such manner as the Lord Chancellor may direct, and the Lord Chancellor may, if he thinks fit, make arrangements for allowing inspection of the records so kept by members of the public in such circumstances and subject to such conditions as he may prescribe.
    (4)   A person duly attending in compliance with a summons under this Act shall be entitled on application to the appropriate officer to a certificate recording that he has so attended.

(5)   In subsection (1) above the words 'served on a jury' refer to service on a jury in any court, including any court of assize or other court abolished by the Courts Act 1971, but excluding service on a jury in a coroner's court.

9.   Excusal for certain persons and discretionary excusal

(1)   A person summoned under this Act shall be entitled, if he so wishes, to be excused from jury service if he is among the persons listed in Part III of Schedule 1 to this Act but, except as provided by that Part of that Schedule in the case of members of the forces and others, a person shall not by this section be exempt from his obligation to attend if summoned unless he is excused from attending under subsection (2) below.

(2)   If any person summoned under this Act shows to the satisfaction of the appropriate officer that there is good reason why he should be excused from attending in pursuance of the summons, the appropriate officer may excuse him from so attending and shall do so if the reason shown is that the person is entitled under subsection (1) above to excusal.

(3)   Crown Court rules shall provide a right of appeal to the court (or one of the courts) before which the person is summoned to attend against any refusal of the appropriate officer to excuse him under subsection (2) above.

(4)   Without prejudice to the preceding provisions of this section, the court (or any of the courts) before which a person is summoned to attend under this Act may excuse that person from so attending.

Sections 1 to 9   SCHEDULE 1

INELIGIBILITY AND DISQUALIFICATION FOR AND EXCUSAL FROM JURY
SERVICE

PART I

PERSONS INELIGIBLE

GROUP A

The Judiciary

Holders of high judicial office within the meaning of the Appellate Jurisdiction Act 1876.
Circuit judges and Recorders.
Masters of the Supreme Court.
Registrars and assistant registrars of any court.
Metropolitan and other stipendiary magistrates.
Justices of the peace.
The Chairman or President, the Vice-Chairman or Vice-President, and the registrar and assistant registrar of any Tribunal.
A person who has at any time been a person falling within any description specified above in this Group.

GROUP B

Others concerned with administration of justice

Barristers and solicitors, whether or not in actual practice as such.
Solicitors' articled clerks.
Barristers' clerks and their assistants.
Legal executives in the employment of solicitors.
The Director of Public Prosecutions and members of his staff.
Officers employed under the Lord Chancellor and concerned wholly or mainly with the day-to-day administration of the legal system or any part of it.
Officers and staff of any court, if their work is wholly or mainly concerned with the day-to-day administration of the court.

Coroners, deputy coroners and assistant coroners.

Justices' clerks and their assistants.

Clerks and other officers appointed under section 15 of the Administration of Justice Act 1964 (Inner London magistrates' courts administration).

Active Elder Brethren of the Corporation of Trinity House of Deptford Strond.

A shorthandwriter in any court.

Governors, chaplains, medical officers and other officers of penal establishments; members of boards of visitors for penal establishments.

('Penal establishment' for this purpose means any prison, remand centre, detention centre or borstal institution).

The warden or a member of the staff of a probation home, probation hostel or bail hostel (within the meaning of the Powers of Criminal Courts Act 1973).

Probation officers and persons appointed to assist them.

Members of the Parole Board; members of local review committees established under the Criminal Justice Act 1967.

A member of any police force (including a person on central service under section 43 of the Police Act 1964); special constables; a member of any constabulary maintained under statute; a person employed in any capacity by virtue of which he has the powers and privileges of a constable.

A member of a police authority within the meaning of the Police Act 1964; a member of any body (corporate or other) with responsibility for appointing members of a constabulary maintained under statute.

Inspectors of Constabulary appointed by Her Majesty; assistant inspectors of constabulary appointed by the Secretary of State.

Civilians employed for police purposes by a police authority; members of the metropolitan civil staffs within the meaning of section 15 of the Superannuation (Miscellaneous Provisions) Act 1967 (persons employed under the Commissioner of Police of the Metropolis, Inner London justices' clerks, etc.).

A person in charge of, or employed in, any forensic science laboratory.

A person who at any time within the last ten years has been a person falling within any description specified above in this Group.

GROUP C

The clergy, etc.

A man in holy orders.

A regular minister of any religious denomination.

A vowed member of any religious order living in a monastery, convent or other religious community.

GROUP D

The mentally ill

(Expressions used in this Group are to be construed in accordance with the Mental Health Act 1959.)

A person who suffers or has suffered from mental illness, subnormality, severe subnormality or psychopathic disorder and on account of that condition either—

    (a)   is resident in a hospital or other similar institution; or

    (b)   regularly attends for treatment by a medical practitioner.

A person who, under Part VIII of the Mental Health Act 1959, has been determined by a judge to be incapable, by reason of mental disorder, of managing and administering his property and affairs.

A person for the time being in guardianship under section 33 of the Mental Health Act 1959.

PART II

PERSONS DISQUALIFIED

A person who has at any time been sentenced in the United Kingdom, the Channel Islands or the Isle of Man—

(a) to imprisonment for life or for a term of five years or more; or

(b) to be detained during Her Majesty's pleasure, during the pleasure of the Secretary of State or during the pleasure of the Governor of Northern Ireland.

A person who at any time in the last ten years has, in the United Kingdom or the Channel Islands or the Isle of Man—

(i)   served any part of a sentence of imprisonment or detention, being a sentence for a term of three months or more; or

(ii)   been detained in a borstal institution.

PART III

PERSONS EXCUSABLE AS OF RIGHT

Parliament

Peers and peeresses entitled to receive writs of summons to attend the House of Lords.
Members of the House of Commons.
Officers of the House of Lords.
Officers of the House of Commons.

The Forces

Full-time serving members of—

any of Her Majesty's naval, military or air forces,
the Women's Royal Naval Service,
Queen Alexandra's Royal Naval Nursing Service, or any Voluntary Aid Detachment serving with the Royal Navy.

(A person excusable under this head shall be under no obligation to attend in pursuance of a summons for jury service if his commanding officer certifies to the officer issuing the summons that it would be prejudicial to the efficiency of the service if the person were required to be absent from duty.)

Medical and other similar professions

The following, if actually practising their profession and registered (including provisionally or temporarily registered), enrolled or certified under the enactments relating to that profession—

medical practitioners,
dentists,
nurses,
midwives,
veterinary surgeons and veterinary practitioners,
pharmaceutical chemists.

JURIES (DISQUALIFICATION) ACT 1984
(1984, c. 34)

An Act to make further provision for disqualification for jury service on criminal grounds.

[12th July 1984]

1. Disqualification for jury service of persons who have served or had imposed on them certain sentences.

(1) The following paragraphs shall be substituted for the second paragraph of Part II of Schedule 1 to the Juries Act 1974 (persons disqualified for jury service)—

'A person who at any time in the last ten years has, in the United Kingdom or the Channel Islands or the Isle of Man—

    (a)   served any part of a sentence of imprisonment, youth custody or detention; or

    (b)   been detained in a Borstal institution; or

    (c)   had passed on him or (as the case may be) made in respect of him a suspended sentence of imprisonment or order for detention; or

    (d)   had made in respect of him a community service order.

A person who at any time in the last five years has, in the United Kingdom or the Channel Islands or the Isle of Man, been placed on probation.'

(2)   This section shall not affect the qualification of any person to serve on a jury in pursuance of any summons to attend for jury service issued under the Juries Act 1974 before the commencement of this Act (whether by notice in accordance with section 2 of that Act or under section 6 of that Act).

2.   Short title, repeal, commencement and extent

(1)   This Act may be cited as the Juries (Disqualification) Act 1984.

(2)   In Schedule 14 to the Criminal Justice Act 1982, paragraph 35(b)(ii) (which amends the second paragraph of Part II of Schedule 1 to the Juries Act 1974), and the word 'and' immediately preceding it, are hereby repealed.

(3)   This Act shall come into force on such day as the Secretary of State may by order made by statutory instrument appoint.

(4)   This Act extends to England and Wales only.

4.4   End of Chapter Assessment Question

It has been said that the numerous excluded and exempt categories of persons who do not have to attend court for jury service, ensure that those people who have the intelligence and experience to try criminal cases are able to avoid jury service, whilst only those members of the public who lack the wit to find an excuse are empanelled in the Crown Court. Discuss this statement, in the light of the provisions of the Juries Acts 1974 and 1984.

4.5   End of Chapter Assessment Outline Answer

Before answering this question, it is worth noting that its scope appears to be confined to the methods of jury selection provided by the Juries Act 1974 and the Juries (Disqualification) Act 1984. The discussion of other methods of altering the composition of the jury i.e. by challenge and by jury vetting, does not appear to be necessary.

The Juries Act 1974 (as amended) defines a person who is potentially qualified to undertake jury service as one who:

(a)   is aged between 18 and 70 (the age limit was raised from 65 to 70 in 1988) and

(b)   is registered as a parliamentary or local government elector and

(c)   has been resident in the United Kingdom for at least 5 years since attaining the age of 13.

However, not all the people who fulfil these criteria will necessarily serve on a jury even if summoned to do so. This is because the Act also identifies groups of people who, as a result of their occupation or their life experience, may avoid jury service. The Act creates four categories of this nature:

(a)   Persons who are **ineligible**. This category comprises judges, barristers, solicitors, and numerous other occupations which are connected with the administration of justice e.g. court officers and probation officers, on the grounds that their expertise and knowledge in this field would sit ill with the notion that the jury is a body comprised of lay-people, unversed in the law. Also included in this category are the mentally ill, and also ministers of religion, and members of religious communities.

(b)   Persons who are **disqualified**. Broadly speaking, this group consists of persons who have at any time been sentenced to life imprisonment, those who have served any part of a prison sentence in the last ten years, or have been the subject of a suspended prison sentence or community service order during that time, or who have been placed on probation during the last five years. The rationale behind this provision is clearly the inappropriateness of allowing those who have contravened the norms of society to judge the guilt or innocence of others.

(c)   Persons who are **excused**. Those whose occupations involve duties to the State e.g. members of the Houses of Parliament, and those who are concerned with the relief of pain and suffering, e.g. doctors, nurses, dentists, veterinary surgeons etc., are excused from jury service as of right, along with those who have served on a jury in the last two years, and those over the age of 65. None of these people need therefore sit on a jury if they do not wish to do so.

This category also includes the possibility of excusal at the discretion of the appropriate officer of the court, with appeal to a Crown Court judge if necessary. Thus if 'good reason' is shown by a person wishing to avoid jury service, that person may be excused at the discretion of the court. Reasons which have been found adequate to excuse service in the past include illness, personal involvement in the case or difficulty in arranging for young children to be cared for, as well as less obvious factors such as holiday commitments and conscientious objection to jury service. Clearly there is some need for the court to have some discretion in these areas, but in the case of holiday commitments for example, this should perhaps only be a justification for deferral of service, rather than excusal.

Selection for attendance at court for jury service operates on the basis of random selection from among the categories of persons eligible, but as the question rightly points out, this excludes significant groups of professionally qualified people. Coupled with the fact that there is no way of assessing the intellectual acumen of jury members, this may call into question the ability of the jury to understand the intricacies of the criminal law. It is perhaps these doubts that have led to proposals for the abolition of jury trial in complex fraud cases.

CHAPTER FIVE

APPEALS IN CIVIL AND CRIMINAL CASES

5.1 Appeals in Civil Proceedings

5.1.1 THE HIGH COURT

ADMINISTRATION OF JUSTICE ACT 1969

(1969, c. 58)

PART II

APPEAL FROM HIGH COURT TO HOUSE OF LORDS

12. Grant of certificate by trial judge

(1) Where on the application of any of the parties to any proceedings to which this section applies the judge is satisfied—

(a) that the relevant conditions are fulfilled in relation to his decision in those proceedings, and

(b) that a sufficient case for an appeal to the House of Lords under this Part of this Act has been made out to justify an application for leave to bring such an appeal, and

(c) that all the parties to the proceedings consent to the grant of a certificate under this section,

the judge, subject to the following provisions of this Part of this Act, may grant a certificate to that effect.

(2) This section applies to any civil proceedings in the High Court which are either—

(a) proceedings before a single judge of the High Court (including a person acting as such a judge under section 3 of the Judicature Act 1925), or

(b) proceedings before a commissioner acting under a commission issued under section 70 of the Judicature Act 1925, or

(c) proceedings before a Divisional Court.

(3) Subject to any Order in Council made under the following provisions of this section, for the purposes of this section the relevant conditions, in relation to a decision of the judge in any proceedings, are that a point of law of general public importance is involved in that decision and that that point of law either—

(a) relates wholly or mainly to the construction of an enactment or of a statutory instrument, and has been fully argued in the proceedings and fully considered in the judgment of the judge in the proceedings, or

(b) is one in respect of which the judge is bound by a decision of the Court of Appeal or of the House of Lords in previous proceedings, and was fully considered in the judgments given by the Court of Appeal or the House of Lords (as the case may be) in those previous proceedings.

(4) Any application for a certificate under this section shall be made to the judge immediately after he gives judgment in the proceedings:

Provided that the judge may in any particular case entertain any such application made at any later time before the end of the period of fourteen days beginning with the date on which that judgment is given or such other period as may be prescribed by rules of court.

(5) No appeal shall lie against the grant or refusal of a certificate under this section.

(6) Her Majesty may by Order in Council amend subsection (3) of this section by altering, deleting, or substituting one or more new paragraphs for, either or both of paragraphs (a) and (b) of that subsection, or by adding one or more further paragraphs.

(7) Any Order in Council made under this section shall be subject to annulment in pursuance of a resolution of either House of Parliament.

(8) In this Part of this Act 'civil proceedings' means any proceedings other than proceedings in a criminal cause or matter, and 'the judge', in relation to any proceedings to which this section applies, means the judge or commissioner referred to in paragraph (a) or paragraph (b) of subsection (2) of this section, or the Divisional Court referred to in paragraph (c) of that subsection, as the case may be.

13. Leave to appeal to House of Lords

(1) Where in any proceedings the judge grants a certificate under section 12 of this Act, then, at any time within one month from the date on which that certificate is granted or such extended time as in any particular case the House of Lords may allow, any of the parties to the proceedings may make an application to the House of Lords under this section.

(2) Subject to the following provisions of this section, if on such an application it appears to the House of Lords to be expedient to do so, the House may grant leave for an appeal to be brought directly to the House; and where leave is granted under this section—

(a) no appeal from the decision of the judge to which the certificate relates shall lie to the Court of Appeal, but

(b) an appeal shall lie from that decision to the House of Lords.

(3) Applications under this section shall be determined without a hearing.

(4) Any order of the House of Lords which provides for applications under this section to be determined by a committee of the House—

(a) shall direct that the committee shall consist of or include not less than three of the persons designated as Lords of Appeal in accordance with section 5 of the Appellate Jurisdiction Act 1876, and

(b) may direct that the decision of the committee on any such application shall be taken on behalf of the House.

(5) Without prejudice to subsection (2) of this section, no appeal shall lie to the Court of Appeal from a decision of the judge in respect of which a certificate is granted under section 12 of this Act until—

(a) the time within which an application can be made under this section has expired, and

(b) where such an application is made, that application has been determined in accordance with the preceding provisions of this section.

ANSWERS TO ACTIVITY 17

The conditions to be satisfied in order for the 'leap-frog' procedure to be used are as follows:

1. The trial judge must be satisfied that the relevant conditions are fulfilled (see below); and

2. The House of Lords gives leave to appeal.

The relevant conditions which the trial judge takes into account are that:

(i)   a point of law of general public importance is involved and that it relates to the construction of an act or statutory instrument; or

(ii)   the point of law is one in which the judge is bound by a previous fully considered decision of the Court of Appeal or House of Lords; and in both (i) and (ii)

(iii)   all the parties consent to this procedure.

PEPPER (INSPECTOR OF TAXES) v HART AND RELATED APPEALS
[1993] 1 All ER 42 (HL)

HOUSE OF LORDS

LORD BRIDGE OF HARWICH, LORD GRIFFITHS, LORD EMSLIE, LORD OLIVER OF AYLMERTON AND LORD BROWNE-WILKINSON

4 FEBRUARY 1991

LORD MACKAY OF CLASHFERN LC, LORD KEITH OF KINKEL, LORD BRIDGE OF HARWICH, LORD GRIFFITHS, LORD ACKNER, LORD OLIVER OF AYLMERTON AND LORD BROWNE-WILKINSON

8–11,17–18 JUNE, 26 NOVEMBER 1992

The taxpayers were nine masters and the bursar at an independent boys' school. Under a concessionary fees scheme operated by the school for members of its teaching staff the taxpayers' sons were educated at the school for one-fifth of the fees ordinarily charged to members of the public. The concessionary fees more than covered the additional cost to the school of educating the taxpayers' sons and since in the relevant years the school was not full to capacity their admission did not cause the school to lose full fees which would otherwise have been paid by the members of the public for the places so occupied. The education of the taxpayers' sons at reduced fees was a taxable benefit under s. 61(1) of the Finance Act 1976 and the taxpayers were assessed to income tax on the 'cash equivalent' of that benefit on the basis that they were liable for a rateable proportion of the expenses in running the school as a whole for all the boys, which proportion was roughly equal to the amount of the ordinary school fees. By s. 63 (1) of the 1976 Act the cash equivalent of the benefit was 'an amount equal to the cost of the benefit' and by s. 63(2) the cost of the benefit was 'the amount of any expense incurred in or in connection with its provision'. The taxpayers appealed against the assessments, claiming that since all the costs of running the school generally would have had to be incurred in any event the only expense incurred by the school 'in or in connection' with the education of their sons was the small additional or marginal cost to the school caused by the presence of their sons, which was covered by the fees they paid, and so the 'cash equivalent of the benefit' was nil. The Crown contended that the 'expense incurred in or in connection with' the provision of education for the taxpayers' sons was exactly the same as the expense incurred in or in connection with the education of all other pupils at the school and accordingly the expense of educating any one child was a proportionate part of the cost of running the whole school. The Special Commissioner allowed the taxpayers' appeals, holding that since the taxpayers' sons occupied only surplus places at the school at the school's discretion and the fees paid by the taxpayers fully covered and reimbursed the cost to the school of educating the taxpayers' sons no tax was payable by the taxpayers. The judge allowed an appeal by the Crown and his decision was affirmed by the Court of Appeal. The taxpayers appealed to the House of Lords, where it became apparent that an examination of the proceedings in Parliament in 1976 which led to the enactment of ss. 61 and 63 might give a clear indication whether Parliament intended that the cost of the benefit, i.e. 'the amount of any expense incurred in or in connection with its provision', in s. 63(2) meant the actual expense incurred by the school in providing the benefit or the average cost of the provision of the benefit, the latter being very close to a market value test. The House then heard submissions on the questions whether it would be appropriate to depart from previous authority prohibiting the courts from referring to parliamentary materials in construing statutory provisions and whether the use of Hansard in such circumstances would be an infringement of s. 1, art. 9 of the Bill of Rights (1688) or a breach of parliamentary privilege.

HELD: (1) (Lord Mackay LC dissenting) Having regard to the purposive approach to construction of legislation the courts had adopted in order to give effect to the true intention of the legislature, the rule prohibiting courts from referring to parliamentary material as an aid to statutory construction should, subject to any question of parliamentary privilege, be relaxed so as to permit reference to parliamentary materials where (a) the legislation was ambiguous or obscure or the literal meaning led to an absurdity, (b) the material relied on consisted of statements by a minister or other promoter of the Bill which lead to the enactment of the legislation together if necessary with such other parliamentary material as was necessary to understand such statements and their effect and (c) the statements relied on were clear. Furthermore, the use of parliamentary material as a guide to the construction of ambiguous legislation would not infringe s.1, art.9 of the Bill of Rights since it would not amount to a 'questioning' of the freedom of speech or parliamentary debate provided counsel and the judge refrained from impugning or criticising the minister's statements or his reasoning, since the purpose of the courts in referring to parliamentary material would be to give effect to, rather than thwart through ignorance, the intentions of Parliament and not to question the processes by which such legislation was enacted or to criticise anything said by anyone in Parliament in the course of enacting it . . .; dictum of Lord Reid in *Warner* v *Metropolitan Police Comr* [1968] 2 All ER 365 at 367, *Pickstone* v *Freemans plc* [1988] 2 All ER 803 and *Brind* v *Secretary of State for the Home Dept* [1991] 1 All ER 720 applied; *Church of Scientology of California* v *Johnson-Smith* [1972] 1 All ER 378 distinguished; dicta of Lord Reid in *Beswick* v *Beswick* [1967] 2 All ER 1197 at 1202, of Lord Reid and Lord Wilberforce in *Black-Clawson International Ltd* v *Papierwerke Waldhof-Aschaffenburg AG* [1975] 1 All ER 810 at 814–815, 828 and of Lord Scarman in *Davis* v *Johnson* [1978] 1 All ER 1132 at 1157 not followed; dictum of Dunn LJ in *R* v *Secretary of State for Trade, ex p Anderson Strathclyde plc* [1983] 2 All ER 233 at 239 overruled.

(2) (Per Lord Keith, Lord Bridge, Lord Griffiths, Lord Ackner, Lord Oliver and Lord Browne-Wilkinson) Section 63(2) of the 1976 Act was clearly ambiguous because the 'expense incurred in or in connection with' the provision of in-house benefits could be interpreted as being either the marginal cost caused by the provision of the benefit in question or a proportion of the total cost incurred in providing the service both for the public and for the employee (the average cost). However, the parliamentary history of the 1976 Act and statements made by the Financial Secretary to the Treasury during the committee stage of the Bill made it clear that Parliament had passed the legislation on the basis that the effect of ss. 61 and 63 was to assess in-house benefits, and particularly concessionary education for teachers' children, on the marginal cost to the employer and not on the average cost of the benefit. Acccordingly (per curiam, Lord Mackay LC so construing the section in any event and Lord Griffiths resolving the ambiguity in the taxpayers' favour) s. 63 should be given that meaning . . .

(3) (Per Lord Keith, Lord Bridge, Lord Griffiths, Lord Ackner, Lord Oliver and Lord Browne-Wilkinson) Since the Crown had not identified or specified the nature of any parliamentary privilege going beyond that protected by the Bill of Rights, there was no defined privilege as to the existence and validity of which the House in its judicial capacity would otherwise have been entitled to make a determination, and it would therefore not be right to withhold from the taxpayers the benefit of a decision to which, in law, they were entitled. Accordingly (Lord Mackay LC concurring) the appeal would be allowed . . .

Decision of the Court of Appeal [1991] 2 All ER 824 reversed.

Consolidated appeals

Dr D M Penter, Messrs H J Campbell-Ferguson, M J P Knott, J P Knee, B B White, W J Denny, J T Hart, T Southall and A J Hunter and the personal representatives of Mr C Nicholls deceased (the taxpayers) appealed with leave of the Court of Appeal from the decision of that court (Slade, Nicholls and Farquharson LJJ) ([1991] 2 All ER 824, [1991] Ch 203) on 13 November 1990 dismissing their appeal from the decision of Vinelott J ([1990] STC 6, [1990] 1 WLR 204) dated 24 November 1989 whereby he allowed an appeal by the Crown by way of case stated (set out at [1990] STC 7–17) by the Commissioner for the Special Purposes of the Income Tax Acts in respect of his decision that the expense incurred in educating and maintaining the taxpayers' sons at the school at which the taxpayers were employed did not add to the general costs of the school but was equal to the direct additional costs involved in so doing. Following a hearing on 4 November 1991 the Appellate Committee decided to invite further argument on the question whether the House should depart from previous authority of the House which forbade reference to parliamentary proceedings leading to the enactment of a statute for the purpose of construing ss. 61 and 63 of the Finance Act 1976. The case was thereupon relisted for further hearing before a freshly constituted committee of seven Lords of Appeal in ordinary, four of whom had sat on the original committee. The facts are set out in the opinion of Lord Browne-Wilkinson.

R v R (RAPE: MARITAL EXEMPTION) [1991] 4 All ER 481 (HL)

HOUSE OF LORDS
LORD KEITH OF KINKEL, LORD BRANDON OF OAKBROOK, LORD GRIFFITHS, LORD ACKNER AND LORD LOWRY
1 JULY, 23 OCTOBER 1991

The rule that a husband cannot be criminally liable for raping his wife if he has sexual intercourse with her without her consent no longer forms part of the law of England since a husband and wife are now to be regarded as equal partners in marriage and it is unacceptable that by marriage the wife submits herself irrevocably to sexual intercourse in all circumstances or that it is an incident of modern marriage that the wife consents to intercourse in all circumstances, including sexual intercourse obtained only by force. In s. 1(1) of the Sexual Offences (Amendment) Act 1976, which defines rape as having 'unlawful' intercourse with a woman without her consent, the word 'unlawful' is to be treated as mere surplusage and not as meaning 'outside marriage', since it is clearly unlawful to have sexual intercourse with any woman without her consent. . .

S v HM Advocate 1989 SLT 469 followed.

Decision of the Court of Appeal [1991] 2 All ER 257 affirmed.

Appeal

The appellant appealed with the leave of the Court of Appeal, Criminal Division against the decision of that court (Lord Lane CJ, Sir Stephen Brown P, Watkins, Neill and Russell LJJ) ([1991] 2 All ER 257, [1991] 2 WLR 1065) on 14 March 1991 dismissing his appeal against his conviction before Owen J in the Crown Court at Leicester on 30 July 1990 ([1991] 1 All ER 747) on charges of attempted rape (count 1) and assault occasioning actual bodily harm (count 2) on his then wife to which he pleaded guilty following the trial judge's ruling that he could be convicted of rape on his wife. The appellant was sentenced to three years' imprisonment on count 1 and to 18 months' imprisonment concurrent on count 2. The Court of Appeal certified under s. 33(2) of the Criminal Appeal Act 1968 that a point of law of general public importance was involved in the decision, namely: whether a husband could be criminally liable for raping his wife. The facts are set out in the opinion of Lord Keith.

5.2   End of Chapter Assessment Question

Turn to *Cases and Materials* where you will find extracts from the following two cases:

(1)   *Pepper* v *Hart* [1993] 1 All ER 42; and

(2)   *R* v *R* [1991] 4 All ER 481.

For both of these cases, describe the route by which these cases progressed through the court system, from the first hearing to the final appeal. Include as much relevant information as possible from the report, i.e. dates and places of hearings and names of judges.

5.3   End of Chapter Assessment Outline Answer

In analysing case law, it is important to be able to trace the progress of a case through the various courts.

Obviously the whole case should be studied, but it is also possible to obtain much valuable information from the section following the headnote which is entitled *Appeal*.

The following information should be included in the answer to this question:

Pepper (Inspector of Taxes) v *Hart*

24 November 1989	Vinelott J (presumably High Court — not specified in report)	Appeal by Crown allowed.
13 November 1990	Court of Appeal Slade, Nicholls and Farquharson LJJ	Taxpayers' appeal dismissed.
4 November 1991	House of Lords Lords Bridge, Griffiths, Emslie, Oliver, Browne-Wilkinson	Decision to invite further argument.
8–11, 17–18 June 26 November 1992	House of Lords Lords Mackay, Keith, Bridge, Griffiths, Ackner, Oliver and Browne-Wilkinson	Taxpayers' appeal allowed.

R v R
(It is assumed that committal proceedings took place before magistrates.)

30 July 1990	Crown Court Leicester Owen J	R convicted
14 March 1991	Court of Appeal (Criminal Division) Lord Lane CJ Sir Stephen Brown P Watkins, Neill and Russell LJJ	Appeal of R dismissed.
1 July 1991 23 October 1991	House of Lords Lords Keith, Brandon, Griffiths, Ackner and Lowry	Decision of Court of Appeal affirmed.

CHAPTER SIX

LEGAL SERVICES

6.1 The Legal Profession

COURTS AND LEGAL SERVICES ACT 1990

17. The statutory objective and the general principle

(1)   The general objective of this Part is the development of legal services in England and Wales (and in particular the development of advocacy, litigation, conveyancing and probate services) by making provision for new or better ways of providing such services and a wider choice of persons providing them, while maintaining the proper and efficient administration of justice.

(2)   In this Act that objective is referred to as 'the statutory objective.'

(3)   As a general principle the question whether a person should be granted a right of audience, or be granted a right to conduct litigation in relation to any court or proceedings, should be determined only by reference to—

(a)   whether he is qualified in accordance with the educational and training requirements appropriate to the court or proceedings;

(b)   whether he is a member of a professional or other body which—

(i)   has rules of conduct (however described) governing the conduct of its members;

(ii)   has an effective mechanism for enforcing the rules of conduct; and

(iii)   is likely to enforce them;

(c)   whether, in the case of a body whose members are or will be providing advocacy services, the rules of conduct make satisfactory provision in relation to the court or proceedings in question requiring any such member not to withhold those services—

(i)   on the ground that the nature of the case is objectionable to him or to any section of the public;

(ii)   on the ground that the conduct, opinions or beliefs of the prospective client are unacceptable to him or to any section of the public;

(iii)   on any ground relating to the source of any financial support which may properly be given to the prospective client for the proceedings in question (for example, on the ground that such support will be available under the Legal Aid Act 1988); and

(d)   whether the rules of conduct are, in relation to the court or proceedings, appropriate in the interests of the proper and efficient administration of justice.

(4)   In this Act that principle is referred to as 'the general principle.'

(5)   Rules of conduct which allow a member of the body in question to withhold his services if there are reasonable grounds for him to consider that, having regard to—

(a)   the circumstances of the case;

(b)   the nature of his practice; or

(c)   his experience and standing,

he is not being offered a proper fee, are not on that account to be taken as being incompatible with the general principle.

37. Authorisation of practitioners

(1) On an application duly made by a person who proposes to provide conveyancing services, the Board shall authorise that person to provide those services, if—

(a) it is satisfied that the applicant's business is, and is likely to continue to be, carried on by fit and proper persons or, in the case of an application by an individual, that he is a fit and proper person; and

(b) it is of the opinion that the applicant will comply with the requirements mentioned in subsection (7).

(2) Any such authorisation shall be given in writing and shall take effect on such date as the Board may specify.

(3) A person so authorised is referred to in this Act as 'an authorised practitioner.'

(4) An application for authorisation must be made in accordance with rules made by the Board, with the approval of the Lord Chancellor, for the purposes of this section.

(5) On making any such application, the applicant shall pay to the Board such fee as may be specified in the rules.

(6) The rules may, in particular, make provision—

(a) as to the form in which any application must be made; and

(b) for the furnishing by applicants of information required by the Board in connection with their applications.

(7) The requirements are that the applicant—

(a) complies with any rules made by the Board and any regulations made under section 40, so far as applicable;

(b) ensures that satisfactory arrangements are at all times in force for covering adequately the risk of any claim made against the applicant in connection with the provision of conveyancing services provided by the applicant, however arising;

(c) maintains satisfactory procedures for—

(i) dealing with complaints made about any aspect of conveyancing services provided by the applicant; and

(ii) the payment of compensation;

(d) has in force satisfactory arrangements to protect the applicant's clients in the event of the applicant ceasing to provide conveyancing services;

(e) is a member of the Conveyancing Ombudsman Scheme.

(8) Where the applicant is—

(a) an institution which is authorised by the Bank of England, under Part I of the Banking Act 1987, to carry on a deposit taking business;

(b) a building society which is authorised by the Building Societies Commission, under section 9 of the Building Societies Act 1986, to raise money from its members; or

(c) an insurance company which is authorised under section 3 or 4 of the Insurance Companies Act 1982,

the Board shall have regard to the fact that it is so authorised in determining whether the Board is satisfied as mentioned in subsection (1)(a).

(9) The Board shall maintain a register of authorised practitioners which shall be open to inspection, at all reasonable times, without charge.

(10) The Lord Chancellor may by order amend the provisions of sub-section (7) by imposing any additional requirement or by varying or removing any requirement.

COURTS AND LEGAL SERVICES ACT 1990

Rights of audience and rights to conduct litigation

27. Rights of audience

(1) The question whether a person has a right of audience before a court, or in relation to any proceedings, shall be determined solely in accordance with the provisions of this Part.

(2) A person shall have a right of audience before a court in relation to any proceedings only in the following cases—

(a) where—

(i) he has a right of audience before that court in relation to those proceedings granted by the appropriate authorised body; and

(ii) that body's qualification regulations and rules of conduct have been approved for the purposes of this section, in relation to the granting of that right;

(b)   where paragraph (a) does not apply but he has a right of audience before that court in relation to those proceedings granted by or under any enactment;

(c)   where paragraph (a) does not apply but he has a right of audience granted by that court in relation to those proceedings;

(d)   where he is a party to those proceedings and would have had a right of audience, in his capacity as such a party, if this Act had not been passed; or

(e)   where—

(i)   he is employed (whether wholly or in part), or is otherwise engaged, to assist in the conduct of litigation and is doing so under instructions given (either generally or in relation to the proceedings) by a qualified litigator; and

(ii)   the proceedings are being heard in chambers in the High Court or a county court and are not reserved family proceedings.

(3)   No person shall have a right of audience as a barrister by virtue of subsection (2)(a) above unless he has been called to the Bar by one of the Inns of Court and has not been disbarred or temporarily suspended from practice by order of an Inn of Court.

(4)   Nothing in this section affects the power of any court in any proceedings to refuse to hear a person (for reasons which apply to him as an individual) who would otherwise have a right of audience before the court in relation to those proceedings.

(5)   Where a court refuses to hear a person as mentioned in subsection (4) it shall give its reasons for refusing.

(6)   Nothing in this section affects any provision made by or under any enactment which prevents a person from exercising a right of audience which he would otherwise be entitled to exercise.

(7)   Where, immediately before the commencement of this section, no restriction was placed on the persons entitled to exercise any right of audience in relation to any particular court or in relation to particular proceedings, nothing in this section shall be taken to place any such restriction on any person.

(8)   Where—

(a)   immediately before the commencement of this section; or

(b)   by virtue of any provision made by or under an enactment passed subsequently, a court does not permit the appearance of advocates, or permits the appearance of advocates only with leave, no person shall have a right of audience before that court, in relation to any proceedings, solely by virtue of the provisions of this section.

(9)   In this section—

'advocate,' in relation to any proceedings, means any person exercising a right of audience as a representative of, or on behalf of, any party to the proceedings;

'authorised body' means—

(a)   the General Council of the Bar;

(b)   the Law Society; and

(c)   any professional or other body which has been designated by Order in Council as an authorised body for the purposes of this section;

'appropriate authorised body,' in relation to any person claiming to be entitled to any right of audience by virtue of subsection (2)(a), means the authorised body—

(a)   granting that right; and

(b)   of which that person is a member;

'family proceedings' has the same meaning as in the Matrimonial and Family Proceedings Act 1984 and also includes any other proceedings which are family proceedings for the purposes of the Children Act 1989;

'qualification regulations,' in relation to an authorised body, means regulations (however they may be described) as to the education and training which members of that body must receive in order to be entitled to any right of audience granted by it;

'qualified litigator' means—

(i)   any practising solicitor ('practising' having the same meaning as in section 19(8)(b));

(ii)   any recognised body; and

(iii)   any person who is exempt from the requirement to hold a practising certificate by virtue of section 88 of the Solicitors Act 1974 (saving for solicitors to public departments and the City of London);

'recognised body' means any body recognised under section 9 of the Administration of Justice Act 1985 (incorporated practices);

'reserved family proceedings' means such category of family proceedings as the Lord Chancellor may, after consulting the President of the Law Society and with the concurrence of the President of the Family Division, by order prescribe; and

'rules of conduct,' in relation to an authorised body, means rules (however they may be described) as to the conduct required of members of that body in exercising any right of audience granted by it.

(10)   Section 20 of the Solicitors Act 1974 (unqualified person not to act as a solicitor) section 22 of that Act (unqualified person not to prepare certain documents etc.) and section 25 of that Act (costs where an unqualified person acts as a solicitor), shall not apply in relation to any act done in the exercise of a right of audience.

6.2   Paying for Legal Services

6.2.1   CONDITIONAL FEE AGREEMENTS AND CONTINGENCY FEE AGREEMENTS

COURTS AND LEGAL SERVICES ACT 1990

Miscellaneous

58.   Conditional fee agreements

(1)   In this section 'a conditional fee agreement' means an agreement in writing between a person providing advocacy or litigation services and his client which—

(a)   does not relate to proceedings of a kind mentioned in subsection (10);

(b)   provides for that person's fees and expenses, or any part of them, to be payable only in specified circumstances;

(c)   complies with such requirements (if any) as may be prescribed by the Lord Chancellor; and

(d)   is not a contentious business agreement (as defined by section 59 of the Solicitors Act 1974).

(2)   Where a conditional fee agreement provides for the amount of any fees to which it applies to be increased, in specified circumstances, above the amount which would be payable if it were not a conditional fee agreement, it shall specify the percentage by which that amount is to be increased.

(3)   Subject to subsection (6), a conditional fee agreement which relates to specified proceedings shall not be unenforceable by reason only of its being a conditional fee agreement.

(4)   In this section 'specified proceedings' means proceedings of a description specified by order made by the Lord Chancellor for the purposes of subsection (3).

(5)   Any such order shall prescribe the maximum permitted percentage for each description of specified proceedings.

(6)   An agreement which falls within subsection (2) shall be unenforceable if, at the time when it is entered into, the percentage specified in the agreement exceeds the prescribed maximum permitted percentage for the description of proceedings to which it relates.

(7)   Before making any order under this section the Lord Chancellor shall consult the designated judges, the General Council of the Bar, the Law Society and such other authorised bodies (if any) as he considers appropriate.

(8)   Where a party to any proceedings has entered into a conditional fee agreement and a costs order is made in those proceedings in his favour, the costs payable to him shall not include any element which takes account of an percentage increase payable under the agreement.

(9)   Rules of court may make provision with respect to the taxing of any costs which include fees payable under a conditional fee agreement.

(10)   The proceedings mentioned in subsection (1)(a) are any criminal proceedings and any proceedings under—

(a)	the Matrimonial Causes Act 1973;
(b)	the Domestic Violence and Matrimonial Proceedings Act 1976;
(c)	the Adoption Act 1976;
(d)	the Domestic Proceedings and Magistrates' Courts Act 1978;
(e)	sections 1 and 9 of the Matrimonial Homes Act 1983;
(f)	Part III of the Matrimonial and Family Proceedings Act 1984;
(g)	Parts I, II or IV of the Children Act 1989; or
(h)	the inherent jurisdiction of the High Court in relation to children.

THAI TRADING CO. (A FIRM) v TAYLOR AND ANOTHER [1998] 3 All ER 65 (CA)

FACTS: The defendant, Mrs T, ordered a bed from the plaintiff company and paid a deposit of £1,500. When the bed was delivered it did not match Mrs T's expectations, and so she rejected it and refused to pay anything more. The plaintiff brought proceedings in the county court for the unpaid balance of the purchase price and Mrs T counterclaimed for the return of the money she had paid. Mrs T employed her husband, who was a solicitor and a sole practitioner, to act for her on the understanding that she would not pay anything if she lost. Mrs T won her case and obtained judgment on her counterclaim and the plaintiff was ordered to pay her costs. In the course of taxation, the plaintiff challenged the amount claimed to be due from it on the ground that there was no liability, as Mrs T was not legally liable to pay her solicitor his profit costs. The judge concluded that he was bound by authority to hold that the agreement, being an agreement for a contingency fee, was contrary to public policy and void, so that there was no legal liability on Mrs T to pay her husband's profit costs and therefore, by virtue of the indemnity principle, no liability on the plaintiff to pay such costs. The husband, as a party entitled to be heard on the taxation proceedings forming the subject of the appeal and who was interested in and prejudiced by the decision, appealed.

HELD: It was not now contrary to public policy for a solicitor acting for a party to litigation to agree to forego all or part of his fee if he lost, provided that he did not seek to recover more than his ordinary profit costs and disbursements if he won. Where however the solicitor contracted for a reward over and above his proper fees if he won, it might well be that the whole retainer was unlawful and the solicitor could recover nothing; but where he contracted for no more than his proper fees if he won, that result did not follow. There was nothing unlawful in the retainer, or in the client's obligation to pay the solicitor's proper costs if he won the case. It followed, in the instant case, that Mrs T was legally liable to pay her solicitor his profit costs and was therefore entitled to recover by way of indemnity from the plaintiff. The appeal would accordingly be allowed.

Appeal
The second defendant, Wilfred David Taylor, appealed from the decision of Judge Nigel Hague QC at Reading County Court on 26 February 1997 whereby he ordered (i) that an agreement between Mrs Margery Taylor and her solicitor (who was also her husband) for a contingency fee was contrary to public policy and so void, and (ii) that, since Mrs Taylor was not legally liable to pay her solicitor his profit costs, there was by virtue of the indemnity principle no liability on the plaintiff, Thai Trading Co., whose directors were Adrian Beard and Timothy Beard, to pay such costs. The facts are set out in the judgment of Millett LJ.

MILLETT LJ: (giving the first judgment at the invitation of Kennedy LJ):
	1.	In June 1991 Mrs Taylor ordered a four-poster Thai carved bed from the plaintiffs for the price of £2,500. She paid a deposit of £1,500. The bed was delivered, but it did not match Mrs Taylor's expectations. She rejected it and refused to pay anything more. The plaintiffs brought proceedings in the Reading County Court for the unpaid balance of the purchase price and Mrs Taylor counterclaimed for the return of the money she had paid.
	2.	The case was a small, run-of-the-mill county court case and should have been disposed of speedily and with relatively little expense. Unfortunately it had a protracted

history and involved a number of court appearances, with the result that the present appeal, which relates to Mrs Taylor's costs, is concerned with a sum which is out of all proportion to the amount originally in issue.

3. Mrs Taylor won her case. The plaintiffs' action was dismissed and Mrs Taylor obtained judgment on her counterclaim. The plaintiffs were ordered to pay Mrs Taylor's costs up to 22 March 1993 and from 25 January 1994 with no order as to costs for the intervening period. This reflected the fact that Mrs Taylor had eventually succeeded on a point not taken before the district judge.

4. In the course of taxation the plaintiffs challenged the amount claimed to be due from them. Mrs Taylor had paid the disbursements out of her own money and the plaintiffs did not dispute their liability for these. But they disputed any further liability on the ground that Mrs Taylor was not legally liable to pay her solicitor his profit costs. It is a well-settled principle that a successful party who has been awarded his costs can recover by way of indemnity only the costs which he is legally liable to pay to his own solicitor or in the case of disbursements to third parties. The principle was established in *Gundry* v *Sainsbury* [1910] 1 KB 645, where the successful party was unable to obtain an order for costs because his solicitor had agreed to act for him without reward.

5. The circumstances which give rise to the allegation that Mrs Taylor was not legally liable to pay her solicitor's profit costs are as follows. Mrs Taylor's husband is a solicitor practising under the firm name of Taylors. He is a sole practitioner. Mrs Taylor works for the firm as an accounts clerk. She naturally employed the firm to act for her in the proceedings brought against her, and it represented her throughout the course of the litigation.

6. Mrs Taylor deposed in an affidavit as follows:

There was no agreement either expressly or by implication between myself and my husband, acting as my solicitor, that he would not render Bills to me. Upon the recovery of costs awarded to me they will be dealt with in the same way as with any client recovering costs following litigation and a Bill will be raised to cover these costs.

7. The judge (Judge Nigel Hague QC) accepted Mrs Taylor's evidence that there was no express agreement between her and her husband in regard to her costs, but he found that there was an understanding that she would not pay anything if she lost. He said:

. . . the common sense of the matter points strongly to the conclusion that Taylors would only be paid by Mrs Taylor if and to the extent that she won the litigation and could recover the costs from the plaintiffs. I cannot believe that Taylors intended or expected to be paid if she lost. The notions that in those circumstances Taylors would have billed Mrs Taylor and that she would have paid such a bill (whether out of her own earnings or savings or out of money provided by her husband), thereby increasing Mr Taylor's profits and his income tax liability, are to my mind fanciful . . . For those reasons, although I reject the plaintiffs' first contention that Mrs Taylor was under no obligation to pay Taylors in any circumstances, I accept their second contention. I find that there was an understanding between Taylors and Mrs Taylor that she would not be liable to them for any profit costs except in the event of success in the litigation and an order for costs in her favour, when she would become liable for their normal profit costs.

8. There is no appeal from this finding, which was based on inference from the primary facts. In my opinion the facts did not warrant the inference that there was any understanding as to Mrs Taylor's legal liability in respect of costs. To my mind the only legitimate inference was that, while Mrs Taylor's legal liability for costs was not affected, save in unforeseen circumstances neither party expected Mr Taylor to demand payment or enforce her liability unless she won her case and to the extent that she recovered costs from the plaintiffs.

9. In a judgment for which I should wish to express my respectful admiration the judge pointed out that, if the law relating to the recovery of contingent fees be put on one side, the so-called indemnity principle did not avail the plaintiffs. Even if there was an express agreement that Mr Taylor would be paid his profit costs only if Mrs Taylor

won her case, she would still be entitled to be indemnified against a legal liability which had been incurred in the events which had happened. The fact that she would have incurred no liability in a different event which had not happened would not affect this.

10.   Had he felt free to do so, the judge would have held that the agreement between Mrs Taylor and her husband which he had found was entered into was a valid and enforceable agreement. But he reluctantly concluded that he was bound by authority, in particular the decisions of the Divisional Court in *British Waterways Board* v *Norman* (1993) 26 HLR 232 and of Garland J in *Aratra Potato Co. Ltd* v *Taylor Joynson Garrett (a firm)* [1995] 4 All ER 695, to hold that the agreement, being an agreement for a contingent fee, was contrary to public policy and so void. Those decisions also showed that the consequence was that there was no legal liability on Mrs Taylor to pay Taylors' profit costs, and hence by virtue of the indemnity principle no liability on the plaintiffs to pay such costs.

11.   The judge felt the injustice of the result which he was constrained by authority to reach. He subjected the two decisions to which I have referred to respectful criticism, but rightly held that he was bound by them. We are not so bound, and are free to examine the underlying principles afresh.

12.   Mrs Taylor has appealed the judge's decision, but has no financial interest in the result of the appeal. Accordingly Mr Taylor has been joined as an additional party to the appeal and argument has been presented on his behalf.

The Solicitors Act 1974

13.   It should be observed at the outset that there is nothing in the Solicitors Act 1974 which prohibits the charging of contingent fees. Section 59(2) merely provides that nothing in the Act shall give validity to arrangements of the kind there specified. It does not legitimise such arrangements if they are otherwise unlawful, but neither does it make them unlawful if they are otherwise lawful.

14.   The Solicitors Practice Rules 1987 by contrast provide that a solicitor engaged in any contentious business shall not enter into any arrangement to receive a contingency fee, that is to say a fee payable only in the event of success in the proceeding. There is now an exception for conditional fee agreements which satisfy the requirements of the Courts and Legal Services Act 1990. Except as there provided, therefore, it is unprofessional conduct for a solicitor to enter into any agreement even for his normal fee where this is dependent on achieving a successful result in litigation. The plaintiffs placed much reliance on this. But the fact that a professional rule prohibits a particular practice does not of itself make the practice contrary to law (see *Picton Jones & Co. Arcadia Developments Ltd* [1989] 1 EGLR 43. Moreover, the Solicitors Rules are based on a perception of public policy derived from judicial decisions the correctness of which is in question in this appeal.

Maintenance and champerty

15.   The law governing contingent fees outside the scope of the Courts and Legal Services Act 1990 is derived from the public policy relating to champerty and maintenance. Until 1967 these were both criminal and tortious. Following the recommendation of the Law Commission on *Proposals to Abolish Certain Ancient Criminal Offences* (Law Com No. 3) the Criminal Law Act 1967 provided that they should no longer be either criminal or tortious. Section 14(2) of the Act, however, preserved the rule of the common law that they are contrary to public policy.

16.   Maintenance was described by Lord Denning MR in *Re Trepca Mines Ltd (Application of Radomir Nicola Pachitch (Pasic))* [1962] 3 All ER 351 at 355, [1963] Ch 199 at 219 as 'improperly stirring up litigation and strife by giving aid to one party to bring or defend a claim without just cause or excuse'. Champerty was described by Scrutton LJ in *Ellis* v *Torrington* [1920] 1 KB 399 at 412, [1918–19] All ER Rep 1132 at 1138 as 'only a particular form of maintenance, namely, where the person who maintains takes as a reward a share in the property recovered'.

17.   This last formulation does not assume that the maintenance is unlawful. There can be no champerty if there is no maintenance; but there can still be champerty even if the maintenance is not unlawful. The public policy which informs the two doctrines is different and allows for different exceptions. In examining the present scope of the

doctrine, it must be remembered that public policy is not static. In recent times the roles of maintenance and champerty have been progressively redefined and narrowed in scope. The current position is stated by the decision of the House of Lords in *Giles* v *Thompson* [1993] 3 All ER 321 at 357, [1994] 1 AC 142 at 161.

Maintenance

18.   The policy underlying the law of maintenance was described by Fletcher Moulton LJ in *British Cash and Parcel Conveyors Ltd* v *Lamson Store Service Co. Ltd* [1908] 1 KB 1006 at 1014, [1908–10] All ER Rep 146 at 150 in terms which were approved by Lord Mustill in *Giles* v *Thompson* [1993] 3 All ER 321 at 357, [1994] 1 AC 142 at 161 as follows:

> It is directed against wanton and officious intermeddling with the disputes of others in which the [maintainer] has no interest whatever, and where the assistance he renders to one or the other party is without justification or excuse.

The language and the policy which it describes are redolent of the ethos of an earlier age when litigation was regarded as an evil and recourse to law was discouraged. It rings oddly in our ears today when access to justice is regarded as a fundamental human right which ought to be readily available to all.

19.   But even in former times maintenance was permissible when the maintainer had a legitimate interest in the outcome of the suit. This was not confined to cases where he had a financial or commercial interest in the result. It extended to other cases where social, family or other ties justified the maintainer in supporting the litigation. In *Neville* v *London Express Newspaper Ltd* [1919] AC 368 at 389, [1918–19] All ER Rep 61 at 71 Viscount Haldane said:

> Such an interest is held to be possessed when in litigation a master assists his servant, or a servant his master, or help is given to an heir, or a near relative, or to a poor man out of charity, to maintain a right which he might otherwise lose.

In *Bradlaugh* v *Newdegate* (1883) 11 QBD 1 at 11 Lord Coleridge CJ spoke of 'the interest which consanguinity or affinity to the suitor give to the man who aids him, or the interest arising from the connection of the parties, eg as master and servant . . .' In *Condliffe* v *Hislop* [1996] 1 All ER 431, [1996] 1 WLR 753 this court held that it was not unlawful for a mother to provide limited funds to finance her bankrupt son's action for defamation.

20.   In the present case the plaintiffs do not contend that Mr Taylor was guilty of unlawfully maintaining his wife's suit. He was doubly justified in doing so; the suitor was both his wife and his employee.

Champerty

21.   In *Giles* v *Thompson* [1993] 3 All ER 321 at 357, [1994] 1 AC 142 at 161 Lord Mustill cited with approval Fletcher Moulton LJ's description of maintenance to which I have already referred, and added: 'This was a description of maintenance. For champerty there must be added the notion of a division of the spoils.'

22.   The public policy which underlies the doctrine of champerty was described by Lord Denning MR in *Re Trepca Mines Ltd* [1962] 3 All ER 351 at 355, [1963] Ch 199 at 219–220:

> The reason why the common law condemns champerty is because of the abuses to which it may give rise. The common law fears that the champertous maintainer might be tempted, for his own personal gain, to inflame the damages, to suppress evidence, or even to suborn witnesses.

Describing champerty as 'a particularly obnoxious form of [maintenance] in *Trendtex Trading Corp* v *Credit Suisse* [1980] 3 All ER 721 at 741, [1980] QB 629 at 654, Lord Denning MR reserved his particular condemnation for the lawyer who charged a contingency fee, that is to say a fee which would be payable only if his client was successful. He said:

> [Champerty] exists when the maintainer seeks to make a profit out of another man's action, by taking the proceeds of it, or part of them, for himself. Modern public policy

condemns champerty in a lawyer whenever he seeks to recover not only his proper costs but also a portion of the damages for himself, *or when he conducts a case on the basis that he is to be paid he wins but not if he loses!* (My emphasis.)

23.   Lord Denning MR was there repeating what he had said in *Wallersteiner* v *Moir (No. 2)* [1975] 1 All ER 849 at 860, [1975] QB 373 at 393:

English law has never sanctioned an agreement by which a lawyer is remunerated on the basis of a 'contingency fee', that is that he gets paid the fee if he wins, but not if he loses. Such an agreement was illegal on the ground that it was the offence of champerty.

Lord Denning MR was prepared nevertheless to authorise the plaintiff in a derivative action to enter into a contingency fee agreement, but the other members of the court (Buckley and Scarman LJJ) thought otherwise. It is, however, clear from the judgments of the majority that they did not have in mind the charging of normal fees contingent on success in the action. Thus Buckley LJ said ([1975] 1 All ER 849 at 867, [1975] QB 373 at 402):

Under a contingency fee agreement the remuneration payable by the client to his lawyer in the event of his success must be higher than it would be if the lawyer were entitled to be remunerated, win or lose: the contingency fee must contain an element of compensation for the risk of having done the work for nothing. It would, it seems to me, be unfair to the opponent of a contingency fee litigant if he were at risk of being ordered to pay higher costs to his opponent in the event of the latter's success in the action than would be the case if there were no contingency fee agreement.

24.   It is understandable that a contingency fee which entitles the solicitor to a reward over and above his ordinary profit costs if he wins should be condemned as tending to corrupt the administration of justice. There is no reason to suppose that Lord Denning MR in *Trendtex Trading Corp* v *Crédit Suisse* or any of the members of the court in *Wallersteiner* v *Moir* had in mind a contingency fee which entitles the solicitor to no more than his ordinary profit costs if he wins. These are subject to taxation and their only vice is that they are more than he will receive if he loses. Such a fee cannot sensibly be described as a 'division of the spoils'. The solicitor cannot obtain more than he would without the arrangement and risks obtaining less. On the principle that 'the worker is worthy of his hire' I would regard the solicitor who enters into such an arrangement, not as charging a fee if he wins, but rather as agreeing to forego his fee if he loses. I question whether this should be regarded as contrary to public policy today, if indeed it ever was.

25.   In *British Waterways Board* v *Norman* the solicitors knew that their client was on income support, advised her to bring a private prosecution without suggesting to her that she would have to pay anything towards the costs, and only expected to be paid by her if she was successful and an order for costs was made against the Board. It never occurred to the client that she would have to pay any costs out of her own pocket. The Divisional Court held that the only possible conclusion from these facts was that there was an understanding amounting in law to a contract that the client would not be liable for their costs if she lost the case. This was in the face of evidence which the magistrates accepted that there was no contractual arrangement with the client that the solicitors would not collect costs from her if the case was lost, that there was no question of a contingency fee, and no agreement express or implied that the solicitors would only be paid if successful. I doubt that the Divisional Court was correct to conclude that there. was only one possible interpretation of the facts. It is not uncommon for solicitors to take on a case for an impecunious client with a meritorious case, knowing that there is no realistic prospect of recovering their costs from the client if the case is lost, without thereby waiving their legal right to their fees in that event. As every debt collector knows, what is legally recoverable and what is recoverable in practice are not the same.

26.   The Divisional Court followed Lord Denning MR's indication of the width of the doctrine in *Trendtex Trading Corp* v *Credit Suisse*. McCowan LJ explained the rationale in *British Waterways Board* v *Norman* (1993) 26 HLR 232 at 242 as follows: 'To put it in a

nutshell, once a lawyer has a personal interest in litigation, his or her objectivity may be affected.' Tuckey J (at 243) said that if it was made clear that the client was liable for costs irrespective of the outcome of the proceedings, there could be no objection to the solicitor agreeing that such liability need not be discharged until the outcome of the proceedings was known. At that stage, *provided it had not formed the basis of any prior agreement with the client*, the solicitor could properly forego his right to be paid to the extent that any of the costs were not recovered from the other party to the proceedings. In the present case the judge described this conclusion as most unsatisfactory. He pointed out, justifiably in my opinion, that it elevates form above substance, and invites solicitors to produce documents evidencing an agreement which both parties know would not be enforced. I agree with the judge's comment that the need for solicitors to engage in a subterfuge of this kind in order to recover their costs in the event of a successful outcome to the litigation shows that the underlying reasoning is unsound.

27.   In *Aratra Potato Co. Ltd* v *Taylor Joynson Garrett (a firm)* [1995] 4 All ER 695 the absurdities to which such reasoning is capable of leading were dramatically exposed. Solicitors were engaged on a retainer which included a term that there would be a 20% reduction from solicitor/client costs for any lost cases. Garland J held that it was champertous and contrary to public policy for solicitors to agree a differential fee dependent on the outcome of litigation; that the entire retainer was unlawful; and accordingly the solicitors could not recover their outstanding fees for work done irrespective of the outcome of the cases and with or without the reduction. The fact that the solicitors were seeking to recover no more (and in respect of lost cases less) than their ordinary profit costs made no difference.

28.   If this is the law then something has gone badly wrong. It is time to step back and consider the matter afresh in the light of modern conditions. I start with three propositions. First, if it is contrary to public policy for a lawyer to have a financial interest in the outcome of a suit this is because (and only because) of the temptations to which it exposes him. At best he may lose his professional objectivity; at worst he may be persuaded to attempt to pervert the course of justice. Secondly, there is nothing improper in a lawyer acting in a case for a meritorious client who to his knowledge cannot afford to pay his costs if the case is lost (see *Singh* v *Observer Ltd (Note)* [1989] 3 All ER 777 and *A Ltd* v *B Ltd* [1996] 1 WLR 665). Not only is this not improper; it is in accordance with current notions of the public interest that he should do so. Thirdly, if the temptation to win at all costs is present at all, it is present whether or not the lawyer has formally waived his fees if he loses. It arises from his knowledge that in practice he will not be paid unless he wins. In my judgment the reasoning in the *British Waterways Board* v *Norman* is unsound.

29.   Accordingly, either it is improper for a solicitor to act in litigation for a meritorious client who cannot afford to pay him if he loses, or it is not improper for a solicitor to agree to act on the basis that he is to be paid his ordinary costs if he wins but not if he loses. I have no hesitation in concluding that the second of these propositions represents the current state of the law.

30.   I reach this conclusion for several reasons. In the first place, I do not understand why it is assumed that the effect of the arrangement being unlawful is that the solicitor is unable to recover his proper costs in any circumstances. Where the solicitor contracts for a reward over and above his proper fees if he wins, it may well be that the whole retainer is unlawful and the solicitor can recover nothing. But where he contracts for no more than his proper fees if he wins, this result does not follow. There is nothing unlawful in the retainer or in the client's obligation to pay the solicitor's proper costs if he wins the case. If there is anything unlawful, it is in the waiver or reduction of the fees if he loses. On ordinary principles the result of holding this to be unlawful is that the client is liable for the solicitor's proper costs even if he loses the case. I regard *Aratra Potato Co. Ltd* v *Taylor Joynson Garrett* as wrongly decided.

31.   In the second place, it is in my judgment fanciful to suppose that a solicitor will be tempted to compromise his professional integrity because he will be unable to recover his ordinary profit costs in a small case if the case is lost. Solicitors are accustomed to withstand far greater incentives to impropriety than this. The solicitor who acts for a multinational company in a heavy commercial action knows that if he loses the case his client may take his business elsewhere. In the present case, Mr Taylor had more at stake

than his profit costs if he lost. His client was his wife; desire for domestic harmony alone must have provided a powerful incentive to win.

32.   Current attitudes to these questions are exemplified by the passage into law of the Courts and Legal Services Act 1990. This shows that the fear that lawyers may be tempted by having a financial incentive in the outcome of litigation to act improperly is exaggerated, and that there is a countervailing public policy in making justice readily accessible to persons of modest means. Legislation was needed to authorise the increase in the lawyer's reward over and above his ordinary profit costs. It by no means follows that it was needed to legitimise the long-standing practice of solicitors to act for meritorious clients without means, and it is in the public interest that they should continue to do so. I observe that the author of *Cook on Costs* (2nd edn, 1995) p. 341 expresses his doubt that it is now against public policy for a solicitor to agree with a client that he will not charge a fee unless a particular result is achieved. I agree with him and would hold that it is not.

Conclusion
In my judgment there is nothing unlawful in a solicitor acting for a party to litigation to agree to forego all or part of his fee if he loses, provided that he does not seek to recover more than his ordinary profit costs and disbursements if he wins. I would accordingly overrule the decisions in *British Waterways Board* v *Norman* and *Aratra Potato Co. Ltd* v *Taylor Joynson Garrett* and allow the appeal.

HUTCHISON LJ: I agree that this appeal should be allowed for the reasons that Millett LJ has given, with which I am in complete agreement.

KENNEDY LJ: I also agree.

Appeal allowed.

6.3   Alternative Means of Resolving Legal Disputes

6.3.1   ARBITRATION

ARBITRATION ACT 1996
(1996, c. 23)

PART I

ARBITRATION PURSUANT TO AN ARBITRATION AGREEMENT

Introductory

1.   General principles
The provisions of this Part are founded on the following principles and shall be construed accordingly—
   (a)   the object of arbitration is to obtain the fair resolution of disputes by an impartial tribunal without unnecessary delay or expense;
   (b)   the parties should be free to agree how their disputes are resolved, subject only to such safeguards as are necessary, in the public interest;
   (c)   in matters governed by this Part the court should not intervene except as provided by this Part.
   For this purpose an applicable law determined in accordance with the parties' agreement, or which is objectively determined in the absence of any express or implied choice, shall be treated as chosen by the parties.

5.   Agreements to be in writing
   (1)   The provisions of this Part apply only where the arbitration agreement is in writing, and any other agreement between the parties as to any matter is effective for the purposes of this Part only if in writing.

The expressions 'agreement', 'agree' and 'agreed' shall be construed accordingly.

(2) There is an agreement in writing—

(a) if the agreement is made in writing (whether or not it is signed by the parties),

(b) if the agreement is made by exchange of communications in writing, or

(c) if the agreement is evidenced in writing.

(3) Where parties agree otherwise than in writing by reference to terms which are in writing, they make an agreement in writing.

(4) An agreement is evidenced in writing if an agreement made otherwise than in writing is recorded by one of the parties, or by a third party, with the authority of the parties to the agreement.

(5) An exchange of written submissions in arbitral or legal proceedings in which the existence of an agreement otherwise than in writing is alleged by one party against another party and not denied by the other party in his response constitutes as between those parties an agreement in writing to the effect alleged.

(6) References in this Part to anything being written or in writing include its being recorded by any means.

8. Whether agreement discharged by death of a party

(1) Unless otherwise agreed by the parties, an arbitration agreement is not discharged by the death of a party and may be enforced by or against the personal representatives of that party.

(2) Subsection (1) does not affect the operation of any enactment or rule of law by virtue of which a substantive right or obligation is extinguished by death.

Stay of legal proceedings

9. Stay of legal proceedings

(1) A party to an arbitration agreement against whom legal proceedings are brought (whether by way of claim or counterclaim) in respect of a matter which under the agreement is to be referred to arbitration may (upon notice to the other parties to the proceedings) apply to the court in which the proceedings have been brought to stay the proceedings so far as they concern that matter.

(2) An application may be made notwithstanding that the matter is to be referred to arbitration only after the exhaustion of other dispute resolution procedures.

(3) An application may not be made by a person before taking the appropriate procedural step (if any) to acknowledge the legal proceedings against him or after he has taken any step in those proceedings to answer the substantive claim.

(4) On an application under this section the court shall grant a stay unless satisfied that the arbitration agreement is null and void, inoperative, or incapable of being performed.

(5) If the court refuses to stay the legal proceedings, any provision that an award is a condition precedent to the bringing of legal proceedings in respect of any matter is of no effect in relation to those proceedings.

13. Application of Limitation Acts

(1) The Limitation Acts apply to arbitral proceedings as they apply to legal proceedings.

(2) The court may order that in computing the time prescribed by the Limitation Acts for the commencement of proceedings (including arbitral proceedings) in respect of a dispute which was the subject matter—

(a) of an award which the court orders to be set aside or declares to be of no effect, or

(b) of the affected part of an award which the court orders to be set aside in part, or declares to be in part of no effect,

the period between the commencement of the arbitration and the date of the order referred to in paragraph (a) or (b) shall be excluded.

(3) In determining for the purposes of the Limitation Acts when a cause of action accrued, any provision that an award is a condition precedent to the bringing of legal proceedings in respect of a matter to which an arbitration agreement applies shall be disregarded.

(4)   In this Part 'the Limitation Acts' means—

(a)   in England and Wales, the Limitation Act 1980, the Foreign Limitation Periods Act 1984 and any other enactment (whenever passed) relating to the limitation of actions;

(b)   in Northern Ireland, the Limitation (Northern Ireland) Order 1989, the Foreign Limitation Periods (Northern Ireland) Order 1985 and any other enactment (whenever passed) relating to the limitation of actions.

14.   Commencement of arbitral proceedings

(1)   The parties are free to agree when arbitral proceedings are to be regarded as commenced for the purposes of this Part and for the purposes of the Limitation Acts.

(2)   If there is no such agreement the following provisions apply.

(3)   Where the arbitrator is named or designated in the arbitration agreement, arbitral proceedings are commenced in respect of a matter when one party serves on the other party or parties a notice in writing requiring him or them to submit that matter to the person so named or designated.

(4)   Where the arbitrator or arbitrators are to be appointed by the parties, arbitral proceedings are commenced in respect of a matter when one party serves on the other party or parties notice in writing requiring him or them to appoint an arbitrator or to agree to the appointment of an arbitrator in respect of that matter.

(5)   Where the arbitrator or arbitrators are to be appointed by a person other than a party to the proceedings, arbitral proceedings are commenced in respect of a matter when one party gives notice in writing to that person requesting him to make the appointment in respect of that matter.

The arbitral tribunal

15.   The arbitral tribunal

(1)   The parties are free to agree on the number of arbitrators to form the tribunal and whether there is to be a chairman or umpire.

(2)   Unless otherwise agreed by the parties, an agreement that the number of arbitrators shall be two or any other even number shall be understood as requiring the appointment of an additional arbitrator as chairman of the tribunal.

(3)   If there is no agreement as to the number of arbitrators, the tribunal shall consist of a sole arbitrator.

16.   Procedure for appointment of arbitrators

(1)   The parties are free to agree on the procedure for appointing the arbitrator or. arbitrators, including the procedure for appointing any chairman or umpire.

(2)   If or to the extent that there is no such agreement, the following provisions apply.

(3)   If the tribunal is to consist of a sole arbitrator, the parties shall jointly appoint the arbitrator not later than 28 days after service of a request in writing by either party to do so.

(4)   If the tribunal is to consist of two arbitrators, each party shall appoint one arbitrator not later than 14 days after service of a request in writing by either party to do so.

(5)   If the tribunal is to consist of three arbitrators—

(a)   each party shall appoint one arbitrator not later than 14 days after service of a request in writing by either party to do so, and

(b)   the two so appointed shall forthwith appoint a third arbitrator as the chairman of the tribunal.

(6)   If the tribunal is to consist of two arbitrators and an umpire—

(a)   each party shall appoint one arbitrator not later than 14 days after service of a request in writing by either party to do so, and

(b)   the two so appointed may appoint an umpire at any time after they themselves are appointed and shall do so before any substantive hearing or forthwith if they cannot agree on a matter relating to the arbitration.

(7)   In any other case (in particular, if there are more than two parties) section 18 applies as in the case of a failure of the agreed appointment procedure.

17. Power in case of default to appoint sole arbitrator

(1)   Unless the parties otherwise agree, where each of two parties to an arbitration agreement is to appoint an arbitrator and one party ('the party in default') refuses to do so, or fails to do so within the time specified, the other party, having duly appointed his arbitrator, may give notice in writing to the party in default that he proposes to appoint his arbitrator to act as sole arbitrator.

(2)   If the party in default does not within 7 clear days of that notice being given—

   (a)   make the required appointment, and

   (b)   notify the other party that he has done so,

the other party may appoint his arbitrator as sole arbitrator whose award shall be binding on both parties as if he had been so appointed by agreement.

(3)   Where a sole arbitrator has been appointed under subsection (2), the party in default may (upon notice to the appointing party) apply to the court which may set aside the appointment.

(4)   The leave of the court is required for any appeal from a decision of the court under this section.

18. Failure of appointment procedure

(1)   The parties are free to agree what is to happen in the event of a failure of the procedure for the appointment of the arbitral tribunal.

There is no failure if an appointment is duly made under section 17 (power in case of default to appoint sole arbitrator), unless that appointment is set aside.

(2)   If or to the extent that there is no such agreement any party to the arbitration agreement may (upon notice to the other parties) apply to the court to exercise its powers under this section.

(3)   Those powers are—

   (a)   to give directions as to the making of any necessary appointments;

   (b)   to direct that the tribunal shall be constituted by such appointments (or any one or more of them) as have been made;

   (c)   to revoke any appointments already made;

   (d)   to make any necessary appointments itself.

(4)   An appointment made by the court under this section has effect as if made with the agreement of the parties.

(5)   The leave of the court is required for any appeal from a decision of the court under this section.

24. Power of court to remove arbitrator

(1)   A party to arbitral proceedings may (upon notice to the other parties, to the arbitrator concerned and to any other arbitrator) apply to the court to remove an arbitrator on any of the following grounds—

   (a)   that circumstances exist that give rise to justifiable doubts as to his impartiality;

   (b)   that he does not possess the qualifications required by the arbitration agreement;

   (c)   that he is physically or mentally incapable of conducting the proceedings or there are justifiable doubts as to his capacity to do so;

   (d)   that he has refused or failed—

      (i)   properly to conduct the proceedings, or

      (ii)   to use all reasonable despatch in conducting the proceedings or making an award,

and that substantial injustice has been or will be caused to the applicant.

(2)   If there is an arbitral or other institution or person vested by the parties with power to remove an arbitrator, the court shall not exercise its power of removal unless satisfied that the applicant has first exhausted any available recourse to that institution or person.

(3)   The arbitral tribunal may continue the arbitral proceedings and make an award while an application to the court under this section is pending.

(4)   Where the court removes an arbitrator, it may make such order as it thinks fit with respect to his entitlement (if any) to fees or expenses, or the repayment of any fees or expenses already paid.

(5)   The arbitrator concerned is entitled to appear and be heard by the court before it makes any order under this section.

(6)   The leave of the court is required for any appeal from a decision of the court under this section.

47.   Awards on different issues

(1)   Unless otherwise agreed by the parties, the tribunal may make more than one award at different times on different aspects of the matters to be determined.

(2)   The tribunal may, in particular, make an award relating—

   (a)   to an issue affecting the whole claim, or

   (b)   to a part only of the claims or cross-claims submitted to it for decision.

(3)   If the tribunal does so, it shall specify in its award the issue, or the claim or part of a claim, which is the subject matter of the award.

48.   Remedies

(1)   The parties are free to agree on the powers exercisable by the arbitral tribunal as regards remedies.

(2)   Unless otherwise agreed by the parties, the tribunal has the following powers.

(3)   The tribunal may make a declaration as to any matter to be determined in the proceedings.

(4)   The tribunal may order the payment of a sum of money, in any currency.

(5)   The tribunal has the same powers as the court—

   (a)   to order a party to do or refrain from doing anything;

   (b)   to order specific performance of a contract (other than a contract relating to land);

   (c)   to order the rectification, setting aside or cancellation of a deed or other document.

6.4   End of Chapter Assessment Question

Refer to *Cases and Materials* (**6.2.1**) and read the case of *Thai Trading Co. (a firm)* v *Taylor and another* then answer the following question: What particular features of the English legal system today have led to the decision in this case, and what are the implications for the future?

6.5   End of Chapter Assessment Outline Answer

This question reveals a number of features of the modern English legal system which have led to the decision in the case in question, and also illustrates the way in which the law develops and changes over the years.

It is at present apparent that the cost of consulting a solicitor or barrister deters members of the public from seeking legal advice. This is particularly so where litigation is concerned, for the legal costs can be considerable, no guarantees can be given concerning the outcome of a case, and generally speaking the loser of the case has to pay the costs of the successful party.

In the past 50 years, the legal aid scheme has been available to enable those on a limited income to have access to both legal advice and representation in court. But the increasingly strict financial limits on the provision of legal aid have meant that a 'middle income not eligible for legal aid' trap has developed. Potential litigants whose income and capital exceed the financial criteria for the provision of legal aid, but who do not have the resources needed to fund a court action therefore find that access to the legal system is denied them.

It is in circumstances such as these that the type of situation which was revealed in the *Thai Trading Co.* case can arise. Here, a dispute concerning goods which the buyer, Mrs Taylor, found unsatisfactory, developed into a court action when Mrs Taylor refused to pay for the goods. The sum of money involved was £1,500, which meant that the case was not suitable for reference to arbitration as a small claim. The case therefore fell to be heard in the County Court, with the consequence that higher fees and costs would be incurred.

Mrs Taylor's husband, who happened to be a solicitor, represented her in the case, and she succeeded in her counterclaim against the plaintiffs, who were ordered to pay her costs. The plaintiffs alleged, however, that as Mrs Taylor was not legally liable to her husband to pay his profit costs, then they were not liable to indemnify her. The County Court judge was persuaded by this argument, and held that there was between Mrs Taylor and her husband an arrangement in the nature of a contingency which was contrary to public policy and therefore void.

The Court of Appeal led by Millett LJ was clearly minded to change the perception of public policy on this point, in order to bring it into line with modern practices. Millett LJ pointed out that in the past, the rules relating to maintenance and champerty had governed this area of conduct. These rules has been developed at a time when 'litigation was regarded as an evil, and recourse to the law to be discouraged'. The offence of maintenance was thus developed in order to prevent persons intermeddling with legal disputes in which they had no valid interest, and champerty was intended to prevent persons from making a profit out of the legal action of another by claiming all or some of the proceeds. Supposedly, the continuing justification for this rule was based on the fear that if a solicitor took a financial interest in the litigation of his or her client, then the solicitor's objectivity might be affected, and he or she might attempt to pervert the course of justice in order to win at any cost.

Millett LJ pointed out, however, that public policy is not static, and that modern conditions required a different approach. For example, one of the aims of the Courts and Legal Services Act 1990 was to make justice more readily accessible to persons of modest means. The Act therefore sanctioned the use of conditional fee agreements in certain prescribed circumstances. Given this background, Millett LJ was of the opinion that it could not be improper for a solicitor to act for a meritorious client on the basis that the solicitor would be paid the ordinary costs if the case were won, but nothing if it were lost. This, he said, would be in accordance with modern notions of public interest.

The two case precedents by which the County Court judge had felt himself bound were therefore overruled, and the Court of Appeal declared that in the conditions prevailing in the modern legal system, it was in the interests of access to justice for this type of agreement between solicitor and client to be lawful.

CHAPTER SEVEN

STATUTORY INTERPRETATION (OR STATUTORY CONSTRUCTION)

7.1 Understanding Statute Law: Interpretation and Construction

7.1.1 THE GENERALITY OF STATUTE LAW

OBSCENE PUBLICATIONS ACT 1959

(7 & 8 Eliz. 2, c. 66)

An Act to amend the law relating to the publication of obscene matter; to provide for the protection of literature; and to strengthen the law concerning pornography.

[29th July, 1959]

1. Test of obscenity

(1) For the purposes of this Act an article shall be deemed to be obscene if its effect or (where the article comprises two or more distinct items) the effect of any one of its items is, if taken as a whole, such as to tend to deprave and corrupt persons who are likely, having regard to all relevant circumstances, to read, see or hear the matter contained or embodied in it.

(2) In this Act 'article' means any description of article containing or embodying matter to be read or looked at or both, any sound record, and any film or other record of a picture or pictures.

(3) For the purposes of this Act a person publishes an article who—

(a) distributes, circulates, sells, lets on hire, gives, or lends it, or who offers it for sale or for letting on hire; or

(b) in the case of an article containing or embodying matter to be looked at or a record, shows, plays or projects it:

Provided that paragraph (b) of this subsection shall not apply to anything done in the course of a cinematograph exhibition (within the meaning of the Cinematograph Act, 1952), other than one excluded from the Cinematograph Act 1909, by subsection (4) of section seven of that Act (which relates to exhibitions in private houses to which the public are not admitted), or to anything done in the course of television or sound broadcasting.

2. Prohibition of publication of obscene matter

(1) Subject as hereinafter provided, any person who, whether for gain or not, publishes an obscene article shall be liable—

(a) on summary conviction to a fine not exceeding one hundred pounds or to imprisonment for a term not exceeding six months;

(b) on conviction on indictment to a fine or to imprisonment for a term not exceeding three years or both.

(2) Notwithstanding anything in section one hundred and four of the Magistrates' Courts Act 1952, summary proceedings for an offence against this section may be brought at any time within twelve months from the commission of the offence; and paragraph 16 of the First Schedule to the Magistrates' Courts Act 1952 (under which an offence at common law of publishing, exhibiting or selling obscene articles may be tried summarily) is hereby repealed.

(3) A prosecution on indictment for an offence against this section shall not be commenced more than two years after the commission of the offence.

(4) A person publishing an article shall not be proceeded against for an offence at common law consisting of the publication of any matter contained or embodied in the article where it is of the essence of the offence that the matter is obscene.

(5) A person shall not be convicted of an offence against this section if he proves that he had not examined the article in respect of which he is charged and had no reasonable cause to suspect that it was such that his publication of it would make him liable to be convicted of an offence against this section.

(6) In any proceedings against a person under this section the question whether an article is obscene shall be determined without regard to any publication by another person unless it could reasonably have been expected that the publication by the other person would follow from publication by the person charged.

7.2 The Approaches to Statutory Interpretation or Construction

7.2.1 THE LITERAL RULE (THE ORDINARY MEANING APPROACH)

DUPORT STEELS LTD AND OTHERS v *SIRS AND OTHERS* [1980] 1 All ER 529 (HL)

LORD DIPLOCK: My Lords, as recently as 13 December 1979, this House decided in *Express Newspapers Ltd* v *MacShane* [[1980] 1 All ER 65] that on the true interpretation of s. 13(1) of the Trade Union and Labour Relations Act 1974, as substituted by s. 3(2) of the Trade Union and Labour Relations (Amendment) Act 1976, the test whether an act was 'done by a person in contemplation or furtherance of a trade dispute' and so entitled him to immunity from a part of the common law of tort, is purely subjective: i.e. provided that the doer of the act honestly thinks at the time he does it that it may help one of the parties to a trade dispute to achieve their objectives and does it for that reason, he is protected by the section.

That conclusion as to the meaning of words that have been used by successive Parliaments since the Trade Disputes Act 1906, to describe acts for which the doer is entitled to immunity from the law of tort over an area that has been much extended by the 1974 and 1976 Acts, is (as I pointed out in the *MacShane* case) one which is intrinsically repugnant to anyone who has spent his life in the practice of the law or the administration of justice. Sharing those instincts it was a conclusion that I myself reached with considerable reluctance, for given the existence of a trade dispute, it involves granting to trade unions a power, which has no other limits than their own self-restraint, to inflict by means which are contrary to the general law, untold harm to industrial enterprises unconcerned with the particular dispute, to the employees of such enterprises, to members of the public and to the nation itself, so long as those in whom the control of the trade union is vested honestly believe that to do so may assist it, albeit in a minor way, in achieving its objectives in the dispute.

My Lords, at a time when more and more cases involving the application of legislation which gives effect to policies that are the subject of bitter public and parliamentary controversy, it cannot be too strongly emphasised that the British Constitution, though largely unwritten, is firmly based on the separation of powers: Parliament makes the laws, the judiciary interpret them. When Parliament legislates to remedy what the majority of its members at the time perceive to be a defect or a lacuna in the existing law (whether it be the written law enacted by existing statutes or the unwritten common law as it has been expounded by the judges in decided cases), the role of the judiciary is confined to ascertaining from the words that Parliament has approved as expressing its intention what that intention was, and to giving effect to it. Where the meaning of the statutory words is plain and unambiguous it is not for the judges to invent fancied ambiguities as an excuse for failing to give effect to its plain meaning because they themselves consider that the consequences of doing so would be inexpedient, or even unjust or immoral. In controversial matters such as are involved in industrial relations there is room for differences as to what is expedient, what is just and what is morally justifiable. Under our Constitution it is Parliament's opinion on these matters that is paramount.

A statute passed to remedy what is perceived by Parliament to be a defect in the existing law may in actual operation turn out to have injurious consequences that Parliament did not anticipate at the time the statute was passed; if it had, it would have made some provision in the Act in order to prevent them. It is at least possible that Parliament, when the 1974 and 1976 Acts were passed, did not anticipate that so widespread and crippling use as has in fact occurred would be made of sympathetic withdrawals of labour and of secondary blacking and picketing in support of sectional interests able to exercise 'industrial muscle'. But if this be the case it is for Parliament, not the judiciary, to decide whether any changes should be made to the law as stated in the Acts, and if so, what are the precise limits that ought to be imposed on the immunity from liability for torts committed in the course of taking industrial action. These are matters on which there is a wide legislative choice, the exercise of which is likely to be influenced by the political complexion of the government and the state of public opinion at the time amending legislation is under consideration.

It endangers continued public confidence in the political impartiality of the judiciary, which is essential to the continuance of the rule of law, if judges, under the guise of interpretation, provide their own preferred amendments to statutes which experience of their operation has shown to have had consequences that members of the court before whom the matter comes consider to be injurious to the public interest. The frequency with which controversial legislation is amended by Parliament itself (as witness the 1974 Act, which was amended in 1975 as well as in 1976) indicates that legislation, after it has come into operation, may fail to have the beneficial effects which Parliament expected or may produce injurious results that Parliament did not anticipate. But, except by private or hybrid Bills, Parliament does not legislate for individual cases. Public Acts of Parliament are general in their application; they govern all cases falling within categories of which the definitions are to be found in the wording of the statute. So in relation to s. 13(1) of the 1974 Act, for a judge (who is always dealing with an individual case) to pose himself the question, 'Can Parliament really have intended that the acts that were done in this particular case should have the benefit of the immunity?' is to risk straying beyond his constitutional role as interpreter of the enacted law and assume a power to decide at his own discretion whether or not to apply the general law to a particular case. The legitimate questions for a judge in his role as interpreter of the enacted law are, 'How has Parliament, by the words that it has used in the statute to express its intentions, defined the category of acts that are entitled to the immunity? Do the acts done in this particular case fall within that description?'

. . .

7.2.2   THE GOLDEN RULE — AN APPROACH TO INTERPRETATION TO AVOID ABSURDITY

ADLER v *GEORGE* [1964] 1 All ER 628 (QBD)

This was an appeal by way of Case Stated from a decision of the justices for the County of Norfolk sitting at Downham Market, whereby they convicted the appellant, Frank Adler, of an offence contrary to s. 3 of the Official Secrets Act 1920, in that on May 11 1963, being in the vicinity of a prohibited place, namely Marham Royal Air Force Station, he obstructed a member of Her Majesty's Forces engaged in security duty in relation to the said prohibited place. The respondent to the appeal was Police Superintendent Albert George.

LORD PARKER CJ: Section 3 of the Official Secrets Act 1920, provides that:

> No person in the vicinity of any prohibited place shall obstruct, knowingly mislead or otherwise interfere with or impede, the chief officer or a superintendent or other officer of police, or any member of His Majesty's forces engaged on guard, sentry, patrol, or other similar duty in relation to the prohibited place, and, if any person acts in contravention of, or fails to comply with, this provision, he shall be guilty of a misdemeanour.

In the present case the appellant had obtained access—it matters not how—to, and was on, Marham Royal Air Force station on May 11 1963, and it was found that he there and then obstructed a member of Her Majesty's Royal Air Force.

The sole point here, and a point ably argued by the appellant, is that if he was on the station he could not be in the vicinity of the station, and that it is an offence under this section to obstruct a member of Her Majesty's forces only while the accused is in the vicinity of the station. The appellent has referred to the natural meaning of 'vicinity', which I take to be quite generally the state of being near in space, and he says that it is inapt and does not cover being in fact on the station in the present case. For my part I am quite satisfied that this is a case where no violence is done to the language by reading the words 'in the vicinity of' as meaning 'in or in the vicinity of'. Here is a section in an Act of Parliament designed to prevent interference with, amongst others, members of Her Majesty's forces who are engaged on guard, sentry, patrol or other similar duty in relation to a prohibited place such as this station. It would be extraordinary, and I venture to think that it would be absurd, if an indictable offence was thereby created when the obstruction took place outside the precincts of the station, albeit in the vicinity, and no offence at all was created if the obstruction occurred on the station itself. It is to be observed that if the appellant is right, the only offence committed by him in obstructing such a member of the Air Force would be an offence contrary to s. 193 of the Air Force Act 1955, which creates a summary offence, the maximum sentence for which is three months, whereas s. 3 of the Official Secrets Act 1920 is, as one would expect, dealing with an offence which can be tried on indictment and for which under s. 8 the maximum sentence of imprisonment is one of two years. There may be of course many contexts in which 'vicinity' must be confined to its literal meaning of 'being near in space', but, under this section, I am quite clear that the context demands that the words should be construed in the way which I have stated. I would dismiss this appeal.

PAULL J: I agree.

WIDGERY J: I agree also.

7.2.3 THE MISCHIEF RULE — INTERPRETATION ACCORDING TO THE STATUTORY PURPOSE

ROYAL COLLEGE OF NURSING OF THE UNITED KINGDOM v DEPARTMENT OF HEALTH AND SOCIAL SECURITY [1981] 1 All ER 545 (QBD)

Prior to 1967 it was an offence under ss. 58 and 59 of the Offences against the Person Act 1861 for any person, including doctors and nurses, unlawfully to use any means to procure the miscarriage of a woman. However, a doctor who carried out an abortion to save a pregnant woman's life or because the consequence of the continuation of the pregnancy would make her 'a physical or mental wreck' apparently had a defence at common law to a charge under s. 58 or s. 59 of the 1861 Act. In 1967 s. 1(1) of the Abortion Act 1967 enacted that no offence was committed 'when a pregnancy [was] terminated by a registered medical practitioner' in specified circumstances. The Act further provided, by s. 1(3), that 'any treatment for the termination of pregnancy' was to be carried out in a national health service hospital or an approved clinic. In 1972 surgical methods of carrying out abortions in hospitals were replaced by the medical induction method which involved pumping a chemical fluid into the mother's womb to induce premature labour. There were two stages in medical induction, the first being the insertion of a catheter into the womb and the second the administration of the fluid into the womb via the catheter by means of a pump or drip apparatus. The first stage was carried out by a doctor and the second by nurses under the doctor's instructions but in his absence, although he would be on call. The causative factor in inducing labour and thus in terminating the pregnancy was the administration of the fluid, which was done by the nurses and not the doctor. The Department of Health and Social Security issued a circular to the nursing profession stating that no offence was committed by nurses who terminated a pregnancy by medical induction if a doctor decided on the termination, initiated it and remained responsible throughout for its overall conduct and control. The department took the view that in such circumstances the pregnancy was 'terminated by a registered medical practitioner' within s. 1(1) of the 1967 Act. The Royal College of Nursing disputed that view, and sought a declaration as against the department that the advice in the circular was wrong and that the acts carried out by nurses in terminating pregnancies by medical induction contravened s. 58 of the 1861 Act. The judge held that the department's advice did not involve the performance of unlawful acts by nurses, and granted the department a declaration to that effect. The college appealed to the Court of Appeal which reversed the judge's decision, holding that the whole process of medical induction had to be carried out by a doctor and not merely under a doctor's instructions if it was to come within s. 1(1) of the 1967 Act. The department appealed to the House of Lords.

HELD (Lord Wilberforce and Lord Edmund-Davies dissenting): The 1967 Act was to be construed in the light of the fact that it was intended to amend and clarify the unsatisfactory and uncertain state of the law previously existing and in the light of the policy of the Act, which was to broaden the grounds on which abortions might lawfully be obtained and to ensure that abortions were carried out with proper skill in hygienic conditions in ordinary hospitals as part of ordinary medical care and in accordance with normal hospital practice in which tasks forming part of the treatment were entrusted as appropriate to nurses and other members of the staff under the instructions of the doctor in charge of the treatment. Accordingly, provided a doctor prescribed the treatment for the termination of a pregnancy, remained in charge and accepted responsibility throughout, and the treatment was carried out in accordance with his directions, the pregnancy was 'terminated by a registered medical practitioner' for the purposes of the 1967 Act and any person taking part in the termination was entitled to the protection afforded by s. 1(1). The appeal would therefore be allowed. . .

5 February. The following written opinions were given.

LORD WILBERFORCE: My Lords, on 27 October 1967 Parliament passed the Abortion Act 1967. Its long title describes it as an Act 'to amend and clarify the law *relating to termination of pregnancy by registered medical practitioners*'.

Before the Act was passed it was an offence (sc felony) for *any person* with intent to procure the miscarriage of any woman, whether she be or be not with child, unlawfully to administer to her or cause to be taken by her any poison or other noxious thing or unlawfully to use any instrument or other means whatsoever with the like intent (see the Offences against the Person Act 1861, s. 58). Further, the Infant Life (Preservation) Act 1929 created the offence of child destruction in relation to a child capable of being born alive. These provisions thus affected not only doctors, but nurses, midwives, pharmacists and others; they were in operation in 1967, subject only to the defence judicially given to the doctor in *R v Bourne* [1938] 3 All ER 615, [1939] 1 KB 687.

Section 1 of the 1967 Act created a new defence, available to any person who might be liable under the existing law. It is available (i) *'when a pregnancy is terminated by a registered medical practitioner'* (these are the words of the Act), (ii) when certain other conditions are satisfied, including the expressed opinion of two registered medical practitioners as to the risks (specified in paras (a) and (b)) to mother, or child, or existing children, and the requirement that the treatment for the termination of pregnancy must be carried out in a national health service hospital or other approved place. The present case turns on the meaning to be given to condition (i).

The issue relates to a non-surgical procedure of medical induction by the use of a drug called prostaglandin. This operates on the mother's muscles so as to cause contractions (similar to those arising in normal labour) which expel the fetus from the womb. It is used during the second trimester. The question has been raised by the Royal College of Nursing as to the participation of nurses in this treatment, particularly since nurses can be called on (subject to objections of conscience which are rarely invoked) to carry it out. They have felt, and express grave concern as to the legality of doing so and seek a declaration, that a circular issued by the Department of Health and Social Security, asserting the lawfulness of the nurses' participation, is wrong in law.

There is an agreed statement as to the nature of this treatment and the part in it played by the doctors and the nurses or midwives. Naturally this may vary somewhat from hospital to hospital, but, for the purpose of the present proceedings, the assumption has to be made of maximum nurse participation, i.e. that the nurse does everything which the doctor is not required to do . . .

On these facts the question has to be answered: has the pregnancy been terminated by the doctor; or has it been terminated by the nurse; or has it been terminated by doctor and nurse? I am not surprised that the nurses feel anxiety as to this.

In attempting to answer it, I start from the point that in 1967, the date of the Act, the only methods used to produce abortions were surgical methods; of these there were several varieties, well enough known. One of these was by intra-amniotic injection, i.e. the direct injection of glucose or saline solutions into the amniotic sac. It was not ideal or, it appears, widely used. Parliament must have been aware of these methods and cannot have had in mind a process where abortifacient agents were administered by nurses. They did not exist. Parliament's concern must have been to prevent existing methods being carried out by unqualified persons and to insist that they should be carried out by doctors. For these reasons Parliament no doubt used the words, in s. 1(1), 'termination of pregnancy by a registered medical practitioner'.

Extra-amniotic administration of prostaglandin was first reported in 1971, and was soon found to have advantages. It involves, or admits, as shown above, direct and significant participation by nurses in the abortifacient steps. Is it covered by the critical words?

In interpreting an Act of Parliament it is proper, and indeed necessary, to have regard to the state of affairs existing, and known by Parliament to be existing, at the time. It is a fair presumption that Parliament's policy or intention is directed to that state of affairs. Leaving aside cases of omission by inadvertence, this being not such a case when a new state of affairs, or a fresh set of facts bearing on policy, comes into existence, the courts have to consider whether they fall within the parliamentary intention. They may be held to do so if they fall within the same genus of facts as those to which the expressed policy has been formulated. They may also be held to do so if there can be detected a clear purpose in the legislation which can only be fulfilled if the extension is made. How liberally these principles may be applied must depend on the nature of the enactment, and the strictness or otherwise of the words in which it has been expressed. The courts should be less willing to extend expressed meanings if it is clear that the Act in question was designed to be restrictive or circumscribed in its operation rather than liberal or permissive. They will be much less willing to do so where the new subject matter is different in kind or dimension from that for which the legislation was passed. In any event there is one course which the courts cannot take under the law of this country; they cannot fill gaps; they cannot by asking the question, 'What would Parliament have done in this current case, not being one in contemplation, if the facts had been before it?', attempt themselves to supply the answer, if the answer is not to be found in the terms of the Act itself.

In my opinion this Act should be construed with caution. It is dealing with a controversial subject involving moral and social judgments on which opinions strongly differ. It is, if ever an Act was, one for interpreting in the spirit that only that which Parliament has authorised on a fair reading of the relevant sections should be held to be within it. The new (post-1967) method of medical induction is clearly not just a fresh species or example of something already authorised. The Act is not one for 'purposive' or 'liberal' or 'equitable' construction. This is a case where the courts must hold that anything beyond the legislature's fairly expressed authority should be left for Parliament's fresh consideration.

Having regard particularly to the Act's antecedents and the state of affairs existing in 1967, which involved surgical action requiring to be confined to termination by doctors alone, I am unable to read the words 'pregnancy terminated by a registered medical practitioner' as extended or extensible to cover cases where other persons, whether nurses, or midwives, or even lay persons, play a significant part in the process of termination. That a process in which they do so may be reliable, and an improvement on existing surgical methods, may well be the case, we do not in fact even know this. It may be desirable that doctors' time should be spared from directly participating in all the stages of the abortifacient process; it may be (though there are very many hospitals and nursing homes in the United Kingdom, not all with the same high standards) that nurses, midwives etc may be relied on to carry out the doctor's instructions accurately and well. It may be that doctors, though not present, may always be available on call. All this may, though with some reservation, be granted, but is beside the point. With nurse, etc, participation, to the degree mentioned, a new dimension has been introduced; this should not be sanctioned by judicial decision, but only by Parliament after proper consideration of the implications and necessary safeguards.

The department contend that the Act is framed in sufficiently wide terms to authorise what they say is lawful.

Their contention, or that which they were willing to accept as their contention during argument, was that the words 'pregnancy is terminated by a registered medical practitioner' means 'pregnancy is terminated by treatment of a registered medical practitioner in accordance with recognised medical practice'. But, with all respect, this is not construction: it is rewriting. And, moreover, it does not achieve its objective. I could perhaps agree that a reference to treatment could fairly be held to be implied; no doubt treatment is necessary. But I do not see that this alone carries the matter any further: it must still be treatment by the registered medical practitioner. The additional words, on the other hand, greatly extend the enactment, and it is they which are supposed to introduce nurse participation. But I cannot see that they do this. For a nurse to engage in abortifacient acts cannot, when first undertaken, be in accordance with recognised practice, when it is the legality of the practice that is in question. Nor can the recognised practice (if such there is, though the agreed statements do not say so) by which nurses connect up drips to supply glucose or other life-giving or preserving substances cover connecting up drips etc giving substances designed to destroy life, for that is what they are. The added words may well cover the provision of swabs, bandages or the handing up of instruments; that would only be common sense. They cannot be used as cover for a dimensional extension of the Act.

The argument for the department is carried even further than this, for it is said that the words 'when a pregnancy is terminated by a registered medical practitioner' mean 'when treatment for the termination of pregnancy is carried out by a registered medical practitioner'. This is said to be necessary in order to cover the supposed cases where the treatment is unsuccessful, or where there is no pregnancy at all. The latter hypothesis I regard as fanciful; the former, if it was Parliament's contemplation at all in 1967 (for failures under post-1967 methods are not in point), cannot be covered by any reasonable reading of the words. Termination is one thing; attempted and unsuccessful termination wholly another. I cannot be persuaded to embark on a radical reconstruction of the Act by reference to a fanciful hypothesis or an improbable casus omissus.

It is significant, as Lord Denning MR has pointed out, that recognised language exists and has been used, when it is desired that something shall be done by doctors with nurse participation. This takes the form 'by a registered medical practitioner or by a person acting in accordance with the directions of any such practitioner'. This language has been used in four Acts of Parliament (listed by Lord Denning MR), three of them prior to the 1967 Act, all concerned with the administration of substances, drugs or medicines which may have an impact on the human body. It has not been used, surely deliberately, in the present Act. We ought to assume that Parliament knew what it was doing when it omitted to use them.

In conclusion, I am of opinion that the development of prostaglandin induction methods invites, and indeed merits, the attention of Parliament. It has justly given rise to perplexity in the nursing profession. I doubt whether this will be allayed when it is seen that a majority of the judges who have considered the problem share their views. On this appeal I agree with the judgments in the Court of Appeal that an extension of the 1967 Act so as to include all persons, including nurses, involved in the administration of prostaglandin is not something which ought to, or can, be effected by judicial decision. I would dismiss the appeal.

LORD DIPLOCK: My Lords, this appeal arises out of a difference of opinion between the Royal College of Nursing of the United Kingdom and the Department of Health and Social Security about the true construction of the Abortion Act 1967, and, in particular, whether it renders lawful the part played by hospital nurses in the treatment for terminating pregnancies by a method known as medical induction. This comparatively modern method, which was unknown as a means of bringing about an abortion at the time of the passing of the Act, has come into increasing use for terminating pregnancies in the second trimester (i.e. between the 12th and 24th weeks), when it presents less risk to the patient than those methods more exclusively surgical in character that were formerly employed. The treatment takes considerably longer than the purely surgical methods; the average duration is 18 hours with a maximum of 30 hours and the part played by nurses in the treatment is of greater importance as well as longer than when a purely surgical method is employed.

The Abortion Act 1967 which it falls to this House to construe is described in its long title as 'An Act to amend and clarify the law relating to termination of pregnancy by registered medical practitioners'. The legalisation of abortion, at any rate in circumstances in which the termination of the pregnancy is not essential in order to save the mother's life, is a subject on which strong moral and religious convictions are held; and these convictions straddle the normal party political lines. That, no doubt, is why the Act, which incorporates a 'conscience clause' that I shall be quoting later, started its parliamentary life as a private member's Bill and, maybe for that reason, it lacks that style and consistency of draftsmanship both internal to the Act itself and in relation to other statutes which one would expect to find in legislation that had its origin in the office of parliamentary counsel.

Whatever may be the technical imperfections of its draftsmanship, however, its purpose in my view becomes clear if one starts by considering what was the state of the law relating to abortion before the passing of the Act, what was the mischief that required amendment, and in what respects was the existing law unclear.

The Abortion Act 1967 applies to England and to Scotland; but your Lordships are not concerned with Scotland in the instant case. In England the 'law relating to abortion' which it was the purpose of the Act to amend and clarify, is defined in s. 6 of the Act itself as meaning 'sections 58 and 59 of the Offences against the Person Act 1861'. The relevant section, which it is desirable to set out verbatim, is s. 58. (Section 59 deals with supplying abortifacients and instruments for use in unlawful abortions.) Section 58 provides:

Every Woman, being with Child, who, with Intent to procure her own Miscarriage, shall unlawfully administer to herself any Poison or other noxious Thing, or shall unlawfully use any Instrument or other Means whatsoever with the like Intent, and whosoever, with intent to procure the Miscarriage of any Woman, whether she be or be not with Child, shall unlawfully administer to her or cause to be taken by her any Poison or other noxious Thing, or shall unlawfully use any Instrument or other Means whatsoever with the like Intent, shall be guilty of Felony, and being convicted thereof shall be liable to be kept in Penal Servitude for Life.

An offence under the section is committed whether the woman was in fact pregnant or not, and, if pregnant, whether or not the attempt to terminate it was in fact successful. The section on the face of it draws no distinction between terminations of pregnancies carried out on the advice of medically-qualified gynaecologists or obstetricians and those 'back-street abortions' that figured so commonly in the calendars of assizes in the days when I was trying crime; but the requirement that in order to constitute the offence the abortifacient must be administered or the instrument used 'unlawfully', indicated that there might be circumstances in which it would be lawful to bring about an abortion.

It has long been generally accepted that abortion was lawful where it was necessary to save the pregnant woman's life; but what circumstances, if any, short of this, legitimised termination of a pregnancy does not appear to have attracted judicial notice until, in 1938, the matter was put to a sagaciously selected test by Mr Aleck Bourne, a well-known obstetrical surgeon at St Mary's Hospital, London. He there performed an abortion on a 14-year old girl who was seven weeks pregnant as a consequence of being the victim of a particularly brutal rape. He invited prosecution for having done so. The evidence at his trial was that if the girl had been allowed to bear the child she would 'be likely to have become a mental wreck'.

The summing up by Macnaghten J in *R* v *Bourne* [1938] 3 All ER 615, [1939] 1 KB 687 resulted in an acquittal. So the correctness of his statement of the law did not undergo examination by any higher authority. It still remained in 1967 the only judicial pronouncement on the subject. No disrespect is intended to that eminent judge and former head of my old chambers if I say that his reputation is founded more on his sturdy common sense than on his lucidity of legal exposition. Certainly his summing up, directed as it was to the highly exceptional facts of the particular case, left plenty of loose ends and ample scope for clarification. For instance, his primary ruling was that the onus lay on the Crown to satisfy the jury that the defendant did not procure the miscarriage of the woman in good faith for the purpose only of 'preserving her life' but this requirement he suggested to the jury they were entitled to regard as satisfied if the probable consequence of the continuance of the pregnancy would be to 'make the woman a physical or mental wreck', a vivid phrase borrowed from one of the witnesses but unfortunately lacking in precision. The learned judge would appear to have regarded the defence as confined to registered medical practitioners, and there is a passage in his summing up which suggests that it is available only where the doctor's opinion as to the probable dire consequences of the continuance of the pregnancy was not only held bona fide, but also based on reasonable grounds and adequate knowledge, an objective test which it would be for the jury to determine whether, on the evidence adduced before them, it was satisfied or not.

Such then was the unsatisfactory and uncertain state of the law that the Abortion Act 1967 was intended to amend and clarify. What the Act sets out to do is to provide an exhaustive statement of the circumstances in which treatment for the termination of a pregnancy may be carried out lawfully. That the statement, which is contained in s. 1. is intended to be exhaustive appears from s. 5(2):

> For the purposes of the law relating to abortion, anything done with intent to procure the miscarriage of a woman is unlawfully done unless authorised by section 1 of this Act.

This sets aside the interpretation placed by Macnaghten J in *R* v *Bourne*, on the word 'unlawfully' in ss. 58 and 59 of the Offences against the Person Act 1861.

The 'conscience clause' which I have already mentioned is also worth citing before coming to the crucial provisions of s. 1. It is s. 4(1) and so far as is relevant for the present purposes it reads:

> . . . no person shall be under any duty, whether by contract or by any statutory or other legal requirement, to participate in any treatment authorised by this Act to which he has a conscientious objection . . .

Section 1 itself needs to be set out *in extenso*:

> (1) Subject to the provisions of this section, a person shall not be guilty of an offence under the law relating to abortion when a pregnancy is terminated by a registered medical practitioner if two registered medical practitioners are of the opinion, formed in good faith—(a) that the continuance of the pregnancy would involve risk to the life of the pregnant woman, or of injury to the physical or mental health of the pregnant woman or any existing children of her family, greater than if the pregnancy were terminated; or (b) that there is a substantial risk that if the child were born it would suffer from such physical or mental abnormalities as to be seriously handicapped.
>
> (2) In determining whether the continuance of a pregnancy would involve such risk of injury to health as is mentioned in paragraph (a) of subsection (1) of this section,

account may be taken of the pregnant woman's actual or reasonably foreseeable environment.

(3) Except as provided by subsection (4) of this section, any treatment for the termination of pregnancy must be carried out in a hospital vested in the Minister of Health or the Secretary of State under the National Health Service Acts, or in a place for the time being approved for the purposes of this section by the said Minister or the Secretary of State.

(4) Subsection (3) of this section, and so much of subsection (1) as relates to the opinion, of two registered medical practitioners, shall not apply to the termination of a pregnancy by a registered medical practitioner in a case where he is of the opinion, formed in good faith, that the termination is immediately necessary to save the life or to prevent grave permanent injury to the physical or mental health of the pregnant woman.

My Lords, the wording and structure of the section are far from elegant, but the policy of the Act, it seems to me, is clear. There are two aspects to it: the first is to broaden the grounds on which abortions may be lawfully obtained; the second is to ensure that the abortion is carried out with all proper skill and in hygienic conditions. Subsection (1) which deals with the termination of pregnancies other than in cases of dire emergency consists of a conditional sentence of which a protasis, which is a condition precedent to be satisfied in order to make the abortion lawful at all, is stated last: 'if two registered medical practitioners are of the opinion etc'. It is this part of the subsection which defines the circumstances which qualify a woman to have pregnancy terminated lawfully. They are much broader than the circumstances stated in R v Bourne; and, since they depend on comparative risks of injury to the physical or mental health of the pregnant woman or existing children of the family and to the possibility of abnormalities in the yet unborn child, they are matters of expert medical opinion. The Act leaves them to be decided not by the jury on expert evidence after the event, as in R v Bourne, but in advance by two registered medical practitioners whose opinion as to the existence of the required circumstances, if formed in good faith and duly certified under s. 2(a), renders treatment for the termination of the pregnancy lawful if it is carried out in accordance with the requirements of the Act.

I have spoken of the requirements of the Act as to the way in which 'treatment for the termination of the pregnancy' is to be carried out rather than using the word 'termination' or 'terminated' by itself, for the draftsman appears to use the longer and the shorter expressions indiscriminately, as is shown by a comparison between sub-ss (1) and (3) of s. 1, and by the reference in the conscience clause to 'treatment authorised by this Act'. Furthermore, if 'termination' or 'terminated' meant only the event of miscarriage and not the whole treatment undertaken with that object in mind, lack of success, which apparently occurs in 1% to 2% of cases, would make all who had taken part in the unsuccessful treatment guilty of an offence under s. 58 or s. 59 of the Offences against the Person Act 1861. This cannot have been the intention of Parliament.

The requirement of the Act as to the way in which the treatment is to be carried out, which in my view throws most light on the second aspect of its policy and the true construction of the phrase in sub-s. (1) of s. 1 which lies at the root of the dispute between the parties to this appeal, is the requirement in sub-s. (3) that, except in cases of dire emergency, the treatment must be carried out in a national health service hospital (or private clinic specifically approved for that purpose by the minister). It is in my view evident that, in providing that treatment for termination of pregnancies should take place in ordinary hospitals Parliament contemplated that (conscientious objections apart) like other hospital treatment, it would be undertaken as a team effort in which, acting on the instructions of the doctor in charge of the treatment, junior doctors, nurses, paramedical and other members of the hospital staff would each do those things forming part of the whole treatment which it would be in accordance with accepted medical practice to entrust to a member of the staff possessed of their respective qualifications and experience.

Subsection (1) although it is expressed to apply only 'when a pregnancy is terminated by a registered medical practitioner' (the subordinate clause that although introduced by 'when' is another protasis and has caused the differences of judicial opinion in the instant case) also appears to contemplate treatment that is in the nature of a team effort and to extend its protection to all those who play a part in it. The exoneration from guilt is not confined to the registered medical practitioner by whom a pregnancy is terminated, it extends to any person who takes part in the treatment for its termination.

What limitation on this exoneration is imposed by the qualifying phrase, 'when a pregnancy is terminated by a registered medical practitioner'? In my opinion, in the context of the Act, what it requires is that a registered medical practitioner, whom I will refer to as a doctor, should accept responsibility for all stages of the treatment for the termination of the pregnancy. The particular method to be used should be decided by the doctor in charge of the treatment for termination of the pregnancy; he should carry out any physical acts, forming part of the treatment, that in accordance with accepted medical practice are done only by qualified medical practitioners, and should give specific instructions as to the carrying out of such parts of the treatment as in accordance with accepted medical practice are carried out by nurses or other members of the hospital staff without medical qualifications. To each of them, the doctor, or his substitute, should be available to be consulted or called on for assistance from beginning to end of the treatment. In other words, the doctor need not do everything with his own hands; the requirements of the subsection are satisfied when the treatment for termination of a pregnancy is one prescribed by a registered medical practitioner carried out in accordance with his directions and of which a registered medical practitioner remains in charge throughout.

My noble and learned friend Lord Wilberforce has described the successive steps taken in the treatment for termination of pregnancies in the third trimester by medical induction; and the parts played by registered medical practitioners and nurses respectively in the carrying out of the treatment. This treatment satisfies the interpretation that I have placed on the requirements of s. 1 of the Act. I would accordingly allow the appeal and restore the declaration made by Woolf J.

LORD EDMUND-DAVIES: My Lords, this House is presently concerned with the task of interpreting the Abortion Act 1967, and of applying the interpretation to the termination of pregnancy by a certain type of medical induction. It is well known that the Act was the outcome of a private member's Bill dealing with a highly controversial topic and, as enacted, it is the product of considerable compromise between violently opposed and emotionally charged views. In its preamble it is described as an Act 'to amend and clarify the law relating to termination of pregnancy by registered medical practitioners', and, far from simply enlarging the existing abortion facilities, in the true spirit of compromise it both relaxed and restricted the existing law.

Before turning to the 1967 Act, reference must be made to the still-extant s. 58 of the Offences against the Person Act 1861, which provides as follows: . . .
Section 1 of the Abortion Act 1967 is in these terms: . . .

Although no reference to an act done 'for the purpose only of preserving the life of the mother' appears in the 1861 Act, it does appear in the Infant Life (Preservation) Act 1929, s. 1. And in *R v Bourne* [1938] 3 All ER 615, [1939] 1 KB 687 Macnaghten J expressed the view that it represented the common law and should be read into the earlier Act by reason of the inclusion of the adverb 'unlawfully' in s. 58. In that case a surgeon had aborted a girl who had been shockingly raped and, although there was no immediate danger to her life, he claimed that she would have become a physical and mental wreck had her pregnancy been allowed to continue. Directing the jury on a charge of contravening s. 58, the learned judge said of 'preserving the life of the mother' that the words—

ought to be construed in a reasonable sense, and, if the doctor is of opinion, on reasonable grounds and with adequate knowledge, that the probable consequence of the continuance of the pregnancy will be to make the woman a physical or mental wreck, the jury are quite entitled to take the view that the doctor, who, in those circumstances, and in that honest belief, operates, is operating for the purpose of preserving the life of the woman.

(See [1938] 3 All ER 615 at 619, [1939] 1 KB 687 at 693–694.)

Following the acquittal in that case, the courts did not closely scrutinise the evidence of danger to life itself: see, for example, *R v Newton and Stungo* [1958] Crim LR 469 where, on a s. 58 charge of unlawfully using an instrument, Ashworth J directed the jury that—

'Such use of an instrument is unlawful unless the use is made in good faith for the purpose of preserving the life *or health* of the woman.' When I say health I mean not only her physical health but also her mental health.

My Lords, such was the law and practice when the Abortion Act reached the statute book in 1967, s. 6 thereof providing that the phrase 'the law relating to abortion' used in ss. 1(1) and 5(2) thereof means 'sections 58 and 59 of the Offences against the Person Act 1861, and any rule of law relating to the procurement of abortion'. And s. 5(2) itself provided:

For the purposes of the law relating to abortion, anything done with intent to procure the miscarriage of a woman is unlawfully done unless authorised by section 1 of this Act.

Details of the termination of pregnancy by administering prostaglandin are the subject of a helpful agreed statement prepared by the parties to this litigation. This has been examined in the speech of my noble and learned friend Lord Wilberforce, and it is sufficient for me to say that the Royal College of Nursing, while adopting a neutral role, were and remain deeply disturbed as to the legality of the marked degree of participation by nurses in the challenged method of induction and therefore sought clarification and guidance from the court. They must ruefully regard such judicial illumination as has hitherto been vouchsafed them, Woolf J pronouncing 'without any doubt at all' that the prostaglandin procedure is permissible within the terms of s. 1 of the 1967 Act, while the Court of Appeal unanimously held that it is not, Lord Denning MR declaring emphatically that 'the continuous act of administering prostaglandin from the moment it is started until the unborn child is expelled from the mother's body . . . must be done by the doctor personally. It is not sufficient that it is done by a nurse when he is not present.'
. . .
My Lords, I have already commented that it would be quite wrong to regard the 1967 Act as wholly permissive in character, for it both restricted and amplified the existing abortion law. It amplified 'the law relating to abortion' as declared in *R v Bourne* by extending it in s. 1(1)(a) to cases where—

the continuance of the pregnancy would involve risk to the . . . physical or mental health of . . . any existing children of [the pregnant woman's] family, greater than if the pregnancy were terminated . . .

and in s.1(1)(b) by including the case of—

substantial risk that if the *child* were born it would suffer from such physical or mental abnormalities as to be seriously handicapped.

On the other hand, the Act also restricted the *Bourne* law in several ways. The pregnancy must now be terminated 'by a registered medical practitioner', and this even if, in the words of s. 1(4), '. . . the termination is immediately necessary to save the life or to prevent grave permanent injury to the physical or mental health of the pregnant woman', whereas *Bourne* imposed no such restriction in the cases predicated, and a qualified doctor who was not a registered medical practitioner could have invoked the decision in that case. And, save in those circumstances of urgency, abortive treatment is required under the Act to be carried out in such premises as are designated in ss. 1(3) and 3. Again, in the forefront is the requirement in s. 1(1) of the opinion of two doctors that the risks indicated in para (a) or para (b) are involved if pregnancy were allowed to go full term. And a further practical (though not legal) restriction was imposed by the requirement under s. 2 that the—

registered medical practitioner who terminated a pregnancy [must] give notice of the termination and such other information relating to the termination as may be . . . prescribed.

My Lords, the opening words of s. 1(1) are clear and simple, clear to understand and simple to apply to the only abortive methods professionally accepted in 1967 when the Act was passed. Save in grave emergency, only a qualified doctor or surgeon could then lawfully perform the orthodox surgical acts, and the statute could have had no other person in mind. Then should s. 1 be interpreted differently now that abortive methods undreamt of in 1967 have since been discovered and become widely applied? The answer must be that its simple words must not be distorted in order to bring under the statutory umbrella medical procedures to which they cannot properly be applied, however desirable such an extension may be thought to be. The extra-amniotic procedure first reported in 1971 has already been described by my noble and learned friend Lord Wilberforce, and it is sufficient for my present purpose to quote merely the final paragraph of the 'Agreed statement as to clinical background':

It will be appreciated that in the medical induction process the causative factor in inducing the labour and hence the termination of pregnancy is the effect of the administration of prostaglandin and/or oxytocin and not any mechanical effect from the insertion of the catheter or cannula. In that the nurse does, on the instructions of the doctor, commence or augment the flow of prostaglandin or oxytocin, and even sometimes effect the connection between the already inserted catheter and the prostin pump and the already intravenous cannula and the oxytocin infusion, her role in the process does include acts which have, and are intended to have, an abortifacient effect. Such acts are, however, always carried out in accordance with the specific instructions of the registered medical practitioner.

In my judgment, it is quite impossible to regard an abortion resulting from such procedure as one 'terminated by a registered medical practitioner', for the acts indispensable to termination are in many such cases performed not by the doctor but by the nurses over a long period of hours after the doctor last saw the pregnant woman. And, despite the claims of the Solicitor General that he sought simply to give the statutory words 'their plain and ordinary meaning', he substantially departed from that approach by submitting that they should be read as meaning 'terminated by treatment for the termination of pregnancy carried out by a registered medical practitioner in accordance with recognised medical practice'. My Lords, this is redrafting with a vengeance. And, even were it permissible, it would still remain to consider what *part* the doctor played in the treatment, in order to ensure that it was not so remote from the termination as to make it impossible to say in any realistic sense that it was *he* who terminated the pregnancy. I am in respectful agreement with Brightman LJ, who said of the extra-amniotic procedure (see pp 559–560, ante):

. . . it would be a misuse of language . . . to describe such a treatment for termination of a pregnancy as 'carried out by' a registered medical practitioner, however detailed and precise the written instructions given by the registered medical practitioner to the nurse . . . The true analysis is that the doctor *has provided the nurse with the means* to terminate the pregnancy, not that the doctor has terminated the pregnancy. (Brightman LJ's emphasis.)

It is true that the word 'treatment' is to be found in several places in the Act, and that the phrase 'treatment of the termination of pregnancy' appears both in s. 1(3) and in s. 3(1), but both are significantly different from the language of s. 1(1). And, had Parliament been minded to legislate on the lines which the appellants submit was its aim, Lord Denning MR demonstrated by reference to several earlier statutes in the medical field that the legislature had ready to hand suitable words which would have rendered unnecessary any such expansive interpretation as that favoured in the present instance by the Solicitor General.

My Lords, at the end of the day the appellants were driven to rely on a submission that, were s. 1(1) given its literal meaning, such absurd consequences would follow that a liberal construction is unavoidable if the 1967 Act is to serve a useful purpose. In the foreground was the submission that, were a termination of pregnancy embarked on when (as it turned out) the woman was not pregnant, the Act would afford no defence to a doctor prosecuted under the 1861 Act. And it was secondly urged that he would be equally defenceless even where he personally treated a pregnant woman throughout if, for some reason, the procedure was interrupted and the pregnancy not terminated. I have respectfully to say that in my judgment it is these objections which are themselves absurd. Lawful termination under the Act predicates the personal services of a doctor operating in s. 1(3) premises and armed with the opinion of two medical practitioners. But where termination is nevertheless not achieved the appellants invite this House to contemplate the doctor and his nursing staff being prosecuted under s. 58 of the 1861 Act, the charge being, of course, not the unlawful termination of pregnancy (for ex hypothesi there was *no* termination) but one of unlawfully administering a noxious thing or unlawfully using an instrument with intent to procure miscarriage. And on *that* charge unlawfulness has still to be established and the prosecution would assuredly fail. For the circumstances predicated themselves establish the absence of any mens rea in instituting the abortive treatment, and its initial lawfulness could not be rendered unlawful either by the discovery that the woman was not in fact pregnant or by non-completion of the abortive treatment. Were it otherwise, the unavoidable conclusion is that doctors and nurses could in such cases be convicted of what in essence would be the extraordinary crime of attempting to do a *lawful* act.

My Lords, it was after drafting the foregoing that I happened on the following passage in Smith and Hogan's Criminal Law (4th Edn, 1978. p 346) which I now gratefully adopt, for it could not be more apposite:

. . . the legalisation of an abortion must include the steps which are taken towards it. Are we really to say that these are criminal until the operation is complete, when they are retrospectively authorised, or alternatively that they are lawful until the operation is discontinued or the woman is discovered not to be pregnant when, retrospectively, they become unlawful? When the conditions of the Act are otherwise satisfied, it is submitted that [the doctor] is not unlawfully administering, etc., and that this is so whether the pregnancy be actually terminated or not.

I am in this way fortified in my conclusion that the 'absurdities' on which the Solicitor General relies are in reality non-existent and that there is no reason for not giving the specific words of s. 1 of the 1967 Act their plain and ordinary meaning. Doing just that, the prostaglandin treatment presently adopted requires the nursing staff to participate unlawfully in procedures necessitating their personally performing over a period of several hours a series of acts calculated to bring about a termination of pregnancy. This they cannot lawfully do, and in my judgment the Royal College of Nursing were entitled to a declaration in those terms.

My Lords, I express no view regarding this result, save that I believe it to be inevitable on the facts of the case, and this despite my awareness that several thousand extra-amniotic terminations are now performed annually. If it is sought to render such medical induction lawful, the task must be performed by Parliament. But under the present law it is a registered medical practitioner who must terminate pregnancy. I would therefore affirm the unanimous view of the Court of Appeal and dismiss this appeal.

7.3   Aids to Statutory Interpretation or Construction

7.3.1   INTERNAL AIDS

LAW OF PROPERTY ACT 1925

205.   General definitions

(1)   In this Act unless the context otherwise requires, the following expressions have the meanings hereby assigned to them respectively, that is to say:—

(i)   'Bankruptcy' includes liquidation by arrangement; also in relation to a corporation means the winding up thereof;

(ii)   'Conveyance' includes a mortgage, charge, lease, assent, vesting declaration, vesting instrument, disclaimer, release and every other assurance of property or of an interest therein by any instrument, except a will; 'convey' has a corresponding meaning; and 'disposition' includes a conveyance and also a devise, bequest, or an appointment of property contained in a will; and 'dispose of' has a corresponding meaning;

(iii)   'Building purposes' include the erecting and improving of, and the adding to, and the repairing of buildings; and a 'building lease' is a lease for building purposes or purposes connected therewith;

[(iii A)   'the county court limit', in relation to any enactment contained in this Act, means the amount for the time being specified by an Order in Council under section 145 of the County Courts Act 1984 as the county court limit for the purposes of the enactment (or, where no such Order in Council has been made, the corresponding limit specified by Order in Council under section 192 of the County Courts Act 1959);]

(iv)   'Death duty' means estate duty [. . .] and every other duty reviable or payable on a death;

(v)   'Estate owner' means the owner of a legal estate, but an infant is not capable of being an estate owner;

(vi)   'Gazette' means the London Gazette;

(vii)   'Incumbrance' includes a legal or equitable mortgage and a trust for securing money, and a lien, and a charge of a portion, annuity, or other capital or annual sum; and 'incumbrancer' has a meaning corresponding with that of incumbrance, and includes every person entitled to the benefit of an incumbrance, or to require payment or discharge thereof;

(viii)   'Instrument' does not include a statute, unless the statute creates a settlement;

(ix)   'Land' includes land of any tenure, and mines and minerals, whether or not held apart from the surface, buildings or parts of buildings (whether the division is horizontal, vertical or made in any other way) and other corporeal hereditaments, also a manor, an advowson, and a rent and other incorporeal hereditaments, and an easement, right, privilege, or benefit in, over, or derived from land; but not an undivided share in land; and 'mines and minerals' include any strata or seam of minerals or substances in or under any land, and powers of working and getting the same but not an undivided share thereof; and 'manor' includes a lordship, and reputed manor or lordship; and 'hereditament' means any real property which on an intestacy occurring before the commencement of this Act might have devolved upon an heir;

(x)   'Legal estates' mean the estates, interests and charges, in or over land (subsisting or created at law) which are by this Act authorised to subsist or to be created as legal estates; 'equitable interests' means all the other interests and charges in or over land or in the proceeds of sale thereof; an equitable interest 'capable of subsisting as a legal estate' means such as could validly subsist or be created as a legal estate under this Act;

(xi)   'Legal powers' include the powers vested in a chargee by way of legal mortgage or in an estate owner under which a legal estate can be transferred or created; and 'equitable powers' mean all the powers in or over land under which equitable interests or powers only can be transferred or created;

(xii)   'Limitation Acts' mean the Real Property Limitation Acts, 1833, 1837 and 1874, and 'limitation' includes a trust;

[(xiii)   'Mental disorder' has the meaning assigned to it by [section one of the Mental Health Act, 1983], and 'receiver', in relation to a person suffering from mental disorder, means a receiver appointed for that person under [Part VIII of the Mental Health Act 1959 or Part VII of the said Act of 1983];]

(xiv)   A 'mining lease' means a lease for mining purposes, that is, the searching for, winning, working, getting, making merchantable, carrying away, or disposing of mines and minerals, or purposes connected therewith, and includes a grant or licence for mining purposes;

(xv)   'Minister' means the 'Minister of Agriculture and Fisheries and Food';

(xvi)   'Mortgage' includes any charge or lien on any property for securing money or money's worth; 'legal mortgage' means a mortgage by demise or subdemise or a charge by way of legal mortgage and 'legal mortgagee' has a corresponding meaning;

'mortgage money' means money or money's worth secured by a mortgage; 'mortgagor' includes any person from time to time deriving title under the original mortgagor or entitled to redeem a mortgage according to his estate interest or right in the mortgaged property; 'mortgagee' includes a chargee by way of legal mortgage and any person from time to time deriving title under the original mortgagee; and 'mortgagee in possession' is, for the purposes of this Act, a mortgagee who, in right of the mortgage, has entered into and is in possession of the mortgaged property; and 'right of redemption' includes an option to repurchase only if the option in effect creates a right of redemption;

(xvii)   'Notice' includes constructive notice;

(xviii)   'Personal representative' means the executor, original or by representation, or administrator for the time being of a deceased person, and as regards any liability for the payment of death duties includes any person who takes possession of or inter-meddles with the property of a deceased person without the authority of the personal representatives or the court;

(xix)   'Possession' includes receipt of rents and profits or the right to receive the same, if any; and 'income' includes rents and profits;

(xx)   'Property' includes any thing in action, and any interest in real or personal property;

(xxi)   'Purchaser' means a purchaser in good faith for valuable consideration and includes a lessee, mortgagee or other person who for valuable consideration acquires an interest in property except that in Part I of this Act and elsewhere where so expressly provided 'purchaser' only means a person who acquires an interest in or charge on property for money or money's worth; and in reference to a legal estate includes a chargee by way of legal mortgage; and where the context so requires 'purchaser' includes an intending purchaser; 'purchase' has a meaning corresponding with that of 'pur-chaser'; and 'valuable consideration' includes marriage but does not include a nominal consideration in money;

(xxii)   'Registered land' has the same meaning as in the Land Registration Act, 1925, and 'Land Registrar' means the Chief Land Registrar under that Act;

(xxiii)   'Rent' includes a rent service or a rentcharge, or other rent, toll, duty, royalty, or annual or periodical payment in money or money's worth, reserved or issuing out of or charged upon land, but does not include mortgage interest; 'rentcharge' includes a fee farm rent; 'fine' includes a premium or foregift and any payment, consideration, or benefit in the nature of a fine, premium or foregift; 'lessor' includes an underlessor and a person deriving title under a lessor or underlessor; and 'lessee' includes an underlessee and a person deriving title under a lessee or underlessee, and 'lease' includes an underlease or other tenancy;

(xxiv)   'Sale' includes an extinguishment of manorial incidents, but in other respects means a sale properly so called;

(xxv)   'Securities' include stocks, funds and shares;

(xxvi)   'Tenant for life,' 'statutory owner,' 'settled land,' 'settlement,' 'vesting deed,' 'subsidiary vesting deed,' 'vesting order,' 'vesting instrument,' 'trust instrument,' 'capital money,' and 'trustees of the settlement' have the same meanings as in the Settled Land Act, 1925;

(xxvii)   'Term of years absolute' means a term of years (taking effect either in possession or in reversion whether or not at a rent) with or without impeachment for waste, subject or not to another legal estate, and either certain or liable to determination by notice, re-entry, operation of law, or by a provision for cesser on redemption, or in any other event (other than the dropping of a life, or the determination of a determinable life interest); but does not include any term of years determinable with life or lives or with the cesser of a determinable life interest, nor, if created after the commencement of this Act, a term of years which is not expressed to take effect in possession within twenty-one years after the creation thereof where requried by this Act to take effect within that period; and in this definition the expression 'term of years' includes a term for less than a year, or for a year or years and a fraction of a year or from year to year;

(xxviii)   'Trust Corporation' means the Public Trustee or a corporation either appointed by the court in any particular case to be a trustee or entitled by rules made under subsection (3) of section four of the Public Trustee Act, 1906, to act as custodian trustee; . . .

PEPPER (INSPECTOR OF TAXES) v *HART AND RELATED APPEALS* [1993] 1 All ER
42 (HL)

Their Lordships took time for consideration.

26 November 1992. The following opinions were delivered.

LORD MACKAY OF CLASHFERN LC: My Lords, I have had the advantage of reading
in draft the speech of my noble and learned friend Lord Browne-Wilkinson. I respectfully
adopt his narrative of the proceedings in this appeal and his account of the statutory
provisions by reference to which it falls to be decided. . .

For these reasons I would allow these appeals. I should perhaps add that I was not a
member of the committee who heard these appeals in the first hearing, since I became
involved only when your Lordships who sat in the first hearing suggested a second
hearing under my chairmanship and accordingly I have not been asked to consider this
matter apart from the discussion of the extracts from Hansard which have been put
before us in this appeal. However, this is the conclusion that I would have reached apart
altogether from considering Hansard.

But much wider issues than the construction of the Finance Act 1976 have been raised
in these appeals and for the first time this House has been asked to consider a detailed
argument on the extent to which reference can properly be made before a court of law
in the United Kingdom to proceedings in Parliament recorded in Hansard.

For the taxpayers Mr Lester QC submits that it should now be appropriate for the
courts to look at Hansard in order to ascertain the intention of the legislators as expressed
in the proceedings on the Bill which has then been enacted in the statutory words
requiring to be construed. This submission appears to me to suggest a way of making
more effective proceedings in Parliament by allowing the court to consider what has been
said in Parliament as an aid to resolving an ambiguity which may well have become
apparent only as a result of the attempt to apply the enacted words to a particular case.
It does not seem to me that this can involve any impeachment, or questioning, of the
freedom of speech and debates or proceedings in Parliament; accordingly I do not see
how such a use of Hansard can possibly be thought to infringe s. 1, art. 9 of the Bill of
Rights (1688) and I agree with my noble and learned friend's more detailed consideration
of that matter.

The principal difficulty I have on this aspect of the case is that in Mr Lester's
submission reference to parliamentary material as an aid to interpretation of a statutory
provision should be allowed only with leave of the court and where the court is satisfied
that such a reference is justifiable (a) to confirm the meaning of a provision as conveyed
by the text, its object and purpose, (b) to determine a meaning where the provision is
ambiguous or obscure or (c) to determine the meaning where the ordinary meaning is
manifestly absurd or unreasonable.

I believe that practically every question of statutory construction that comes before the
courts will involve an argument that the case falls under one or more of these three
heads. It follows that the parties' legal advisers will require to study Hansard in
practically every such case to see whether or not there is any help to be gained from it.
I believe this is an objection of real substance. It is a practical objection, not one of
principle, and I believe that it was the fundamental reason that Lord Reid, for example,
considered the general rule to be a good one as he said in the passage my noble and
learned friend has cited from *Beswick* v *Beswick* [1967] 2 All ER 1197 at 1202, [1968] AC
58 at 74. Lord Reid's statement is, I think, worthy of particular weight since he was a
parliamentarian of great experience as well as a very distinguished judicial member of
your Lordships' House. It is significant that in the following year, in his dissenting
speech in *Warner* v *Metropolitan Police Comr* [1968] 2 All ER 366–367, [1969] 2 AC 256 at
279, he, while agreeing with the general rule, was prepared to consider an exception from
it although the time was not right to do so. But the exception he contemplated was in
respect of a particular type of statute, namely a statute creating criminal liability in which
the question was whether or not a guilty intention was required to create liability. Now
that type of exception would mean that the practical difficulties to which he referred
would not arise except in the comparatively few cases that arise of the particular type.

The submission which Mr Lester makes on the other hand is not restricted by reference to the type of statute and indeed the only way in which it could be discovered whether help was to be given is by considering Hansard itself. Such an approach appears to me to involve the possibility at least of an immense increase in the cost of litigation in which statutory construction is involved. It is of course easy to overestimate such cost but it is I fear equally easy to underestimate it. Your Lordships have no machinery from which any estimate of such cost could be derived. Two inquiries with such machinery available to them, namely that of the Law Commission and the Scottish Law Commission, in their joint report on *Interpretation of Statutes* (Law Com no. 21; Scot Law Com no. 11 (1969)), and the Renton Committee report on *Preparation of Legislation* (Cmnd 6053 (1975)) advised against a relaxation on the practical grounds to which I have referred. I consider that nothing has been laid before your Lordships to justify the view that their advice based on this objection was incorrect.

In his very helpful and full submissions Mr Lester has pointed out that there is no evidence of practical difficulties in the jurisdictions where relaxations of this kind have already been allowed, but I do not consider that, full as these researches have been, they justify the view that no substantial increase resulted in the cost of litigation as a result of these relaxations, and, in any event, the parliamentary processes in these jurisdictions are different in quite material respects from those in the United Kingdom.

Your Lordships are well aware that the costs of litigation are a subject of general public concern and I personally would not wish to be a party to changing a well established rule which could have a substantial effect in increasing these costs against the advice of the Law Commissions and the Renton Committee unless and until a new inquiry demonstrated that that advice was no longer valid.

I do not for my part find the objections in principle to be strong and I would certainly be prepared to agree the rule should no longer be adhered to were it not for the practical consideration to which I have referred and which my noble and learned friend agrees to be of real substance. Reference to proceedings in Parliament has already been allowed in *Pickstone* v *Freemans plc* [1988] 2 All ER 803, [1989] AC 66 without, I think, any argument on whether or not it was permissible for ascertaining the purpose of subordinate legislation and also in other cases for ascertaining the purpose for which a power to make subordinate legislation was used. I believe that such statements are likely to be readily identified in parliamentary proceedings and the cases in which they are relevant will be determined by the nature of the subject matter. Allowing reference to Hansard in such cases does not have the large practical consequences to which I have referred. If reference to parliamentary material is permitted as an aid to the construction of legislation which is ambiguous, or obscure or the literal meaning of which leads to an absurdity, I believe as I have said that in practically every case it will be incumbent on those preparing the argument to examine the whole proceedings on the Bill in question in both Houses of Parliament. Questions of construction may be involved on what is said in Parliament and I cannot see how if the rule is modified in this way the parties' legal advisers could properly come to court without having looked to see whether there was anything in the Hansard report on the Bill which could assist their case. If they found a passage which they thought had a bearing on the issue in this case, that passage would have to be construed in the light of the proceedings as a whole.

I fully appreciate and feel the force of the narrowness of the distinctions which are taken between what is admissible and what is not admissible, but the exception presently proposed is so extensive that I do not feel able to support it in the present state of our knowledge of its practical results in this jurisdiction. For these reasons, I agree that these appeals should be allowed, although I cannot agree on the main issue for the discussion of which this further hearing was arranged.

LORD BRIDGE OF HARWICH:. . .

It should, in my opinion, only be in the rare cases, where the very issue of interpretation which the courts are called on to resolve has been addressed in parliamentary debate and where the promoter of the legislation has made a clear statement directed to that very issue, that reference to Hansard should be permitted. Indeed, it is only in such cases that reference to Hansard is likely to be of any assistance to the courts. Provided the relaxation of the previous exclusionary rule is so limited, I find it difficult to suppose that the additional cost of litigation or any other ground of objection can justify the court continuing to wear blinkers which, in such a case as this, conceal the vital clue to the intended meaning of an enactment. I recognise that practitioners will in some cases incur fruitless costs in the search for such a vital clue where none exists. But, on the other hand, where Hansard does provide the answer, it should be so clear to both parties that they will avoid the cost of litigation.

I would allow the appeal.

LORD BROWNE-WILKINSON: My Lords, the underlying subject matter of these tax appeals is the correct basis for valuing benefits in kind received by the taxpayers, who are schoolmasters. However, in the circumstances which I will relate, the appeals have also raised two questions of much wider importance. The first is whether in construing ambiguous or obscure statutory provisions your Lordships should relax the historic rule that the courts must not look at the parliamentary history of legislation or Hansard for the purpose of construing such legislation. The second is whether, if reference to such materials would otherwise be appropriate, it would contravene s. 1, art. 9 of the Bill of Rights (1688) or parliamentary privilege so to do.

. . .

The case was originally argued before a committee of five of your Lordships without reference to any parliamentary proceedings. After the conclusion of the first hearing, it came to your Lordships' attention that an examination of the proceedings in Parliament in 1976 which led to the enactment of ss. 61 and 63 of the 1976 Act might give a clear indication which of the two rival contentions represented the intention of Parliament in using the statutory words. Your Lordships then invited the parties to consider whether they wished to present further argument on the question whether it was appropriate for the House (under *Note* [1966] 3 All ER 77, [1966] 1 WLR 1234) to depart from previous authority of this House which forbids reference to such material in construing statutory provisions and, if so, what guidance such material provided in deciding the present appeal. The taxpayers indicated that they wished to present further argument on these points. The case was listed for rehearing before a committee of seven members not all of whom sat on the original committee.

At the start of the further hearing, the Attorney General, who appeared for the Crown, drew our attention to a letter addressed to him by the Clerk of the House of Commons suggesting that any reference to Hansard for the purpose of construing the 1976 Act might breach the privileges of that House. Until 31 October 1980 the House of Commons took the view that any reference to Hansard in court proceedings would constitute a breach of its privileges and required a petition for leave to use Hansard to be presented in each case. On 31 October 1980 the House of Commons resolved as follows:

That this House, while re-affirming the status of proceedings in Parliament confirmed by article 9 of the Bill of Rights, gives leave for reference to be made in future court proceedings to the Official Report of Debates and to the published Reports and evidence of Committees in any case in which, under the practice of the House, it is required that a petition for leave should be presented and that the practice of presenting petitions for leave to refer to Parliamentary papers be discontinued.

The letter of 5 June 1992 from the Clerk of the House of Commons starts by saying:

My attention has been drawn to the fact that the House of Lords may be asked to hear argument in this case based on the meaning or significance of words spoken during proceedings on a Bill in the House of Commons.

The letter then sets out the text of the resolution of 31 October 1980, and continues:

In my opinion, the use proposed for the Official Report of Debates in this case is beyond the meaning of the 'reference' contemplated in the Resolution of October 1980. If a court were minded in particular circumstances to permit the questioning of the proceedings of the House in the way proposed, it would be proper for the leave of the House to be sought first by way of petition so that, if leave were granted, no question would arise of the House regarding its Privileges as having been breached.

The reference in that letter to 'questioning' the proceedings of the House of Commons plainly raised the issue whether the proposed use of parliamentary materials without the leave of the House of Commons would breach s. 1, art. 9 of the Bill of Rights, which provides:

That the freedome of speech and debates or proceedings in Parlyament ought not to be impeached or questioned in any court or place out of Parlyament.

The Attorney General, while submitting that such use of parliamentary material would breach art. 9, accepted that it was for the courts to determine the legal meaning and effect of art. 9. However, the Attorney General warned your Lordships that, even if reference in this case to parliamentary materials did not infringe art. 9, the House of Commons might take the view the House enjoyed some wider privilege which we would be infringing and might well regret that its views on the point had not been sought before a decision was reached by your Lordships. Whilst strictly maintaining the privileges of the House of Commons, the Attorney General uses the parliamentary materials in this case as an illustration of the dangers of so doing. Moreover, in order to assist us, whilst still maintaining the privileges of the House of Commons, he made submissions as to the effect of such material on the construction of s. 63 if, contrary to his contentions and advice, we decided this appeal with the assistance of such material.

In the result, the following issues arise. (1) Should the existing rule prohibiting any reference to Hansard in construing legislation be relaxed and, if so, to what extent? (2) If so, does this case fall within the category of cases where reference to parliamentary proceedings should be permitted? (3) If reference to parliamentary proceedings is permissible, what is the true construction of the statutory provisions? (4) If reference to the parliamentary proceedings is not permissible what is the true construction of the statutory provisions? (5) If the outcome of this case depends on whether or not reference is made to Hansard, how should the matter proceed in the face of the warnings of the Attorney General that such references might constitute a breach of parliamentary privilege?

. . .

1. SHOULD THE RULE PROHIBITING REFERENCES TO PARLIAMENTARY PRIVILEGE BE RELAXED?

Under present law, there is a general rule that references to parliamentary material as an aid to statutory construction is not permissible (the exclusionary rule) (see *Davis v Johnson* [1978] 1 All ER 1132, [1979] AC 264 and *Hadmor Productions Ltd v Hamilton* [1981] 2 All ER 724, [1983] 1 AC 191). This rule did not always apply but was judge-made. Thus, in *Ash v Abdy* (1678) 3 Swan 664, 36 ER 1014 Lord Nottingham LC took judicial notice of his own experience when introducing the Bill in the House of Lords. The exclusionary rule was probably first stated by Willes J in *Millar v Taylor* (1769) 4 Burr 2303 at 2332, 98 ER 201 at 217. However, *Re Mew and Thorne* (1862) 31 LJ Bcy 87 shows that even in the middle of the last century the rule was not absolute: in that case Lord Westbury LC in construing an Act had regard to its parliamentary history and drew an inference as to Parliament's intention in passing the legislation from the making of an amendment striking out certain words.

The exclusionary rule was later extended so as to prohibit the court from looking even at reports made by commissioners on which legislation was based (see *Salkeld v Johnson* (1848) 2 Exch 256 at 273, 154 ER 487 at 495). This rule has now been relaxed so as to permit reports of commissioners, including Law Commissioners, and white papers to be looked at for the purpose solely of ascertaining the mischief which the statute is intended to cure but not for the purpose of discovering the meaning of the words used by Parliament to effect such cure (see *Eastman Photographic Materials Co Ltd v Comptroller-General of Patents Designs and Trade-marks* [1898] AC 571 and *Assam Railways and Trading Co Ltd v IRC* [1935] AC 445 at 457–458, [1934] All ER Rep 646 at 655). Indeed, in *Factortame Ltd v Secretary of State for Transport* [1989] 2 All ER 692, [1990] 2 AC 85 your Lordships' House went further than this and had regard to a Law Commission report not only for the purpose of ascertaining the mischief but also for the purpose of drawing an inference as to parliamentary intention from the fact that Parliament had not expressly implemented one of the Law Commission's recommendations.

Although the courts' attitude to reports leading to legislation has varied, until recently there was no modern case in which the court had looked at parliamentary debates as an aid to construction. However, in *Pickstone* v *Freemans plc* [1988] 2 All ER 803, [1989] AC 66 this House, in construing a statutory instrument, did have regard to what was said by the minister who initiated the debate on the regulations. Lord Keith after pointing out that the draft regulations were not capable of being amended when presented to Parliament, said that it was 'entirely legitimate for the purpose of ascertaining the intention of Parliament to take into account the terms in which the draft was presented by the responsible minister and which formed the basis of its acceptance' (see [1988] 2 All ER 803 at 807, [1989] AC 66 at 112). Lord Templeman also referred to the minister's speech, although possibly only by way of support for a conclusion he had reached on other grounds (see [1988] 2 All ER 803 at 814, [1989] AC 66 at 121–122). Lord Brandon and Lord Jauncey agreed with both those speeches. This case therefore represents a major inroad on the exclusionary rule (see also *Owens Bank Ltd* v *Bracco* [1992] 2 All ER 193, [1992] 2 AC 443).

Mr Lester QC, for the taxpayers, did not urge us to abandon the exclusionary rule completely. His submission was that where the words of a statute were ambiguous or obscure or were capable of giving rise to an absurd conclusion it should be legitimate to look at the parliamentary history, including the debates in Parliament, for the purpose of identifying the intention of Parliament in using the words it did use. He accepted that the function of the court was to construe the actual words enacted by Parliament so that in no circumstances could the court attach to words a meaning that they were incapable of bearing. He further accepted that the court should only attach importance to clear statements showing the intention of the promoter of the Bill, whether a minister or private member; there could be no dredging through conflicting statements of intention with a view to discovering the true intention of Parliament in using the statutory words.

In *Beswick* v *Beswick* [1967] 2 All ER 1197 at 1202, [1968] AC 58 at 74 Lord Reid said:

> For purely practical reasons we do not permit debates in either House to be cited: it would add greatly to the time and expense involved in preparing cases involving the construction of a statute if counsel were expected to read all the debates in Hansard, and it would often be impractical for counsel to get access to at least the older reports of debates in select committees of the House of Commons; moreover, in a very large proportion of cases such a search, even if practicable, would throw no light on the question before the court . . .

In *Black-Clawson International Ltd* v *Papierwerke Waldhof-Aschaffenburg AG* [1975] 1 All ER 810 at 814–815, [1975] AC 591 at 613–615 Lord Reid said:

> We often say that we are looking for the intention of Parliament, but that is not quite accurate. We are seeking the meaning of the words which Parliament used. We are seeking not what Parliament meant but the true meaning of what they said . . . I have more than once drawn attention to the practical difficulties . . . but the difficulty goes deeper. The questions which give rise to debate are rarely those which later have to be decided by the courts. One might take the views of the promoters of a Bill as an indication of the intention of Parliament but any view the promoter may have had about questions which later come before the court will not often appear in Hansard and often those questions have never occurred to the promoters. At best we might get material from which a more or less dubious inference might be drawn as to what the promoters intended or would have intended if they had thought about the matter, and it would, I think, generally be dangerous to attach weight to what some other members of either House may have said . . . in my view, our best course is to adhere to present practice.

In the same case Lord Wilberforce said ([1975] 1 All ER 810 at 828, [1975] AC 591 at 629):

> The second [reason] is one of constitutional principle. Legislation in England is passed by Parliament, and put in the form of written words. This legislation is given legal effect on subjects by virtue of judicial decisions, and it is the function of the courts to say what the application of the words used to particular cases or individuals is to be

. . . it would be a degradation of that process if the courts were to be merely a reflecting mirror of what some other interpretation agency might say.

In *Fothergill* v *Monarch Airlines Ltd* [1980] 2 All ER 696 at 705, [1981] AC 251 at 279 Lord Diplock said:

The constitutional function performed by courts of justice as interpreters of the written law laid down in Acts of Parliament is often described as ascertaining 'the intention of Parliament'; but what this metaphor, though convenient, omits to take into account is that the court, when acting in its interpretative role, as well as when it is engaged in reviewing the legality of administrative action, is doing so as mediator between the state in the exercise of its legislative power and the private citizen for whom the law made by Parliament constitutes a rule binding upon him and enforceable by the executive power of the state. Elementary justice or . . . the need for legal certainty, demands that the rules by which the citizen is to be bound should be ascertainable by him (or, more realistically, by a competent lawyer advising him) by reference to identifiable sources that are publicly accessible.

In *Davis* v *Johnson* [1978] 1 All ER 1132 at 1157, [1979] AC 264 at 350 Lord Scarman said:

. . . such material is an unreliable guide to the meaning of what is enacted. It promotes confusion, not clarity. The cut and thrust of debate and the pressures of executive responsibility, the essential features of open and responsible governments, are not always conducive to a clear and unbiased explanation of the meaning of statutory language. And the volume of parliamentary and ministerial utterances can confuse by its very size.

Thus the reasons put forward for the present rule are, first, that it preserves the constitutional proprieties, leaving Parliament to legislate in words and the courts (not parliamentary speakers) to construe the meaning of the words finally enacted, second, the practical difficulty of the expense of researching parliamentary material which would arise if the material could be looked at, third, the need for the citizen to have access to a known defined text which regulates his legal rights and, fourth, the improbability of finding helpful guidance from Hansard.
. . .

My Lords, I have come to the conclusion that, as a matter of law, there are sound reasons for making a limited modification to the existing rule (subject to strict safeguards) unless there are constitutional or practical reasons which outweigh them. In my judgment, subject to the questions of the privileges of the House of Commons, reference to parliamentary material should be permitted as an aid to the construction of legislation which is ambiguous or obscure or the literal meaning of which leads to an absurdity. Even in such cases references in court to parliamentary material should only be permitted where such material clearly discloses the mischief aimed at or the legislative intention lying behind the ambiguous or obscure words. In the case of statements made in Parliament, as at present advised I cannot foresee that any statement other than the statement of the minister or other promoter of the Bill is likely to meet these criteria.
. . .

I therefore reach the conclusion, subject to any question of parliamentary privilege, that the exclusionary rule should be relaxed so as to permit reference to parliamentary materials where: (a) legislation is ambiguous or obscure, or leads to an absurdity; (b) the material relied on consists of one or more statements by a minister or other promoter of the Bill together if necessary with such other parliamentary material as is necessary to understand such statements and their effect; (c) the statements relied on are clear. Further than this, I would not at present go.
. . .

7.4   End of Chapter Assessment Question

Refer to *Cases and Materials* where you will find extracts from the speeches of the House of Lords in *Pepper* v *Hart*.

You will have already looked at part of this case in an earlier exercise in Chapter 4. Now read the extracts again, with a view to answering the following questions:

(a)   What reasons are given for the former rule which prohibited reference to Hansard as an aid to statutory interpretation?

(b)   What conditions are imposed by the Law Lords on those who wish to consult Hansard as an aid to statutory interpretation?

(c)   What implications does this have for modern methods of statutory interpretation?

7.5   End of Chapter Assessment Outline Answer

(a)   For many years, Hansard was not regarded as a legitimate aid to the construction of legislation.

A number of reasons were cited for this rule in the case of *Pepper* v *Hart*. Lord Mackay was concerned that in practical terms, legal advisers would have to study Hansard in practically every case of statutory interpretation, to ascertain whether any assistance could be derived from it. This would add greatly to the cost of litigation.

Lord Browne-Wilkinson identified three further reasons for the rule; first, that it preserves constitutional proprieties, secondly, the practical difficulty and expense of researching parliamentary material, thirdly, the need for the citizen to have access to a known text which regulates his legal rights and fourthly the improbability of finding helpful guidance from Hansard.

(b)   Reference to Hansard for the purpose of statutory intrepretation is now permitted where:

(i)   legislation is ambiguous or obscure or leads to an absurdity; and

(ii)   the material relied on consists of one or more statements by a minister or other promoter of the Bill; and

(iii) the statements relied on are clear.

(c)   The speech of Lord Browne-Wilkinson suggests that the use of Hansard (subject to the conditions set out above) is acceptable in cases where the Court adopts a purposive approach to the construction of legislation. Thus where the literal rule has failed, because its use leads to an absurdity or because the words of the statute are ambiguous or obscure, the court may wish to utilise an approach to interpretation based on the mischief rule. This then enables the Court to examine the purpose of the legislation and its history, and reference to Hansard will thus be of assistance in these cases. Lord Browne-Wilkinson's words suggest that the literal approach may still be the first method adopted by the Court in cases of statutory interpretation, but that the purposive approach is valuable where the literal rule fails.

CHAPTER EIGHT

LEGAL REASONING

8.1 Facts and Evidence

R v STRATFORD-UPON-AVON HOUSING BENEFIT REVIEW BOARD, EX PARTE WHITE, The Times, 23 April 1998 (CA)

Members of a religious community who were required to give all their capital and income to the order and lived as licensees in a house owned by the order were not living under an arrangement which had been contrived to take advantage of the Housing Benefit (General) Regulations (SI 1987 No. 1971) pursuant to regulation 7(1) and were entitled to receive housing benefit.

The Court of Appeal so held in allowing an appeal by Richard Walter Wellstood White, a member of the Jesus Fellowship Church, against the dismissal by Mr Justice Dyson of his application for judicial review of the decision of the Stratford-upon-Avon Housing Benefit Review Board that he was not entitled to housing benefit.

LORD JUSTICE OTTON said that the Christian ideal which called for payment of the whole income, including housing benefit, into the common pool did not extinguish the legal relationship or diminish the appellant's separate obligation to pay board and lodging for himself and his family.

The obligation was separate and binding, predated the application for housing benefit and still prevailed at the time of the hearing before the board.

Clearly if there was evidence from which the council could infer that there had been an abuse of the system or, that the applicant had behaved improperly through bad faith then they could readily infer that the liability had been created to take advantage of the housing benefit scheme.

However, where there was no evidence to show that the person whose liability to make payments had so behaved the council would be less ready or able to come to a conclusion adverse to the tenant.

In the instant case, the appellant had not created such an arrangement to take advantage of the scheme or been a party to it. He had merely submitted himself to the discipline of the religious order and agreed to be bound by the conditions of residence.

The precise language of regulation 7(1)(b) indicated that there had to have been some purposive conduct on the part of those seeking benefit, the liability had to appear 'to have been created to take advantage'. That connoted that something had been contrived or devised for the purpose of taking advantage of or exploiting the scheme.

There was no evidence to suggest that the appellant or his landlord had behaved in such a manner or been motivated by dubious ingenuity to create the liability. Thus the council could not reasonably have concluded that the liability had been created to take advantage of the scheme.

His Lordship went on to consider points raised by the secretary of state in a respondent's notice and concluded that because there was some spiritual element it did not deprive the rest of the arrangement of its legally enforceable character. Nor did the spiritual obligations overwhelm those that were legally enforceable.

LORD JUSTICE PETER GIBSON, agreeing, said that he agreed with Mr Justice Black-burne's decision in *R* v *Sheffield City Council Housing Benefit Review Board, Ex parte Smith* ((1994) 93 LGR 139) that the terms and conditions of residence in the community houses were intended to create a legally enforceable relationship imposing on members occupying dwellings a liability to make payment for that occupation.

SIR CHRISTOPHER SLADE agreed.

8.2 Facts and Law

CLARKE v *KATO AND OTHERS, The Times,* 11 December 1996 (CA)

The regular and incontrovertible use of a car park as a pedestrian route to a parade of shops was sufficient for the route to qualify as a road for the purposes of the Road Traffic Act 1988 and further consideration of whether or not use of the route by prams and bicycles amounted to vehicular use was unnecessary.

The Court of Appeal so held when dismissing an appeal by the Motor Insurers' Bureau, from Mr Assistant Recorder Goodchild at Great Grimsby County Court on 20 July 1995 whereby he determined a preliminary issue that the car park at the rear of the shopping precinct at Waltham Road/Springfield Road, Grimsby, in which the respondent, Ellen Katie Clark, had been injured, was a road within s. 192 of the Road Traffic Act 1988.

Pursuant to the Motor Insurers' Bureau (Compensation of Victims of Uninsured Drivers) Agreement made on 21 December 1988 the MIB was required to satisfy judgments against uninsured drivers in respect of any 'relevant liability' which was defined in the agreement as 'a liability in respect of which a policy of insurance must insure a person in order to comply with Part IV of the Road Traffic Act [1988].'

The respondent, who had been walking through the car park on her way home, had been struck by a car driven by Paul Kato, who was not insured to drive or possessed of any covering insurance. He was with Jarred Smith who had allowed him to drive the car. The respondent had brought an action against Kato, Smith and the MIB for personal injury and consequential loss.

Section 192 of the 1988 Act provides:

(1)   . . . 'road' means any highway and any other road to which the public has access. . .

LORD JUSTICE POTTER said that the car park was situated behind a parade of shops. There was a covered passageway from the car park to the middle of the parade.

The passageway and the ramp leading up to it were together designed for access by pedestrians, wheelchairs and perambulators.

They were not designed for, nor negotiable by cars although it was possible for cyclists to use them. The sole vehicular access to and from the car park was at the northeast corner from a short drive running from a public road. The entrance was effectively open at all times.

Pursuant to s. 143 of the Act a policy of insurance was only compulsory when a vehicle was being used on a road. Thus the liability of the MIB to indemnify the respondent in respect of any judgment against Kato and Smith depended upon whether or not at the time of the accident the car park could properly have been described as a road.

As far as the meaning of the word 'highway' was concerned, its existence depended upon the establishment of a public right of passage whether on foot, on horseback or by vehicle, over the way concerned as a result of dedication or long usage.

However, the argument before the county court had turned entirely upon whether the car park might properly be described or regarded as 'any other road to which the public has access'. The issue was narrower than that since it was accepted that the public had access to the car park. The question was simply whether or not the whole or part of the car park came within the definition or concept of a 'road' at all.

His Lordship considered the relevant case law including the Scottish case of *Harrison* v *Hill* (1932 JC 13) and *Griffin* v *Squires* [1958] 1 WLR 1106).

It was apparent that to qualify as a road to which the public had access it was not necessary that the area concerned should enjoy either the usual appearance or common appellation of a road.

Quite apart from the policy considerations summarised in *Harrison* v *Hill* it seemed to his Lordship that the use of the words 'highways and other roads' in the Act suggested that save for the question of public user as of right as opposed to de facto access the legislative intention was that the words 'highways' and 'roads' should bear equivalent meanings.

On the basis of the authorities a car park could properly be regarded as a road where it was not simply used as such in the sense that the passage of vehicles and pedestrians was not restricted to passage over the surface of the car park for the purpose of obtaining access to and from a parking place but was used for what might be called 'through' traffic, so as to alter its character from that of a car park to one which was also used as or as part of a road.

The county court had found that a line of communication for the public between east and west existed via the passageway, ramp and car park.

The respondent had been able to rely, upon regular and incontrovertible use of that line of communication as a pedestrian route between the hinterland lying to the east of the car park entrance and to the west of the parade of shops.

That being so it seemed to his Lordship that the concern of the assistant recorder as to whether or not use by prams and bicycles amounted to vehicular use sufficient for the route to qualify as a road was unnecessary.

Unrestricted pedestrian user with or without such use by wheeled traffic as the assistant recorder had found to exist, was sufficient to establish a road provided there was sufficient evidence of a definable route in relation to the pedestrian traffic.

There being clear evidence before the assistant recorder on which he could find as he did, the appeal would therefore be dismissed.

Lord Justice McCowan and Lord Justice Waite agreed.

8.3   How to Organise Factual Information

Anderson, T. and Twining, W., *Analysis of Evidence*, London:
Weidenfeld and Nicolson, 1991, p. 105

Chapter 3   Methods of Analysis

A.   INTRODUCTION

The principles of inductive logic are the common tools of practical reasoning and for that reason are important to anyone who must make decisions based upon incomplete data. These tools are specially important in many professions. Society holds professionals to a higher standard of reasoning because, ordinarily, their decisions can significantly affect the interests of individuals or society as a whole, and they are supposed to be competent to make such decisions. In one view, the highest standards may reasonably be required of doctors and lawyers. They undertake to solve problems of great importance for individuals, and their work in the aggregate is critical to society.

Every profession that engages in fact analysis and reasoning must develop ways of recording and organising the data in forms suitable for analysis and use. Analysis must ordinarily precede use, and a system designed to record and organise data in a manner that facilitates analysis will ordinarily differ significantly from a system designed to facilitate the effective, post-analysis use of that data.

This is surely true for lawyers. At every stage, the lawyer must engage in analysis. Has my client provided me with sufficient facts to state a claim for relief? What additional evidence should I seek to test and strengthen my client's case? Given the evidence available to both sides, can the data be marshalled to persuade the relevant decision-maker that my client is entitled to satisfactory relief? The lawyer must have a system for recording and organising the data available at any stage to conduct the analysis necessary to address and respond to questions such as these. The kind of system needed changes, however, when the lawyer and client have decided, on the basis of the analysis, how to proceed. The lawyer then needs a system under which the data can be organised and marshalled for presentation in the appropriate context, be it counselling, negotiation, or trial. Here, the nature of the forum in which the evidence and arguments will be presented dictates the requirement for a system to order and organise the available data for its intended use.

Lawyers have developed a variety of systems for recording and organising data for both purposes — analysis and use. They (or other professionals) have developed sophisticated record management and indexing systems to facilitate analysis, often augmented by computerised support systems. So too, they have developed devices such as the trial book to organise the data for effective presentation to a tribunal in light of the analysis done. The question remains whether there are principles that can guide the construction and application of systems designed for analysis and for use.

In our view, there are essentially three methods of analysis — the 'chart method,' the 'outline method,' and the 'narrative method.' The three methods are complementary rather than rival. Each has special advantages for specific purposes at various stages of a case. For each, the quality of the product can be enhanced by the careful application of a specified set of procedures in its construction. We believe that every lawyer should be familiar with each of the methods, with the purposes for which each is best suited, and with the procedures by which each may be used to maximise its advantages. The present chapter was designed to enable students to achieve those objectives.

8.3.1   ANALYSING FACTUAL INFORMATION USING INDUCTIVE REASONING: THE KEY LIST METHOD

A Murder Investigation (based on exercises contained in *Analysis of Evidence* by *Anderson and Twining*.)

You are a vacation placement student attached to the local office of the Crown Prosecution Service. You have been given the file relating to a murder case which has been investigated by the police.

You have been asked to organise the information contained in the file in such a way that it can be used as the basis of the case for the prosecution in court.

The file reveals the following:

B's body was found on the hard shoulder of the northbound carriage of the motorway at 10.30 pm on 1 February. He had bled to death as a result of several stab wounds to his back.

Witness 1 says that she saw B getting into the passenger seat of a car which had the characteristics X, Y, and Z (none of which characteristics was the registration number) at 9.30 pm on 1 February. The car drove off in the direction of the motorway,

A owns a car which has the characteristics X, Y and Z.

Witness 2 says that at 10.45 pm on 1 February, he saw A (who was known to him) driving erratically away from the motorway exit nearest to the place where B's body was found.

Witness 3 says that on 31 January he heard A and B having a heated argument. Witness 3 heard B say angrily to A, 'You will do this over my dead body'.

A forensic laboratory report states that blood found on A's clothing and in A's car almost certainly belonged to B.

8.3.2   ANALYSING FACTUAL INFORMATION USING INDUCTIVE REASONING: THE NARRATIVE METHOD

Anderson, T. and Twining, W., *Analysis of Evidence*, London: Weidenfeld & Nicolson, 1991, p. 155

C.   OTHER METHODS OF ANALYSIS

1.   Wigmore's Narrative Method

J. Wigmore, The Science of Judicial Proof §36 (1937)

33.   The Narrative Method.   This is the simpler method, more readily used by the beginner, and more akin to the usual way of describing an evidence problem. It calls for the use of the general classification of Evidence employed in the fore-going chapters. And, though it uses the narrative form, it should be so concisely worded, and so paragraphed and italicised, as to exhibit clearly the general connection of all details.

As to *style*, it should ordinarily consist of four parts:

1. An *introductory statement* of the circumstances leading up to the judicial inquiry, — the finding of a dead body, the offering of a disputed will for probate, the filing of a claim for money unpaid, etc. — in short, the stage-setting.

2. Then comes the *recital of the evidence as classified*; this is the main part of the Narrative. Ordinarily this should be presented in two parts, — first, from the plaintiff's or prosecution's point of view, and then from the defence's point of view; i.e., Motive, Design, etc., as evidenced by the first party, and then Alibi, Motive explained away, etc., as evidenced by the opposite party. . . . But occasionally it may be more clear to set forth the evidence of both sides, under each of the main heads, i.e. Motive, both sides, Design, both sides; etc.

In this classification, every piece of significant evidence should be accounted for. Of course, condensation can be used, by referring to groups of witnesses testifying to the same fact. But the feature to be specially avoided is the mere recital of testimony as given by one witness after another. This is an easy, lazy thing to do; and it is a way often used. But it is *not* a classification of evidence; it is a mere journalistic abstract of the proceedings. Classification means the picking apart of the witnesses' testimony and putting each evidential piece in its proper place in the logical scheme of proof. The order in which data may have to be presented through witnesses at the trial is a mere convenience or necessity of the trial, and has nothing inherently to do with the logical scheme, — any more than the departmental arrangement of food-stuffs in a grocery-shop has to do with the relative dietetic values of the different foods. So that style of recital of testimonies of one witness after another is futile, for our present purpose.

This process of Classification was long ago inculcated and admirably described in a truly scientific work on Evidence, once much in vogue, but nowadays undeservedly fallen into neglect:

Alexander M. Burrill, 'A Treatise on Circumstantial Evidence', (1868, p. 598):

The course of illustration, thus far adopted, exhibits the process of constructing a body of evidence out of elementary facts. It is in this way, too, that the [detailed] infirmative considerations [i.e. explanations] which are always necessary to be taken into view are most effectually presented, and, at the same time, most readily expunged from the process.

The theory of judicial investigation, however, requires that the juror should keep his mind wholly free from impression, until *all the facts* are before him in evidence; and that he should then frame his conclusion from *all* these facts, *taken together*.

The difficulty attending this mode of dealing with the elements of evidence (especially in important cases requiring protracted investigation) is that the facts thus surveyed in mass and at one view are apt to confuse, distract, and oppress the mind by their very number and variety, especially as they are only mentally contemplated, with little or no aid of the bodily senses. They are, moreover, necessarily mixed up with remembrances of the mere machinery of their introduction, and the contests (often close and obstinate) attending their proof; in the course of which attempts are sometimes made to suppress or distort the truth, in the very act of its presentation. And the reservation of the use of infirmative hypotheses [explaining away the inferences], as a *final* means of testing a presumption or conclusion provisionally formed, is attended with more or less of danger of overlooking some single hypothesis, which, though not readily suggested, might be at the same time not unreasonable in itself, and might eventually prove to be the absolute truth of the case.

On the other hand, the manner in which the facts of a case are presented before a jury in a trial is attended with advantages peculiar to itself. In order to construct the required body of evidence out of the materials or elements which may be available for the purpose, with the nearest approach to truth, or to the actual case as it occurred, it is requisite not only that *all* the materials should be got *together*, but that they should be *arranged*, as far as possible, in their *proper places*, or in the relative positions which they occupied, or are reasonably supposed to have occupied, in the actual case; it being, in fact, as already observed, a process of reconstructing and representing, with more or less of completeness and truth, the original case itself. These relative positions cannot always be effectually ascertained until all the attainable facts have been brought together, examined, and compared, or adjusted temporarily (as it were) to each other, so as to develop the traces of their former actual connections; much as an architect would proceed who was required to reconstruct a demolished edifice, out of the same materials which originally composed it, with the nearest possible approach to identity in every particular. . . .

The figure which has, thus far, been used in illustrating the process of circumstantial proof, and which has been suggested by the meaning of the word 'circumstance' itself, is that of a *framework* of facts, arranged in certain positions of relation to the fact sought, and connected with it and with each other by lines expressive, at once, of their separate and united significance. Another figure more frequently used as descriptive of the same process, or rather of the body of evidence constructed by it, is that of *a chain* connecting the two great and fundamental points of a case, — the crime committed, and the individual charged with its commission, — the links of such chain answering to the evidentiary facts proved. This figure expresses, with great force and aptness, the historical order of the facts, and the necessity of a continuous connection between them throughout; but it does not represent that other feature of the process, which has been prominently presented in the present section; namely the aggregation of *distinct* elements, or elements drawn from distinct sources into one consistent and homogeneous body. The evidence does not always present a *single line* of continuous and connected circumstances, but often exhibits lines of connection from different points in *collateral* positions. Supposing, however, a chain to be composed of a number of minor and constituent chains, the figure acquires aptness in every sense.

The evidentiary facts, with their inferred and assigned meanings, may also in many cases be very appropriately compared to *strands of a rope or cable*, forming so many lines of connection with the principal fact, each continuous in itself, though weak in its connecting power; but, when woven together in sufficient numbers, constituting a medium of connection which cannot be broken.

Note, finally, that at each step of inference towards the main probanda, the analyser should *record his own conclusion*, as representing *facts*, and should not merely recite the pros and cons. Thus alone will he be prepared at the end to gather together and weigh the various competing data and form his final conclusion.

3. Then comes the statement of the *analyser's final conclusions* from the various chief subordinate facts. These are of course brief. They should ordinarily be reached and stated judicially, i.e. impartially, — at least when preparing the narrative for one's own exercise or for the information of others. But when drawing up a statement preliminary to use in a trial argument, the statement would naturally take another form.

4. Finally, there will be a paragraph or two for recording the *verdict* actually rendered by the jury, with a comment on its fitness, and a notation of any special characteristics giving interest to this particular trial. . . .

BOLITHO (ADMINISTRATRIX OF THE ESTATE OF BOLITHO (DECEASED) v CITY AND HACKNEY HEALTH AUTHORITY [1997] 4 All ER 771 (HL)

On 16 January 1984 a two-year-old boy, P, who had a past history of hospital treatment for croup, was readmitted to hospital under the care of Dr H and Dr R. On the following day he suffered two short episodes at 12.40 pm and 2.00 pm during which he turned white and clearly had difficulty breathing. Dr H was called in the first instance and she delegated Dr R to attend in the second instance but neither attended P, who at both times appeared quickly to return to a stable state. At about 2.30 pm P suffered total respiratory failure and a cardiac arrest, resulting in severe brain damage. He subsequently died and his mother continued his proceedings for medical negligence as administratrix of his estate. The defendant health authority accepted that Dr H had acted in breach of her duty of care to P but contended that the cardiac arrest would not have been avoided if Dr H or some other suitable deputy had attended earlier than 2.30 pm. It was common ground that intubation so as to provide an airway would have ensured that respiratory failure did not lead to cardiac arrest and that such intubation would have had to have been carried out before the final episode. The judge found that the views of P's expert witness and Dr D for the defendants, though diametrically opposed, both represented a responsible body of professional opinion espoused by distinguished and truthful experts. He therefore held that Dr H, if she had attended and not intubated, would have come up to a proper level of skill and competence according to the standard represented by Dr D's views and that it had not been proved that the admitted breach of duty by the defendants had caused the injury which occurred to P. The Court of Appeal dismissed an appeal by P's mother and she appealed to the House of Lords.

HELD: A doctor could be liable for negligence in respect of diagnosis and treatment despite a body of professional opinion sanctioning his conduct where it had not been demonstrated to the judge's satisfaction that the body of opinion relied on was reasonable or responsible. In the vast majority of cases the fact that distinguished experts in the field were of a particular opinion would demonstrate the reasonableness of that opinion. However, in a rare case, if it could be demonstrated that the professional opinion was not capable of withstanding logical analysis, the judge would be entitled to hold that the body of opinion was not reasonable or responsible. The instant case was not such a situation since it was implicit in the judge's judgment that he had accepted Dr D's view as reasonable and although he thought that the risk involved would have called for intubation, he considered that could not dismiss Dr D's views to the contrary as being illogical. The appeal would, accordingly, be dismissed

Appeal
Valerie Margaret Holt (formerly Bolitho), as administratrix of the estate of Patrick Nigel Bolitho, appealed with leave from the decision of the Court of Appeal (Dillon and Farquharson LJJ; Simon Brown LJ dissenting) (13 BMLR 111) on 15 December 1992 dismissing her appeal from the decision of Hutchison J on 15 February 1991 whereby he dismissed a claim for damages for injuries suffered by the deceased allegedly caused by the negligence of a doctor employed by the respondent, City and Hackney Health Authority. The facts are set out in the opinion of Lord Browne-Wilkinson.

LORD BROWNE-WILKINSON: My Lords, this appeal raises two questions relating to liability for medical negligence. The first, which I believe to be more apparent than real, relates to the proof of causation when the negligent act is one of omission. The second concerns the approach to professional negligence laid down in *Bolam* v *Friern Hospital Management Committee* [1957] 2 All ER 118, [1957] 1 WLR 583.

The claim relates to treatment received by Patrick Nigel Bolitho at St Bartholomew's Hospital on 16 and 17 January 1984 when he was two years old. Patrick suffered catastrophic brain damage as a result of cardiac arrest induced by respiratory failure. The issues investigated at trial were wide ranging but as a result of the judge's findings I can state the relevant facts quite shortly.

On 11 January 1984 Patrick was admitted to St Bartholomew's suffering from croup and was treated under the care of the senior paediatric registrar, Dr Janet Horn, and the senior house officer in paediatrics, Dr Keri Rodger. On 15 January he was discharged home. No complaint is made about this episode in his treatment.

On the evening of 16 January his parents became concerned about his condition. He had not slept well and had been restless; further, he seemed to be having increasing difficulty in breathing and was wheezier. As a result he was readmitted to St Bartholomew's on the evening of 16 January. Dr Rodger examined him and was also concerned about his condition. At 8.30 pm she arranged for him to be nursed by a special nurse on a one-to-one basis. On the following morning, 17 January, the medical notes indicated that he was much better but that there was still reduced air entry on the left side. He was seen on the morning round by the consultant who carried out an examination (albeit not a full one) but he was not concerned about his condition. Patrick ate a large lunch.

At around 12.40 pm on 17 January there occurred the first episode. The nurse who was observing Patrick summoned Sister Sallabank, a skilled and experienced nurse. Sister Sallabank described his respiratory sounds as 'awful' but reported that surprisingly he was still talking. He was very white in colour. The sister was sufficiently concerned about his condition to bleep Dr Horn rather than to go through the usual chain of command by first contacting the senior house officer, Dr Rodger. She took this course because she felt something was acutely wrong. Sister Sallabank asked Dr Horn to come and see Patrick straight away as he was having difficulty in breathing and was very white. Dr Horn seemed alarmed that Patrick was in such distress when he had appeared perfectly well a short time before during the consultant's round. Sister Sallabank told Dr Horn that there had been a notable change in Patrick's colour and that he sounded as though something was stuck in his throat. Dr Horn said that she would attend as soon as possible. In the event, neither she nor Dr Rodger came to see Patrick. When Sister Sallabank returned to Patrick she was extremely surprised to see him walking about again with a decidedly pink colour. She requested a nurse to stay with Patrick.

At around 2 pm the second episode occurred. The nurse observing Patrick called Sister Sallabank back to Patrick. Sister Sallabank saw that he was in the same difficulties as he had been in at 12.40 pm and she became very worried. She went off to telephone Dr Horn again. Dr Horn informed Sister Sallabank over the telephone that she was on afternoon clinic and had asked Dr Rodger to come in her place. While the sister was talking to Dr Horn, the nurse reported to her that Patrick was now pink again; the sister then took the opportunity to explain to Dr Horn in detail the episodes which Patrick had experienced. Dr Rodger did not attend Patrick after the second episode. Her evidence was that her bleep was not working because of flat batteries so that she never got the message.

After the second episode, Sister Sallabank instructed Nurse Newbold to sit with Patrick: she was told that the doctors were coming to see him because he had been unwell earlier. Nurse Newbold tried to take Patrick's pulse and rate of respiration but this proved very difficult as he appeared quite well and was jumping about and playing in his cot. She described Patrick as being very chatty and interested in reading the letters on a dish.

At about 2.30 pm the events leading to the final catastrophe began. There was a change in Patrick's condition. Although he retained his colour he became a little agitated and began to cry. Nurse Newbold left a colleague with Patrick and reported to Sister Sallabank who told her to bleep the doctors again. While she was on the telephone to the doctors, the emergency buzzer sounded having been set off by the nurse left with Patrick. Nurse Newbold immediately returned to Patrick. Sister Sallabank also heard the buzzer and sent out a call for the cardiac arrest team. Patrick had collapsed because his respiratory system was entirely blocked and he was unable to breathe. As a result he suffered a cardiac arrest. He was revived but there was a period of some nine to ten minutes before the restoration of respiratory and cardiac functions. In consequence, Patrick sustained severe brain damage. He has subsequently died and these proceedings have been continued by his mother as administratrix of his estate.

The case came on for trial before Hutchison J. There was a conflict of evidence between Sister Sallabank and Dr Horn as to what was said to Dr Horn in the course of the two telephone calls at about 12.40 pm and 2 pm. The judge accepted Sister Sallabank's version (which is the one I have summarised above). On that basis, the defendants accepted that Dr Horn was in breach of her duty of care after receiving such telephone calls not to have attended Patrick or arranged for a suitable deputy to do so.

Negligence having been established, the question of causation had to be decided: would the cardiac arrest have been avoided if Dr Horn or some other suitable deputy had attended as they should have done. By the end of the trial it was common ground, first, that intubation so as to provide an air way in any event would have ensured that the respiratory failure which occurred did not lead to cardiac arrest and, second, that such intubation would have had to be carried out, if at all, before the final catastrophic episode.

The judge identified the questions he had to answer as follows:

[Mr Owen, for the defendants] submitted, therefore, that (if once it was held that Dr Horn was negligent in failing to attend at either 12.40 or 2 o'clock) the sole issue was whether Patrick would on one or other of these occasions have been intubated. In submitting that on this aspect of the case the issue was what would Dr Horn or another competent doctor sent in her place have done had they attended, Mr Owen was, I think, accepting that the real question was what would Dr Horn or that other doctor have done, *or what should they have done*. As it seems to me, if Dr Horn would have intubated, then the plaintiff succeeds, whether or not that is a course which all reasonably competent practitioners would have followed. If however, Dr Horn would not have intubated, then the plaintiff can only succeed if such failure was contrary to accepted medical practice (I am not purporting to consider the legal tests in detail, and merely using shorthand at this stage) . . . Common to both sides is the recognition that I must decide whether Dr Horn would have intubated (or made preparations for intubation), and, *even if she would not, whether such a failure on her part would have been contrary to accepted practice in the profession*. (My emphasis.)

As to the first of those issues, Dr Horn's evidence was that, had she come to see Patrick at 2 pm, she would not have arranged for him to be intubated. The judge accepted this evidence. However, he found that she would have made preparation to ensure that speedy intubation could take place: in the event that proved to be an irrelevant finding since the judge found that such preparations would have made no difference to the outcome. Therefore, the judge answered the first of his two questions by holding that Dr Horn would not herself have intubated if, contrary to the facts, she had attended.

As to the second of the judge's questions (ie whether any competent doctor should have intubated if she had attended Patrick at any time after 2 pm), the judge had evidence from no less than eight medical experts, all of them distinguished. Five of them were called on behalf of Patrick and were all of the view that, at least after the second episode, any competent doctor would have intubated. Of these five, the judge was most impressed by Dr Heaf, a consultant paediatrician in respiratory medicine at the Royal Liverpool Children's Hospital, which is the largest children's hospital in the United Kingdom. On the other side, the defendants called three experts all of whom said that, on the symptoms presented by Patrick as recounted by Sister Sallabank and Nurse Newbold, intubation would not have been appropriate. Of the defendants' experts, the judge found Dr Dinwiddie, a consultant paediatrician in respiratory diseases at the Great Ormond Street Hospital, most impressive.

The views of the plaintiff's experts were largely based on the premise that over the last two hours before the catastrophe Patrick was in a state of respiratory distress progressing inexorably to hypoxia and respiratory failure. The defendants' experts, on the other hand, considered the facts as recounted by Sister Sallabank indicated that Patrick was quite well apart from the two quite sudden acute episodes at 12.40 pm and 2 pm. The judge held that the evidence of Sister Sallabank and Nurse Newbold as to Patrick's behaviour (which he accepted) was inconsistent with a child passing through the stages of progressive hypoxia.

Having made his findings of fact, the judge directed himself as to the law by reference to the speech of Lord Scarman in *Maynard* v *West Midlands Regional Health Authority* [1985] 1 All ER 635 at 639, [1984] 1 WLR 634 at 639:

. . . I have to say that a judge's 'preference' for one body of distinguished professional opinion to another also professionally distinguished is not sufficient to establish negligence in a practitioner whose actions have received the seal of approval of those whose opinions, truthfully expressed, honestly held, were not preferred. If this was the real reason for the judge's finding, he erred in law even though elsewhere in his judgment he stated the law correctly. For in the realm of diagnosis and treatment negligence is not established by preferring one *respectable* body of professional opinion to another. Failure to exercise the ordinary skill of a doctor (in the appropriate speciality, if he be a specialist) is necessary. (My emphasis.)

The judge held that the views of Dr Heaf and Dr Dinwiddie, though diametrically opposed, both represented a responsible body of professional opinion espoused by distinguished and truthful experts. Therefore, he held, Dr Horn, if she had attended and not intubated, would have come up to a proper level of skill and competence, ie the standard represented by Dr Dinwiddie's views. Accordingly, he held that it had not been proved that the admitted breach of duty by the defendants had caused the catastrophe which occurred to Patrick.

An appeal to the Court of Appeal ((1992) 13 BMLR 111) was dismissed by Dillon and Farquharson LJJ, Simon Brown LJ dissenting. I will have to consider some of their reasons hereafter.

The Bolam test and causation

The locus classicus of the test for the standard of care required of a doctor or any other person professing some skill or competence is the direction to the jury given by McNair J in *Bolam* v *Friern Hospital Management Committee* [1957] 2 All ER 118 at 122, [1957] 1 WLR 583 at 587:

> I myself would prefer to put it this way: a doctor is not guilty of negligence if he has acted in accordance with a practice accepted as proper by a responsible body of medical men skilled in that particular art . . . Putting it the other way round, a doctor is not negligent, if he is acting in accordance with such a practice, merely because there is a body of opinion that takes a contrary view.

It was this test which Lord Scarman was repeating, in different words, in Maynard's case in the passage by reference to which the judge directed himself.

Before your Lordships, Mr Brennan QC, for the appellant, submitted, first, that the Bolam test has no application in deciding questions of causation and, secondly, that the judge misdirected himself by treating it as being so relevant. This argument, which was raised for the first time by amendment to the notice of appeal in the Court of Appeal, commended itself to Simon Brown LJ and was the basis on which he dissented. I have no doubt that, in the generality of cases, the proposition of law is correct but equally have no doubt that the judge in the circumstances of the present case was not guilty of any self-misdirection.

Where, as in the present case, a breach of a duty of care is proved or admitted, the burden still lies on the plaintiff to prove that such breach caused the injury suffered (see *Bonnington Castings Ltd* v *Wardlaw* [1956] 1 All ER 615, [1956] AC 613 and *Wilsher* v *Essex Area Health Authority* [1988] 1 All ER 871, [1988] AC 1074). In all cases, the primary question is one of fact: did the wrongful act cause the injury? But in cases where the breach of duty consists of an omission to do an act which ought to be done (e.g. the failure by a doctor to attend) that factual inquiry is, by definition, in the realms of hypothesis. The question is what would have happened if an event which by definition did not occur, had occurred. In a case of non-attendance by a doctor, there may be cases in which there is a doubt as to which doctor would have attended if the duty had been fulfilled. But in this case there was no doubt: if the duty had been carried out it would have either been Dr Horn or Dr Rodger, the only two doctors at St Bartholomew's who had responsibility for Patrick and were on duty. Therefore in the present case, the first relevant question is 'what would Dr Horn or Dr Rodger have done if they had attended?' As to Dr Horn, the judge accepted her evidence that she would not have intubated. By inference, although not expressly, the judge must have accepted that Dr Rodger also would not have intubated: as a senior house officer she would not have intubated without the approval of her senior registrar, Dr Horn.

Therefore the *Bolam* test had no part to play in determining the first question, viz what would have happened? Nor can I see any circumstances in which the *Bolam* test could be relevant to such a question.

However, in the present case, the answer to the question 'what would have happened?' is not determinative of the issue of causation. At the trial the defendants accepted that if the professional standard of care required any doctor who attended to intubate Patrick, Patrick's claim must succeed. Dr Horn could not escape liability by proving that she would have failed to take the course which any competent doctor would have adopted. A defendant cannot escape liability by saying that the damage would have occurred in any event because he would have committed some other breach of duty thereafter. I have no doubt that this concession was rightly made by the defendants. But there is some difficulty in analysing why it was correct. I adopt the analysis of Hobhouse LJ in *Joyce* v *Merton Sutton and Wandsworth Health Authority* (1996) 27 BMLR 124. In commenting on the decision of the Court of Appeal in the present case, he said (at 156):

Thus, a plaintiff can discharge the burden of proof on causation by satisfying the court *either* that the relevant person would in fact have taken the requisite action (although she would not have been at fault if she had not) *or* that the proper discharge of the relevant person's duty towards the plaintiff required that she take that action. The former alternative calls for no explanation since it is simply the factual proof of the causative effect of the original fault. The latter is slightly more sophisticated: it involves the factual situation that the original fault did not itself cause the injury but that this was because there would have been some further fault on the part of the defendants; the plaintiff proves his case by proving that his injuries would have been avoided if proper care had continued to be taken. In *Bolitho* the plaintiff had to prove that the continuing exercise of proper care would have resulted in his being intubated. (Hobhouse LJ's emphasis.)

There were, therefore, two questions for the judge to decide on causation: (1) What would Dr Horn have done, or authorised to be done, if she had attended Patrick? and (2) If she would not have intubated, would that have been negligent? The *Bolam* test has no relevance to the first of those questions but is central to the second.

There can be no doubt that, as the majority of the Court of Appeal held, the judge directed himself correctly in accordance with that approach. The passages from his judgment which I have quoted (and in particular those that I have emphasised) demonstrate this. The dissenting judgment of Simon Brown LJ in the Court of Appeal is based on a misreading of the judge's judgment. He treats the judge as having only asked himself one question, namely the second question. To the extent that Simon Brown LJ noticed the first question — would Dr Horn have intubated? — he said that the judge was wrong to accept Dr Horn's evidence that she would not have intubated. In my judgment, it was for the judge to assess the truth of her evidence on this issue.

Accordingly, the judge asked himself the right questions and answered them on the right basis.

The Bolam test — should the judge have accepted Dr Dinwiddie's evidence?
As I have said, the judge took a very favourable view of Dr Dinwiddie as an expert. He said:

> . . . I have to say of Dr Dinwiddie also, that he displayed what seemed to me to be a profound knowledge of paediatric respiratory medicine, coupled with impartiality, and there is no doubt, in my view, of the genuineness of his opinion that intubation was not indicated.

However, the judge also expressed these doubts:

> Mr Brennan also advanced a powerful argument — which I have to say, as a layman, appealed to me — to the effect that the views of the defendant's experts simply were not logical or sensible. Given the recent as well as the more remote history of Patrick's illness, culminating in these two episodes, surely it was unreasonable and illogical not to anticipate the recurrence of a life-threatening event and take the step which it was acknowledged would probably have saved Patrick from harm? This was the safe option, whatever was suspected as the cause, or even if the cause was thought to be a mystery. The difficulty of this approach, as in the end I think Mr Brennan acknowledged, was that in effect it invited me to substitute my own views for those of the medical experts.

Mr Brennan renewed that submission both before the Court of Appeal (who unanimously rejected it) and before your Lordships. He submitted that the judge had wrongly treated the *Bolam* test as requiring him to accept the views of one truthful body of expert professional advice, even though he was unpersuaded of its logical force. He submitted that the judge was wrong in law in adopting that approach and that ultimately it was for the court, not for medical opinion, to decide what was the standard of care required of a professional in the circumstances of each particular case.

My Lords, I agree with these submissions to the extent that, in my view, the court is not bound to hold that a defendant doctor escapes liability for negligent treatment or diagnosis just because he leads evidence from a number of medical experts who are genuinely of opinion that the defendant's treatment or diagnosis accorded with sound medical practice. In *Bolam*'s case [1957] 2 All ER 118 at 122, [1957] 1 WLR 583 at 587 McNair J stated that the defendant had to have acted in accordance with the practice accepted as proper by a *'responsible* body of medical men' (my emphasis). Later he referred to 'a standard of practice recognised as proper by a competent *reasonable* body of opinion' (see [1957] 2 All ER 118 at 122, [1957] 1 WLR 583 at 588; my emphasis). Again, in the passage which I have cited from *Maynard's* case, Lord Scarman refers to a 'respectable' body of professional opinion. The use of these adjectives — responsible, reasonable and respectable — all show that the court has to be satisfied that the exponents of the body of opinion relied on can demonstrate that such opinion has a logical basis. In particular, in cases involving, as they so often do, the weighing of risks against benefits, the judge before accepting a body of opinion as being responsible, reasonable or respectable, will need to be satisfied that, in forming their views, the experts have directed their minds to the question of comparative risks and benefits and have reached a defensible conclusion on the matter.

There are decisions which demonstrate that the judge is entitled to approach expert professional opinion on this basis. For example, in *Hucks* v *Cole* (1968) (1993) 4 Med LR 393, a doctor failed to treat with penicillin a patient who was suffering from septic places on her skin though he knew them to contain organisms capable of leading to puerperal fever. A number of distinguished doctors gave evidence that they would not, in the circumstances, have treated with penicillin. The Court of Appeal found the defendant to have been negligent. Sachs LJ said (at 397):

> When the evidence shows that a lacuna in professional practice exists by which risks of grave danger are knowingly taken, then, however small the risks, the court must anxiously examine that lacuna — particularly if the risks can be easily and inexpensively avoided. If the court finds, on an analysis of the reasons given for not taking those precautions that, in the light of current professional knowledge, there is no proper basis for the lacuna, and that it is definitely not reasonable that those risks should have been taken, its function is to state that fact and where necessary to state that it constitutes negligence. In such a case the practice will no doubt thereafter be altered to the benefit of patients. On such occasions the fact that other practitioners would have done the same thing as the defendant practitioner is a very weighty matter to be put on the scales on his behalf, but it is not, as Mr Webster readily conceded, conclusive. The court must be vigilant to see whether the reasons given for putting a patient at risk are valid in the light of any well-known advance in medical knowledge, or whether they stem from a residual adherence to out-of-date ideas . . .'

Again, in *Edward Wong Finance Co. Ltd* v *Johnson Stokes & Master (a firm)* [1984] AC 296, [1984] 2 WLR 1, the defendant's solicitors had conducted the completion of a mortgage transaction in 'Hong Kong style' rather than in the old-fashioned English style. Completion in Hong Kong style provides for money to be paid over against an undertaking by the solicitors for the borrowers subsequently to hand over the executed documents. This practice opened the gateway through which a dishonest solicitor for the borrower absconded with the loan money without providing the security documents for such loan. The Privy Council held that even though completion in Hong Kong style was almost universally adopted in Hong Kong and was therefore in accordance with a body of professional opinion there, the defendant's solicitors were liable for negligence because there was an obvious risk which could have been guarded against. Thus, the body of professional opinion, though almost universally held, was not reasonable or responsible.

These decisions demonstrate that in cases of diagnosis and treatment there are cases where, despite a body of professional opinion sanctioning the defendant's conduct, the defendant can properly be held liable for negligence (I am not here considering questions of disclosure of risk). In my judgment that is because, in some cases, it cannot be demonstrated to the judge's satisfaction that the body of opinion relied on is reasonable or responsible. In the vast majority of cases the fact that distinguished experts in the field are of a particular opinion will demonstrate the reasonableness of that opinion. In particular, where there are questions of assessment of the relative risks and benefits of adopting a particular medical practice, a reasonable view necessarily presupposes that the relative risks and benefits have been weighed by the experts in forming their opinions. But if, in a rare case, it can be demonstrated that the professional opinion is not capable of withstanding logical analysis, the judge is entitled to hold that the body of opinion is not reasonable or responsible.

I emphasise that, in my view, it will very seldom be right for a judge to reach the conclusion that views genuinely held by a competent medical expert are unreasonable. The assessment of medical risks and benefits is a matter of clinical judgment which a judge would not normally be able to make without expert evidence. As the quotation from Lord Scarman makes clear, it would be wrong to allow such assessment to deteriorate into seeking to persuade the judge to prefer one of two views both of which are capable of being logically supported. It is only where a judge can be satisfied that the body of expert opinion cannot be logically supported at all that such opinion will not provide the bench mark by reference to which the defendant's conduct falls to be assessed.

I turn to consider whether this is one of those rare cases. Like the Court of Appeal, in my judgment it plainly is not. Although the judge does not in turn say so, it was implicit in his judgment that he accepted that Dr Dinwiddie's view was a reasonable view for a doctor to hold. As I read his judgment, he was quoting counsel's submission when he described the view that intubation was not the right course as unreasonable and illogical'. The appeal of the argument was to the judge 'as a layman' not a conclusion he had reached on all the medical evidence. He refused to 'substitute his own views for those of the medical experts'. I read him as saying that, without expert evidence he would have thought that the risk involved would have called for intubation, but that he could not dismiss Dr Dinwiddie's views to the contrary as being illogical.

Even if this is to put too favourable a meaning on the judge's judgment, when the evidence is looked at it is plainly not a case in which Dr Dinwiddie's views can be dismissed as illogical. According to the accounts of Sister Sallabank and Nurse Newbold, although Patrick had had two severe respiratory crises, he had recovered quickly from both and for the rest presented as a child who was active and running about. Dr Dinwiddie's view was that these symptoms did not show a progressive respiratory collapse and that there was only a small risk of total respiratory failure. Intubation is not a routine, risk-free process. Dr Roberton described it as 'a major undertaking — an invasive procedure with mortality and morbidity attached — it was an assault'. It involves anaesthetising and ventilating the child. A young child does not tolerate a tube easily 'at any rate for a day or two' and the child unless sedated tends to remove it. In those circumstances, it cannot be suggested that it was illogical for Dr Dinwiddie a most distinguished expert to favour running what, in his view, was a small risk of total respiratory collapse rather than to submit Patrick to the invasive procedure of intubation.

Tragic though this case is for Patrick's mother and much as everyone must sympathise with her, I consider that the judge and the Court of Appeal reached the right conclusions on the evidence in this case. I would dismiss the appeal.

LORD SLYNN OF HADLEY: My Lords, I have had the advantage of reading in draft the speech prepared by my noble and learned friend Lord Browne-Wilkinson. I agree with his analysis of the questions which have to be decided in cases of this kind and of the correct approach in law in deciding them. Despite my anxiety as to the result in this particular case, it is to me clear that Hutchison J asked the right questions and did not misdirect himself in answering them. He was entitled, on all the evidence, to accept that of Dr Dinwiddie. Accordingly, I agree that this appeal must be dismissed.

LORD NOLAN: My Lords, I have had the advantage of reading in draft the speech prepared by my noble and learned friend Lord Browne-Wilkinson. For the reasons which he has given, I, too, would dismiss this appeal.

LORD HOFFMANN: My Lords, I have had the advantage of reading in draft the speech prepared by my noble and learned friend Lord Browne-Wilkinson. For the reasons which he has given, I, too, would dismiss this appeal.

LORD CLYDE: My, Lords, I have had the advantage of reading in draft the speech prepared by my noble and learned friend Lord Browne-Wilkinson. For the reasons which he has given, I, too, would dismiss this appeal.

Appeal dismissed.

8.4   End of Chapter Assessment Question

Read the case of *Bolitho (administratrix of the estate of Bolitho deceased)* v *City and Hackney Health Authority* [1997] 4 All ER 771, set out in *Cases and Materials* (8.3.2), noticing how the judge pays particular attention to the facts of the case. Then answer the following questions:

(a)   What do you think was the ultimate proposition which the appellant (i.e. Patrick's mother) wished to prove?

(b)   At the original hearing of the case in the High Court, what do you think were the propositions which the expert witness evidence for the appellant was intended to prove?

(c)   Lord Browne-Wilkinson identified two questions which the trial judge had to decide concerning causation. Were these questions of causation related to the legal or the factual aspects of the case?

(d)   If you had been acting for the defendants in this case (i.e. the Health Authority), what ultimate proposition would you have attempted to prove in this appeal, and what factual evidence and inferences would you have emphasised?

8.5   End of Chapter Assessment Outline Answer

(a)   That Dr Horn's breach of duty was the cause of the injury which led to Patrick's death.

(b)   The propositions were:

■   That in the last two hours before Patrick's death, he was in respiratory distress.

■   That this state of respiratory distress progressed inexorably to hypoxia and respiratory failure.

■   That after receiving the phone calls concerning Patrick's condition, Dr Horn was in breach of her duty of care in neither attending Patrick nor arranging for a suitable deputy to do so.

■   That after the second episode of breathing difficulties, a competent doctor would have intubated Patrick.

■   That Dr Horn, had she attended Patrick, should have intubated him.

(c)   The questions of causation were:

(i)   What would Dr Horn have done, or authorised to be done if she had attended Patrick? This is a question which is concerned with the **factual** aspects of the case, although the answer to it will have legal consequences.

(ii)   If Dr Horn had not intubated Patrick, would that have constituted negligence? This is a **legal** question, involving the application of the *Bolam* test.

(d)   That the breach of duty of Dr Horn was **not** the cause of the injury which led to Patrick's death.

(i)   Evidence:

■ The consultant on the morning round was not concerned about Patrick's condition.

■ Patrick ate a large lunch.

■ Patrick was still talking during the first episode of breathing difficulties.

■ He made a quick recovery from the first episode and was soon walking around looking pink in colour.

■ After the second episode, Patrick very quickly became pink, and the nurse attending Patrick found it difficult to perform any tests on him because he was jumping about, playing in his cot, and trying to read some letters on a dish.

(ii) Inferences (other reasonable inferences are possible from this evidence, but inferences from the standpoint of the defendants are required):

■ That a doctor of the status of consultant was not worried about Patrick's condition.

■ Patrick's appetite was good.

■ The first episode of breathing difficulty was not of sufficient seriousness as to prevent Patrick from speaking.

■ The first episode was over quickly and did not appear to have any lasting effect.

■ The second episode was also over quickly and immediately afterwards Patrick was playing normally and did not appear to be in any distress.

■ There were thus no indications that Patrick's condition warranted intubation.

CHAPTER NINE

THE DOCTRINE OF PRECEDENT

9.1 The Doctrine as Applied in Individual Courts

9.1.1 THE HOUSE OF LORDS

PRACTICE STATEMENT (JUDICIAL PRECEDENT) [1966] 3 All ER 77

NOTE

Judgment—Judicial decision as authority—Stare decisis—House of Lords—Freedom of House of Lords to depart from their previous decisions where right to do so—Doctrine of precedent nevertheless an indispensable foundation of decisions of law.

Before judgments were given in the House of Lords on July 26 1966, LORD GARDINER LC made the following statement on behalf of himself and the Lords of Appeal in Ordinary:

Their lordships regard the use of precedent as an indispensable foundation upon which to decide what is the law and its application to individual cases. It provides at least some degree of certainty upon which individuals can rely in the conduct of their affairs, as well as a basis for orderly development of legal rules.

Their lordships nevertheless recognise that too rigid adherence to precedent may lead to injustice in a particular case and also unduly restrict the proper development of the law. They propose therefore to modify their present practice and, while treating former decisions of this House as normally binding, to depart from a previous decision when it appears right to do so.

In this connexion they will bear in mind the danger of disturbing retrospectively the basis on which contracts, settlements of property and fiscal arrangements have been entered into and also the especial need for certainty as to the criminal law.

This announcement is not intended to affect the use of precedent elsewhere than in this House.

Explanatory note for press:

Since the House of Lords decided the English case of *London Street Tramways* [sic] v *London County Council* in 1898, the House have considered themselves bound to follow their own decisions, except where a decision has been given *per incuriam* in disregard of a statutory provision or another decision binding on them.

The statement made is one of great importance, although it should not be supposed that there will frequently be cases in which the House thinks it right not to follow their own precedent. An example of a case in which the House might think it right to depart from a precedent is where they consider that the earlier decision was influenced by the existence of conditions which no longer prevail, and that in modern conditions the law ought to be different.

One consequence of this change is of major importance. The relaxation of the rule of judicial precedent will enable the House of Lords to pay greater attention to judicial decisions reached in the superior courts of the Commonwealth, where they differ from earlier decisions of the House of Lords. That could be of great help in the development of our own law. The superior courts of many other countries are not rigidly bound by their own decisions and the change in the practice of the House of Lords will bring us more into line with them.

9.1.2 THE COURT OF APPEAL (CIVIL DIVISION)

WILLIAMS v *FAWCETT* [1985] 1 All ER 787 (CA)

The respondent gave an undertaking in court not to molest the applicant nor to return to her house for a specified period. The applicant subsequently alleged that the respondent had breached the undertaking on a number of occasions, and she applied for an order committing the respondent for contempt. Notice was accordingly given to the respondent in Form N 78 of the County Court (Forms) Rules 1982 to show cause why he should not be committed to prison. The notice failed to specify particulars of the breaches alleged and was signed only by the applicant's solicitor. The particulars of the alleged breaches were not provided until the day of the hearing and at the hearing the respondent requested an adjournment. The judge refused the request and made the committal order sought. The respondent appealed, contending, inter alia, that the notice was defective because it failed to specify the alleged breaches and it was required to be signed by a 'proper officer' of the court.
HELD: (1) There was no requirement that a notice in Form N 78 of the 1982 rules requiring the respondent to show cause why he should not be committed for contempt had to be signed by a 'proper officer' of the court. In the circumstances there were exceptional circumstances for not following, as being *per incuriam*, previous decisions of the Court of Appeal which held that a proper officer was required to sign the notice, those circumstances being (a) that the growth of the error in the previous cases could be clearly detected, (b) that the cases concerned the liberty of the subject and (c) that the cases were of such a nature that it was unlikely that any of them would reach the House of Lords, so giving the House an opportunity of correcting the error which had crept into the law. Accordingly the previous decisions of the Court of Appeal would not be followed . . . ; dicta of Lord Greene MR in *Young* v *Bristol Aeroplane Co. Ltd* [1944] 2 All ER at 300 and of Evershed MR in *Morelle Ltd* v *Wakeling* [1955] 1 All ER at 718 applied; *Gagnon* v *McDonald* (1984) Times, 14 November and *Lee* v *Walker* [1985] 1 All ER 781 not followed.
(2) However, it was wholly wrong to ask the respondent to answer allegations as serious as were breaches of an undertaking given to the court without giving him reasonable notice, and the offer of an adjournment could not cure that defect. Accordingly, on that ground and on the ground that the notice had failed to specify the breaches alleged, the appeal would be allowed and the committal order quashed. . .
PER CURIAM: It is undesirable, but not fatal, for a notice to be addressed to the registrar or other proper officer of the court, or for the notice to be signed by the applicant's solicitor unless he qualifies his signature with a statement to the effect that the notice is made on the application of the applicant or his solicitor, thereby removing any ambiguity whether the notice was an order of the court. The County Court Rules Committee should consider amending Form N 78 to accommodate applicants' solicitors whose practice is to sign the forms. . . .
(2) Form N 79, the committal form, should be amended in order to provide an appropriate space for recording any dispensation pursuant to CCR 1981 Ord. 29, r. 1(6) and (7) . . .

SIR JOHN DONALDSON MR: This is an appeal by Mr William Fawcett (the respondent) against an order made by his Honour Judge Forrester-Paton QC on 9 January 1985 committing him to prison for various terms, totalling in all four months, for five breaches of an undertaking not to molest the respondent to this appeal, Angela Williams (the applicant), and not to return to her house at 60 Tennyson Avenue, Grangetown, Middlesbrough.
    The appeal raises two issues. First, should the committal order be set aside for procedural errors? Second, is there any requirement that a notice to show cause why a

respondent should not be committed to prison be signed by 'the proper officer' of the court? At the conclusion of the argument we quashed the order, and I now give my reasons for that decision. . .

So far I have not referred to the authorities, and there are four decisions of this court which require consideration. . .

If we are bound by these decisions, and we are unless they can be treated as having been reached *per incuriam*, they represent a very considerable change in the law for which, so far as I can see, there is absolutely no warrant. The change to which I refer is, of course, a requirement that these notices shall be signed by the proper officer. The rule of stare decisis is of the very greatest importance, particularly in an appellate court, such as this, which sits in six or seven divisions simultaneously. But for this rule, the law would not only bifurcate; it would branch off in six or seven different directions.

That of course has been stresed over and over again. It was emphasised in the classic case of *Young* v *Bristol Aeroplane Co Ltd* [1944] 2 All ER 293, [1944] KB 718 and in *Morelle Ltd* v *Wakeling* [1955] 1 All ER 708, [1955] 2 QB 379, which considered *Young's* case. But in each of those cases, as I will demonstrate briefly, the court retained the power in an exceptional case to depart from its previous decisions. Thus in *Young's* case [1944] 2 All ER 293 at 300, [1944] KB 718 at 729 Lord Greene MR said:

> Where the court has construed a statute or a rule having the force of a statute, its decision stands on the same footing as any other decision on a question of law. But where the court is satisfied that an earlier decision was given in ignorance of the terms of a statute or a rule having the force of a statute the position is very different. It cannot, in our opinion, be right to say that in such a case the court is entitled to disregard the statutory provision and is bound to follow a decision of its own given when that provision was not present to its mind. Cases of this description are examples of decisions given *per incuriam*. We do not think that it would be right to say that there may not be other cases of decisions given *per incuriam* in which this court might properly consider itself entitled not to follow an earlier decision of its own. Such cases would obviously be of the rarest occurrence and must be dealt with in accordance with their special facts.

Morelle's case was a five-judge Court of Appeal, although I hasten to add that it is now well-established that a five-judge Court of Appeal has no more authority than a three-judge Court of Appeal. It consisted of Evershed MR, Denning, Jenkins, Morris and Romer LJJ. I read from the judgment ([1955] 1 All ER 708 at 718, [1955] 2 QB 379 at 406):

> As a general rule the only cases in which decisions should be held to have been given *per incuriam* are those of decisions given in ignorance or forgetfulness of some inconsistent statutory provision or of some authority binding on the court concerned: so that in such cases some part of the decision or some step in the reasoning on which it is based is found, on that account, to be demonstrably wrong. This definition is not necessarily exhaustive, but cases not strictly within it which can properly be held to have been decided *per incuriam* must, in our judgment, consistently with the stare decisis rule which is an essential feature of our law, be, in the language of Lord Greene MR, of the rarest occurrence. In the present case, it is not shown that any statutory provision or binding authority was overlooked. . . As we have already said, it is, in our judgment, impossible to fasten on any part of the decision under consideration, or on any step in the reasoning on which the judgments were based, and to say of it: 'Here was a manifest slip or error'.

In my judgment, one *can* say that in so far as the authorities which I have cited decide that a notice to show cause must be signed by 'the proper officer' there was a manifest slip or error. There is no warrant for that proposition whatsoever either in the rules or in the statute. So I ask myself: is this case exceptional? I remind myself of the danger of treating a decision as given *per incuriam* simply on the ground that it can be demonstrated to be wrong, even if the error is fairly clear on an examination of the authorities. However, for my part I think there are very exceptional features about the four decisions of this court to which I have referred and they are these.

There is, first of all, the clearness with which the growth of the error can be detected if the decisions are read consecutively. Second, these cases are all concerned with the liberty of the subject. It is true that if we were to leave the law as it has been declared to be, namely that these notices have to be signed by the proper officer, there are a number of subjects who would have to be released forthwith, because it is almost unknown for any notice to show cause to be signed by the proper officer. The change would, therefore, be beneficial to some subjects. But the other side of the coin is that these cases are also concerned with the maintenance of the authority of the courts to insist on obedience to their orders. They are therefore in a very special category. They are also, as I have said, cases which appear to be by no means unusual. Unfortunately there are a number of committals for contempt, particularly in the field of domestic violence. They are cases which are most unlikely to reach the House of Lords, which, if we do not act, is alone able to correct the error which has crept into the law.

I say that such a case is unlikely to reach the House of Lords because if the law is to be left as it has evolved, then this court would quash the committal order and it would be for the respondent to take the case to the House of Lords. I doubt whether any respondents would take that course, bearing in mind that there would be a substantial delay before the appeal to the House of Lords was heard and that he or she would, probably rightly, consider it unlikely that the House of Lords would require the contemnor to return to prison to complete his sentence.

I would like to conclude by summarising the position as I see it. First, a notice in form N 78 does not have to be signed by the proper officer and, in so far as decisions of this court suggest the contrary, they should not be followed. Second, the notice has to be addressed to the respondent, but it is undesirable that it should be addressed in addition to the registrar or to the proper officer. On the other hand, if this is done, it should not be regarded as fatal but should be accepted as a reflection of the fact that these documents start life as, in effect, requests to the court to issue the notice. It is an undesirable practice, but it is not a ground for refraining from making a committal order. Third, I think that it is equally undesirable, for the same reason, namely that it may cause the respondent to wonder whether or not the notice is the order of the court, that the notice should be signed by the applicant's solicitor unless he qualifies his signature with some such rubric as 'This order is made on the application of', But, again, I do not think his failure so to qualify his signature is a ground for refusing to make a committal order. Fourth, particulars of the alleged breaches must appear in the notice. This has been said over and over again by this court, and I mention it merely to reaffirm it. Fifth, the notice must be in Form N 78 and must call on the respondent to show cause why he should not be committed to prison. Again, that is merely a reaffirmation of the law as it has been stated on many occasions. Sixth, I think that the County Court Rule Committee should consider amending Form N 78 to accommodate the many applicant's solicitors whose practice is to sign these forms. I do not suggest that solely for the convenience of those solicitors, but because I believe that the practice may be a convenience to respondents. If they have any objection to the notice, they can take it up with the applicants' solicitors straight away, and it may in some cases save further proceedings. Seventh, and last, I would invite the County Court Rule Committee to consider amending Form N 79, which is the committal form itself, in order to provide an appropriate space for recording any dispensation pursuant to Ord. 29, r. 1(6) or (7).

DILLON LJ: I agree. I feel that it would be very desirable in view of the amount of uncertainty in the differences in practice in the field that Form N 78 should be amended by the addition of some such wording as Sir John Donaldson MR suggested. It is ironic that very similar wording was suggested by his Honour Judge Forrester-Paton QC himself in a Practice Direction for the Middlesbrough County Court, unfortunately issued too late for the notice to show cause in the present case, in which he suggested that there should be added at the foot of the notice a note to the following effect: 'This notice was issued on the application of [blank] of [blank], solicitors for the [blank].' This would make the situation clear in all cases and would have the advantage of bringing the solicitors' name on to the face of the notice without any confusion as to their function, so that the recipient of the notice can take any necessary steps to put forward his defence or secure an adjournment without difficulty.

MUSTILL J: I agree with both judgments which have been given.

9.1.3   THE COURT OF APPEAL (CRIMINAL DIVISION)

R v TAYLOR [1950] 2 KB 368 (CCA)

On an indictment for bigamy the 'second marriage' within the meaning of s. 57 of the Offences against the Person Act, 1861, with which the court is concerned is that which is the subject of the indictment, and if on the hearing of that charge it is proved that the lawful spouse had been absent for seven years, that defence is available to the person charged notwithstanding that person has previously committed bigamy with some other person or persons.

R v Treanor (1939) 27 Cr App R 35, disapproved.

If, in the opinion of a full Court of Criminal Appeal, it appears that in a previous decision of the court the law has been either misapplied or misunderstood and that, as the result of a judge's having followed that decision, a person has been sentenced and imprisoned for an offence, it is the bounden duty of the court to reconsider its own earlier decision with a view to seeing whether that person was properly convicted.

Appeal against convictions.

In 1925 the appellant, John William Taylor, was married to his wife, Alice Julie Taylor, who was still alive at the time of the present proceedings but who had not been seen by the appellant since 1927 and was not known by him to be alive. In 1927 the appellant went through a form of marriage with another woman, and in 1942, having left that woman, he married a third. In 1944 he was charged with bigamy in respect of this last ceremony and was acquitted by reason of the fact that in those proceedings it was alleged that he had committed bigamy during the lifetime of the woman whom he had married in 1942, who was at that time believed by the prosecution to be his lawful wife. In 1945 he was charged at the Central Criminal Court in respect of his alleged bigamy in 1927 and was again acquitted because the prosecution could not at that time establish that his wife had been alive at the time of that marriage.

In 1946 he went through a ceremony of marriage with one Lilian Smithers and in 1948 with one Olive Briggs. In respect of those two ceremonies he was charged with bigamy at the Central Criminal Court in March, 1949, when he pleaded guilty to both charges and received a sentence of four years imprisonment. He applied for leave to appeal against that sentence. The application came before a court of three judges, who raised the question why, since the appellant had not seen or heard of his wife since 1927, he had not availed himself of the defence of seven years' absence afforded by the proviso to s. 57 of the Offences Against the Person Act, 1861.

The appellant's counsel informed the court that, in view of the decision in *R v Treanor* that the defence of absence for seven years was only available in the case of a second marriage and was not available on any subsequent occasion, he had not felt justified in raising it. The court intimated that in their view the decision in *R v Treanor* should receive further consideration by a full court, and accordingly gave leave to the appellant to appeal against the convictions.

LORD GODDARD CJ stated the facts and the circumstances leading up to the appeal, and continued:—I desire to say a word about the reconsideration of a case by this court. The Court of Appeal in civil matters usually considers itself bound by its own decisions or by decisions of a court of co-ordinate jurisdiction. For instance, it considers itself bound by its own decisions and by those of the Exchequer Chamber; and, as is well known, the House of Lords also always considers itself bound by its own decisions. In civil matters this is essential in order to preserve the rule of stare decisis.

This court, however, has to deal with questions involving the liberty of the subject, and if it finds, on reconsideration, that, in the opinion of a full court assembled for that purpose, the law has been either misapplied or misunderstood in a decision which it has previously given, and that, on the strength of that decision, an accused person has been sentenced and imprisoned it is the bounden duty of the court to reconsider the earlier decision with a view to seeing whether that person had been properly convicted. The exceptions which apply in civil cases ought not to be the only ones applied in such a case as the present; . . .

DAVIS v *JOHNSON* [1978] 1 All ER 1132 (HL)

The appellant and the respondent were joint tenants of a council flat. Although they were not married, they lived together as man and wife. The appellant was the father of the respondent's baby girl who lived with them in the flat. Their relationship was, however, marred by violence. The respondent was frequently beaten by the appellant and subjected in at least two instances to extreme violence of a horrifying nature. As a result she fled with the child, then aged $2\frac{1}{2}$, to a refuge for 'battered wives', and subsequently applied to a county court, under s. 1 of the Domestic Violence and Matrimonial Proceedings Act 1976, for an injunction restraining the appellant from assaulting or molesting her or the child and ordering him to vacate the flat and not return. The injunction was granted. On 26 October, on the appellant's application, another county court judge rescinded so much of the order as required the appellant to leave the flat. The respondent appealed to the Court of Appeal which, having held, by a majority, that the court was not bound by its earlier decisions in *B* v *B* [[1978] 1 All ER 824] and *Cantliff* v *Jenkins* [[1978] 1 All ER 836], allowed the appeal and restored the order requiring the appellant to vacate the flat. The appellant appealed to the House of Lords, contending, inter alia, that s. 1 of the 1976 Act did not confer on a county court jurisdiction to exclude a person from premises in which he had a proprietary interest.

HELD: Section 1 did not affect property rights but it could affect the enjoyment of those rights and, having regard to the clear and unambiguous language of s. 1 and the intention of Parliament in enacting it, i.e. to protect a party to a marriage or a relationship akin to a marriage from domestic violence and conduct by the other party which put at risk the first party's security or sense of security in the home, s. 1(1)(c) was to be construed as investing a county court, when dealing with an originating application alleging domestic violence, with power to grant the applicant an injunction excluding the respondent from the premises in which the parties had been living, irrespective of the respondent's proprietary rights in the premises. The appeal would therefore be dismissed . . . *B* v *B* . . ., and *Cantliff* v *Jenkins*, overruled. . . .

PER CURIAM: (i) Because of the position of the Court of Appeal as an intermediate appellate court, with an increasing membership and number of divisions in which it sits, and the consequent need for the legal certainty resulting from the binding effect of previous decisions, the rule that, subject to certain clearly defined exceptions, the Court of Appeal is bound by its previous decisions should be re-affirmed expressly and unequivocably . . . *Young* v *Bristol Aeroplane Co. Ltd* [1944] 2 All ER 293 approved.

(ii) It has always been a well-established and salutary rule that Hansard can never be relied on by counsel in court and therefore can never be relied on by the court in construing a statute or for any other purpose . . .; dictum of Lord Reid in *Beswick* v *Beswick* [1967] 2 All ER at 1202 applied.

Decision of the Court of Appeal . . . affirmed.

Appeal

On 11 October 1977 the respondent, Jennifer Therese Davis, applied to the Brentford County Court for an injunction under s. 1 of the Domestic Violence and Matrimonial Proceedings Act 1976 containing the following provisions: (i) that the appellant, Nehemiah Johnson, should not assault, threaten, molest or otherwise interfere with the respondent, and (ii) that the appellant should vacate the flat at 13 Nisbet House, Homerton Road, Hackney, London E9 ('the premises') of which the parties were joint tenants and not return thereto. On 11 October his Honour Judge Barr made the order for non-molestation but adjourned the application for the order excluding the appellant from the premises. On 18 October Mr J G Paulusz, sitting as a deputy circuit judge, made an order that the appellant should vacate the premises and not return thereto, and attached a power of arrest to the order. On 24 October, following the decision of the Court of Appeal in *Cantliff* v *Jenkins*, the appellant applied for an order that the order of 18 October excluding him from the premises be suspended and that he be permitted to re-enter. On 26 October his Honour Judge Bernard Lewis rescinded so much of the order of 18 October as required the appellant to vacate the premises and not return thereto. The respondent appealed to the Court of Appeal against the order of 26 October on the ground, inter alia, that the judge had been wrong in law in ruling that the 1976 Act did not give him power to exclude a party from premises of which he was a joint tenant. The appellant filed a cross-notice of appeal against the order of 18 October on the ground that the deputy circuit judge had misdirected himself in holding that he had power to exclude the appellant from the premises. On 28 November 1977 the Court of Appeal (Lord Denning MR, Sir George Baker P and Shaw LJ, Goff and Cumming-Bruce LJJ dissenting) allowed the appeal and restored the order of the deputy circuit judge. The appellant appealed to the House of Lords. The facts are set out in the opinion of Lord Diplock.

Their Lordships took time for consideration.
9 March. The following opinions were delivered.

LORD DIPLOCK: My Lords, this appeal is from a judgment of the Court of Appeal which, by a majority of three out of the five members who sat (Lord Denning MR, Sir George Baker P and Shaw LJ, Goff and Cumming-Bruce LJJ dissenting) purported to overrule two recent previous decisions of its own as to the meaning of a statute.

Put in a nutshell, the basic question of statutory construction that has given rise to so acute a conflict of judicial opinion is whether s. 1 of the Domestic Violence and Matrimonial Proceedings Act 1976 does no more than provide additional, expeditious and more easily available remedies to prevent threatened invasions of existing legal rights originating from other sources, whether statutory or at common law, or whether it also, of itself, creates new legal rights as well as new remedies for threatened invasion of them. The former I will call the 'narrower', the latter the 'broader' meaning. In *B* v *B*, on 13 October 1977, the Court of Appeal consisting of Megaw, Bridge and Waller LJJ decided unanimously that it bore the narrower meaning: it gave additional remedies but created no new legal rights. In *Cantliff* v *Jenkins,* on 20 October 1977, the Court of Appeal then consisting of Stamp, Orr and Ormrod LJJ, while holding itself to be bound by the decision in *B* v *B* since it regarded that case as indistinguishable, took occasion, again unanimously, to express its concurrence with the reasoning of Bridge LJ in *B* v *B* and added, for good measure, an additional reason in support of the narrower meaning placed on the section in that previous judgment. For my part, I think that *Cantliff* v *Jenkins* was distinguishable from *B* v *B* but it is conceded that the facts in the instant case are indistinguishable from those held by the Court of Appeal in *Cantliff* v *Jenkins* to be relevant to its decision in that case. So, when the instant case came before the Court of Appeal, there was a preliminary question which fell to be determined: and that was whether the court was bound by its previous decisions in *B* v *B* and *Cantliff* v *Jenkins*. The view of a majority of three was that it was not so bound, though their individual reasons for so holding were not identical. This opened the way to a fresh consideration of the meaning of the statute by all five members. On this question they were divided four to one. Cumming-Bruce LJ sided with the six Lords Justices who in the two previous cases had adopted the narrower meaning of s. 1; the remainder were of opinion that it bore the wider meaning and did create new legal rights as well as new remedies for threatened violation of them. So, of the members of the Court of Appeal who sit regularly in civil matters (of whom there are now 17) there were seven who had adopted the narrower meaning of the section, three who, together with the President of the Family Division, had preferred the wider meaning, and a silent minority of seven regular members of the Court of Appeal whose views had not been expressed by the conclusion of the hearing of the instant case in the Court of Appeal.

I draw attention to this arithmetic because if the view expressed by Lord Denning MR, Sir George Baker P and Shaw LJ that the Court of Appeal was not bound by its own previous decisions is correct, this would apply to its decision in the instant case: and had there been no appeal to your Lordships' House to cut the Gordian knot, it would have been open to the Court of Appeal in any subsequent cases to give effect to the wider or the narrower construction of s. 1 of the Domestic Violence and Matrimonial Proceedings Act 1976 according to the preference of the majority of the members who happened to be selected to sit on that particular appeal.

My Lords, the difference of judicial opinion as to the true construction of the section has spilled over into this House; for although I agree that on the facts of this case it may be that the order of the Court of Appeal could be upheld, and that the actual decision in *Cantliff* v *Jenkins* was wrong. I nevertheless find myself regretfully compelled to part company with the rest of your Lordships and to align myself with the seven Lords Justices who have expressed their preference for the narrower meaning. This cannot affect the disposition of the instant appeal nor will it affect the application of the 1976 Act in subsequent cases; for the section means what a majority of this House declares it means. But it does make the score of appellate opinions in favour of the broader and the narrower meanings eight all.

Although on the question of the construction of s. 1 of the Domestic Violence and Matrimonial Proceedings Act 1976 this House has not been able to reach unanimity, nevertheless on what in the instant case was the first question for the Court of Appeal, viz whether it was bound by its own previous decisions, I understand us to be unanimous, so I too will deal with it first.

So far as civil matters are concerned the law on this question is now clear and unassailable. It has been so for more than 30 years. I do not find it necessary to trace the origin and development of the doctrine of stare decisis before the present structure of the courts was created in 1875. In that structure the Court of Appeal in civil actions has always played, save in a few exceptional matters, an intermediate and not a final appellate role. The application of the doctrine of stare decisis to decisions of the Court of Appeal was the subject of close examination by a Court of Appeal composed of six of its eight regular members in *Young* v *Bristol Aeroplane Co Ltd* [[1944] 2 All ER 293]. The judgment of the court was delivered by Lord Greene MR. Its effect is summarised accurately in the headnote as being:

> The Court of Appeal is bound to follow its own decisions and those of courts of co-ordinate jurisdiction, and the 'full' court is in the same position in this respect as a division of the court consisting of three members. The only exceptions to this rule are:—(1.) The court is entitled and bound to decide which of two conflicting decisions of its own it will follow; (2.) the court is bound to refuse to follow a decision of its own which, though not expressly overruled, cannot, in its opinion, stand with a decision of the House of Lords; (3.) the court is not bound to follow a decision of its own if it is satisfied that the decision was given *per incuriam*, e.g., where a statute or a rule having statutory effect which would have affected the decision was not brought to the attention of the earlier court.

The rule as expounded in the *Bristol Aeroplane* case was not new in 1944. It had been acted on on numerous occasions and had, as recently as the previous year, received the express confirmation in this House of Viscount Simon LC with whose speech Lord Atkin agreed: see *Perrin* v *Morgan* [[1943] 1 All ER 187]. Although prior to 1944 there had been an occasional deviation from the rule, which was why a court of six was brought together to consider it, there has been none since. It has been uniformly acted on by the Court of Appeal and re-affirmed, notably in a judgment of a Court of Appeal of five, of which Lord Denning MR as Denning LJ was a member, in *Morelle Ltd* v *Wakeling* [[1955] 1 All ER 708]. This judgment emphasised the limited scope of the *per incuriam* exception to the general rule that the Court of Appeal is bound by its own previous decisions. The rule has also been uniformly accepted by this House as being correct. Because until recently it has never been questioned the acceptance of the rule has generally been tacit in the course of recounting the circumstances which have rendered necessary an appeal to your Lordships' House; but occasionally the rule has been expressly referred to, as by Viscount Simon in the *Bristol Aeroplane* case itself and by Lord Morton of Henryton and Lord Porter in *Bonsor* v *Musicians' Union* [[1955] 3 All ER 518].

Furthermore, the provisions of the Administration of Justice Act 1969 which authorise 'leap frog' appeals in civil cases direct from the High Court to this House are based on the tacit assumption that the rule as stated in the *Bristol Aeroplane* case is correct. One of the two grounds on which a High Court judge may authorise a 'leap frog' appeal is if he is satisfied that a point of law of general importance involved in his decision (s. 12(3)(b))—

> is one in respect of which the judge is bound by a decision of the Court of Appeal or of the House of Lords in previous proceedings, and was fully considered in the

judgments given by the Court of Appeal or the House of Lords (as the case may be) in those previous proceedings.

The justification for by-passing the Court of Appeal when the decision by which the judge is bound is one given by the Court of Appeal itself in previous proceedings is because that court also is bound by the decision, if the point of law was fully considered and not passed over *per incuriam*.

So the rule as it had been laid down in the *Bristol Aeroplane* case had never been questioned thereafter until, following on the announcement by Lord Gardiner LC in 1966 that the House of Lords would feel free in exceptional cases to depart from a previous decision of its own, Lord Denning MR conducted what may be described, I hope without offence, as a one-man crusade with the object of freeing the Court of Appeal from the shackles which the doctrine of stare decisis imposed on its liberty of decision by the application of the rule laid down in the *Bristol Aeroplane* case to its previous decisions; or, for that matter, by any decisions of this House itself of which the Court of Appeal disapproved: see *Broome* v *Cassell & Co. Ltd* [[1971] 2 All ER 187]; *Schorsch Meier GmbH* v *Hennin* [[1975] 1 All ER 152]. In his judgment in the instant appeal, Lord Denning MR refers to a number of cases after 1966 in which he suggests that the Court of Appeal has either refused to apply the rule as laid down in the *Bristol Aeroplane* case or has added so many other exceptions to the three that were stated by Lord Greene MR that it no longer operates as a curb on the power of the Court of Appeal to disregard any previous decision of its own which the majority of those members who happen to be selected to sit on a particular appeal think is wrong. Such, however, has not been the view of the two members of the Court of Appeal who were sitting with Lord Denning MR in any of those cases to which he refers. Where they felt able to disregard a previous decision of the Court of Appeal this was only because, in their opinion, it fell within the first or second exception stated in the *Bristol Aeroplane* case. When *Miliangos* v *George Frank (Textiles) Ltd* [[1975] 1 All ER 1076] was before the Court of Appeal Lord Denning MR appears to have reluctantly recanted. That was a case in which Bristow J had held that he was bound by a decision of this House in *Re United Railways of the Havana and Regla Warehouses Ltd* [[1960] 2 All ER 332], despite the fact that the Court of Appeal had purported to overrule it in the Schorsch Meier case. On appeal from this decision Lord Denning MR disposed of the case by holding that the Court of Appeal was bound by its own previous decision in the *Schorsch Meier* case. He added:

> I have myself often said that this court is not absolutely bound by its own decisions and may depart from them just as the House of Lords from theirs: but my colleagues have not gone so far. So that I am in duty bound to defer to their view.

The reasons why his colleagues had not agreed to follow him are plain enough. In an appellate court of last resort a balance must be struck between the need on the one side for the legal certainty resulting from the binding effect of previous decisions and on the other side the avoidance of undue restriction on the proper development of the law. In the case of an intermediate appellate court, however, the second *desideratum* can be taken care of by appeal to a superior appellate court, if reasonable means of access to it are available; while the risk to the first *desideratum*, legal certainty, if the court is not bound by its own previous decisions grows ever greater with increasing membership and the number of three-judge divisions in which it sits, as the arithmetic which I have earlier mentioned shows. So the balance does not lie in the same place as in the case of a court of last resort. That is why Lord Gardiner LC's announcement about the future attitude towards precedent of the House of Lords in its judicial capacity concluded with the words: 'This announcement is not intended to affect the use of precedent elsewhere than in this House.'

Much has been said in the instant case about the delay and expense which would have been involved if the Court of Appeal had treated itself as bound by its previous decisions in *B* v *B* and *Cantliff* v *Jenkins*, so as to make it necessary for the respondent to come to this House to argue that those decisions should be overruled. But a similar reasoning could also be used to justify any High Court or county court judge in refusing to follow a decision of the Court of Appeal which he thought was wrong. It is true that since the appeal in the instant case was from the county court, not the High Court, the 'leap-frog' procedure was not available, but since it was conceded that the instant case was indistinguishable from *Cantliff* v *Jenkins,* there was no need for anything but the briefest of hearings in the Court of Appeal. The appeal to this House could in that event have been heard before Christmas instead of in January; and at less cost. The decision could have been announced at once and the reasons given later.

Of the various ways in which Lord Denning MR's colleagues had expressed the reasons for continuing to regard the rule laid down in the *Bristol Aeroplane* case as salutary in the interest of the administration of justice, I select those given by Scarman LJ, in *Tiverton Estates Ltd* v *Wearwell Ltd* [[1976] 2 All ER 721], in the Court of Appeal:

> The Court of Appeal occupies a central, but, save for a few exceptions, an intermediate position in our legal system. To a large extent, the consistency and certainty of the law depend on it. It sits almost always in divisions of three: more judges can sit to hear a case, but their decision enjoys no greater authority than a court composed of three. If, therefore, throwing aside the restraints of *Young* v *Bristol Aeroplane Co. Ltd,* one division of the court should refuse to follow another because it believed the other's decision to be wrong, there would be a risk of confusion and doubt arising where there should be consistency and certainty. The appropriate forum for the correction of the Court of Appeal's errors is the House of Lords, where the decision will at least have the merit of being final and binding—subject only to the House's power to review its own decisions. The House of Lords, as the court of last resort, needs this power of review: it does not follow that an intermediate appellate court needs it: and, for the reasons I have given, I believe the Court of Appeal is better without it, save in the exceptional circumstances specified in *Young* v *Bristol Aeroplane Co. Ltd.*

. . . In my opinion, this House should take this occasion to re-affirm expressly, unequivocably and unanimously that the rule laid down in the *Bristol Aeroplane* case as to stare decisis is still binding on the Court of Appeal.

I come now to the construction of s. 1 of the Domestic Violence and Matrimonial Proceedings Act 1976 under which the respondent, Miss Davis, sought an injunction against the appellant, Mr Johnson, to exclude him from the council flat in Hackney of which they were joint tenants . . .

I conclude by explaining briefly my own reasons for dismissing this appeal. I understand your Lordships to agree in holding, as I myself would hold, that s. 1(1) leaves the substantive law relating to husbands and wives unchanged. All that it does is to provide them with a simpler, speedier, more widely available and more effective remedy for threatened violation of legal rights either already existing when the Act was passed or newly created by ss. 3 and 4. What I cannot accept is that s. 1(2), in contrast to s. 1(1), was intended to change the substantive law by authorising county court judges to make drastic inroads on the respective legal rights of parties to an illicit union to occupy the premises in which they have been living together as man and wife, yet without any statement in the subsection of the limits, if any, that are imposed on those inroads. Nevertheless under the existing substantive law a mistress is entitled to protection against the tort of assault, and if, as in the instant case, she is joint tenant with her paramour of the premises in which she has been living with him she has a legal right to continue in peaceful occupation of them. This latter right of hers is one that he has no right to disturb, and his own corresponding right of occupation is one that can be lawfully exercised only in a manner that does not interfere with it. Where the county court judge is satisfied that there is grave danger that if the mistress returns to the premises her paramour will assault her or her child then, as ancillary to an injunction against threatened violence, the judge would, in my view, have jurisdiction to make an order under s. 1(1)(c) excluding him from the premises, but such an order could properly continue only so long a there was danger that if permitted to return he would assault his mistress or her child.

It is the mistress's legal right under a joint tenancy to continue in occupation of the premises that distinguishes the instant case from *B* v *B*. The same distinction could have been drawn in *Cantliff* v *Jenkins,* which for this reason, I think was wrongly decided.

For these reasons I too would dismiss this appeal.

9.2   End of Chapter Assessment Question

Read the extracts from the case of *Davis* v *Johnson* [1978] 1 All ER 1132 in *Cases and Materials*, or read the original report at the reference given, if you have access to a law library, and then answer the following questions.

1.   What were the central factual issues in the case?

2.   What preliminary question of law had to be determined, and what was the question of statutory interpretation which had to be decided?

3.   Explain the route through the court system by which the case reached the House of Lords.

4.   Did the House of Lords as a whole favour the narrower or the broader view of construction of s. 1 of the Domestic Violence and Matrimonial Proceedings Act 1976? Did Lord Diplock agree with this?

5.   According to Lord Diplock, what is the rule which governs precedent in the Court of Appeal, when that court is reviewing one of its own previous decisions? How does that rule operate?

6.   What are the reasons for the rule mentioned in question 5?

7.   How did Lord Denning attempt to alter that rule? Did he succeed?

9.3   End of Chapter Assessment Outline Answer

The following notes provide an outline of the answers which might be expected to the questions on the case-reading exercise. They are not to be regarded as definitive answers, but as an indication of the facts and issues which might be included.

1.   A man, woman and their baby were cohabiting in a flat of which the man and woman were joint tenants. The man was repeatedly violent towards the woman, and she sought an injunction under s. 1 Domestic Violence and Matrimonial Proceedings Act 1976 to restrain him from assaulting her and also to exclude him from the flat.

2.   Preliminary question of law:

Was the Court of Appeal bound by its own previous decisions in *B* v *B* and *Cantliff* v *Jenkins*?

Question of statutory interpretation:

In interpreting s. 1 of the Domestic Violence and Matrimonial Proceedings Act 1976 was it appropriate to take a narrow view — i.e. that s. 1 merely proved more expeditious and easily available remedies to prevent invasion of existing legal rights; or a broader view — i.e. that s. 1 created new legal rights and conferred on the county court jurisdiction to exclude a person from premises in which he had a proprietory interest?

3.   11.10.77 Davis applied to Brentford County Court for injunction.
     Barr J made non-molestation order; adjourned application for exclusion order.
     18.10.77 Mr J G Paulusz made exclusion order with power of arrest.

24.10.77 Johnson applied for suspension of exclusion order.
26.10.77 Bernard Lewis J rescinded exclusion part of order.
Davis appealed; Johnson cross-appealed.
28.11.77 Court of Appeal — Denning MR; Sir George Baker P, Shaw LJ, Goff and Cumming-Bruce LJJ dissenting — allowed appeal; restored order of 18.10.77

4. House of Lords as a whole favoured broader view.
    Diplock disagreed — favoured narrow view.

5. The rule in *Young* v *Bristol Aeroplane Co. Ltd.*, defines the way in which the doctrine of precedent operates in the Court of Appeal. Known as the 'self-binding' rule it states that the Court is bound to follow its own decisions with three exceptions:

(1) it is entitled to decide which of two conflicting decisions of its own it will follow;

(2) it is bound to refuse to follow a decision of its own which cannot stand with a decision of the House of Lords;

(3) it is not bound to follow a decision of its own if it is satisfied that the decision was given *per incuriam*.

6. The self-binding rule reflects the need for legal certainty. This could be endangered if judges in the Court of Appeal gave conflicting decisions. The rule also reflects the need for consistency and to avoid the risk of confusion and doubt. The House of Lords view is that the Court of Appeal is better without the power to review its own decisions.

7. Lord Denning conducted a 'one-man crusade' to free the Court of Appeal.

    (a) in respect of rule in *Young* v *Bristol Aeroplane*

    (b) in respect of decisions of House of Lords of which the Court of Appeal disapproved.

He did not succeed.

INDEX